Chinese Middlemen in Hong Kong's Colonial Economy, 1830–1890

The traditional view of the Hong Kong colonial economy is that it was dominated by Western companies, notably the great British merchant houses, and that these firms enlisted support from Chinese middlemen – the compradors – who were effectively agents working for the Western firms. This book, which presents a comprehensive overview of the compradors and their economic and social functions over the full period of colonial rule in Hong Kong, puts forward a different view. It shows that compradors existed before the beginning of British rule in 1842, discusses their economic and social roles in the colonial economy, roles which included activities for Western firms, for the government and to support compradors' own commercial activities, and outlines how the comprador system evolved. Overall, the book demonstrates that the compradors played a key role in the formation and development of Hong Kong's economy and society, that they were active participants, not just passive servants of Western companies.

Kaori Abe is a former postdoctoral fellow of Nanyang Technological University, Singapore, and has a PhD in History from the University of Bristol. Her main research areas are the history of Hong Kong, modern China and the British Empire in the nineteenth and twentieth centuries.

Routledge Studies in the Modern History of Asia

For a full list of available titles please visit: https://routledge.com/Routledge-Studies-in-the-Modern-History-of-Asia/book-series/MODHISTASIA

120. **Constitution Making in Asia**
Decolonisation and State-Building in the Aftermath of the British Empire
H. Kumarasingham

121. **Neutrality in Southeast Asia**
Concepts and Contexts
Nicholas Tarling

122. **Britain's Retreat from Empire in East Asia, 1905–1980**
Edited by Antony Best

123. **The Dismantling of Japan's Empire in East Asia**
Deimperialization, Postwar Legitimation and Imperial Afterlife
Edited by Barak Kushner and Sherzod Muminov

124. **Public Health and the Modernization of China, 1910–2015**
Liping Bu

125. **The Economy of Colonial Malaya**
Administrators versus Capitalists
Sivachandralingam Sundara Raja

126. **Secularism, Decolonisation, and the Cold War in South and Southeast Asia**
Engaging the Believers
Clemens Six

127. **Chinese Middlemen in Hong Kong's Colonial Economy, 1830–1890**
Kaori Abe

Chinese Middlemen in Hong Kong's Colonial Economy, 1830–1890

Kaori Abe

Routledge
Taylor & Francis Group
LONDON AND NEW YORK

First published 2018
by Routledge

2 Park Square, Milton Park, Abingdon, Oxfordshire OX14 4RN
52 Vanderbilt Avenue, New York, NY 10017

Routledge is an imprint of the Taylor & Francis Group, an informa business

First issued in paperback 2019

British Library Cataloguing-in-Publication Data
A catalogue record for this book is available from the British Library

Library of Congress Cataloging-in-Publication Data
Names: Abe, Kaori, author.
Title: Chinese middlemen in Hong Kong's colonial economy, 1830–1890 / Kaori Abe.
Description: Abingdon, Oxon ; New York, NY : Routledge, 2018. |
Series: Routledge studies in the modern history of Asia ; 127 |
Includes bibliographical references and index.
Identifiers: LCCN 2017014673| ISBN 9781138684409 (hardback) |
ISBN 9781315543949 (ebook)
Subjects: LCSH: Compradors—China—Hong Kong—History—19th century. | Hong Kong (China)—Commerce—History—19th century. | Hong Kong (China)—Economic conditions—19th century. | Hong Kong (China)—History—19th century.
Classification: LCC HF3852 .A24 2018 | DDC 381—dc23
LC record available at https://lccn.loc.gov/2017014673

ISBN: 978-1-138-68440-9 (hbk)
ISBN: 978-0-367-87807-8 (pbk)

Typeset in Times New Roman
by Florence Production Ltd, Stoodleigh, Devon, UK

For My Parents

Contents

Illustrations

Figures

Tables

Acknowledgement

This monograph is based on my PhD research on the history of Hong Kong, which was supported by many people in various organisations. First and foremost, my deepest thanks goes to my PhD supervisor, Robert Bickers of the University of Bristol, who has generously spent so much of his time providing encouragement, advice, and useful material for this research. Without his support, it would have been impossible to complete this project. I also would like to greatly thank John Mark Carroll of the University of Hong Kong for supporting my research while I visited Hong Kong. Many thanks also to Lars Laamann of the School of Oriental and African Studies (SOAS), University of London, and Kikuchi Hideaki of International Christian University, Tokyo, for encouraging me to take on this PhD project. Financially, the Mytton scholarship of the University of Bristol provided partial assistance for my research, and the Universities' China Committee in London (UCCL) provided a grant for a research trip to Hong Kong in March 2012.

My research has been furthered by many archivists and librarians in the United Kingdom, the United States, Japan and Hong Kong. Jardine, Matheson & Co. and the Hongkong and Shanghai Banking Corporation generously allowed me to use their historical materials. Archivists at SOAS helped me to access the materials of the John Swire & Sons collections. I sincerely appreciate support from staff in the Baker Library (Harvard Business School), the Tung Wah Hospital Archives, the Po Leung Kuk Museum, the Special Collections (University of Hong Kong), Hong Kong Public Record Office, the National Archives (London), the British Library and Toyo Bunko (Tokyo). I also would like to thank Andrew Hillier and Ip Kung Sau for sharing their family materials with me.

I am heavily indebted to my friends and colleagues who provide me with inspiration, encouragement and advice for this research. It is hard to mention everyone in this limited space. I would like to thank all the friends I met in Hong Kong, especially Tommy To, Kayi Fung, To Wai Nar and Yosuke Ishizuka, for continuously encouraging me to conduct research on the history of Hong Kong. Those who provided comments on my research in conferences, workshops, seminars and other occasions greatly helped develop my research. In this capacity, I would like to thank, Jonathan Saha, Henrietta Harrison, Christopher Munn, Elizabeth Sinn, Lee Pui Tak, Calvin Hoito Wong, Gary Luk Chi Hung, Koji Hirata, Chan Yang, Sabrina Fairchild, Jon Chappell, Jim Williams, Gordon Barrett, Sara

Shipway, Yuqun Gao, Helena Lopes, Kent Wan, Jonathan Howlett, Isabella Jackson, Sinae Hyun, Peidong Yang and Harry Yi-Jui Wu. For support in the translation of primary materials and for reading my draft, I am indebted to my friends and proofreaders, including Hsia-yang Liu, Yun-Hsin Chang, Yvonne Kong, Fion So, Sally Herd, Jack Liou, Li-Chao Chen, Michel West, Kang Yinchen and James Disley. My most heartfelt thanks go to Ho-wan To and all the members of my family, especially my parents who tirelessly support my long-term research.

Abbreviations

BPP	British Parliamentary Papers
CO	Colonial Office Records
DG	Year of Daoguang
FO	Foreign Office Records
GX	Year of Guangxu
HKPRO	The Hong Kong Public Record Office
HSBC	The Hongkong and Shanghai Banking Corporation
JMA	Jardine Matheson Archive
NCH	The North-China Herald
P&O	The Peninsular and Oriental Steam Navigation Company
SOAS	The School of Oriental and African Studies
TNA	The National Archives, London
TWM	The Tung Wah Museum
XHRB	Xunhuan Ribao (Universal Circulating Herald)
YPZZ	Zhongguo diyi lishi danganguan (First Historical Archives of China) (ed.), *Yapian zhanzheng dangan ziliao* (Archival materials of the Opium War), Vol. 1–7 (Shanghai: Shanghai renmin chuban she, 1987–1992).

Note on Romanisation

In most places, the Chinese names of places and people in Hong Kong have been transliterated from the Cantonese pronunciation according to common usage or in the way they appear in contemporary Western-language documents. The Romanisation of Chinese titles, names and places follows the standard Pinyin system in most cases. Japanese names are Romanised in accordance with the Hepburn system. The English translations of Chinese and Japanese titles of books and articles are provided in the bibliography. The glossary in the back of the book provides a list of traditional Chinese and Japanese characters of Romanised vocabularies, in alphabetical order.

Note on currencies

A wide variety of currencies was circulated in Canton and Hong Kong throughout the nineteenth century. In early nineteenth-century Canton, Spanish dollars were used for trade, as were other foreign coins including Mexican dollars, Chinese taels and British pounds. In Hong Kong, Silver Mexicans and Spanish dollars were commonly utilised for trade but a diverse range of other foreign and Chinese silver and copper coins was also in circulation. The colonial accounts and the salaries of the civil servants were managed in pounds sterling before the introduction of the Hong Kong silver dollar in 1862. In 1856, Morrison's *Commercial Guide*, a trade guidebook for foreign merchants in South China at that time, recorded that $1000 was approximately 718–720 taels.[1] In 1864, the colonial government converted 1 dollar to 4 shillings and 2 pence.[2] In Christopher Munn's estimation, in the average currency exchange rate from the 1840s and 1880s, 1 pound was about equal to 4.80 dollars or 3.33 taels.[3]

Notes

1 Williams, *Chinese Commercial Guide*, 291.
2 *Ordinances of Hongkong*, 289–290.
3 Munn, *Anglo-China*, xiv.

Introduction

The rise of the compradors in Hong Kong

'Compradors formed an important part of Hong Kong history. What were compradors?' In 1991, the *South China Morning Post*, an English newspaper in Hong Kong, asked this question to readers in its quiz section.[1] In the 1990s, before the handover of Hong Kong to China from Britain in 1997, historical memories of the compradors were fading, yet still existed in Hong Kong society. The compradors, *maiban* in Chinese, were Chinese intermediaries serving foreign institutions and individuals in nineteenth- and twentieth-century China. In Hong Kong, they had pivotal roles in the development of the Hong Kong economy. Through working in foreign firms and in the departments of the colonial government from the 1830s to the 1880s, the compradors facilitated an archetype of Hong Kong society, a system of intermediation that is still in place today. Examples of this are the continued presence of Sino-foreign joint ventures, the prosperity of family businesses, the participation of wealthy businessmen in public affairs, and their intricate relationship with the political authorities.

In the nineteenth century, it was common for Western merchants in Chinese ports to hire local intermediaries, called 'compradors', who could speak English and who would be able to support the Western merchants' commercial activities in China. This was necessary mainly because of the shortage of foreign personnel familiar who understood the local languages, customs and business conditions of the complex Chinese market.[2] For most Western traders and entrepreneurs, the diversity of currencies and dialects of China, and the local business practices were major impediments to doing business deals directly with their Chinese counterparts. The compradors filled the demand for economic middlemen.[3]

After the First Opium War and the conclusion of the Treaty of Nankjing in 1842, the crown colony of Hong Kong and five treaty ports – Shanghai, Foochow, Canton, Ningpo and Amoy – were opened to foreigners.[4] Thereafter, foreign merchants started to settle in Hong Kong and the treaty ports. In 1844, in the British settlement in Shanghai, there were 11 British and American firms. By 1854, this number had increased to more than 120.[5] In addition to European foreigners, Chinese natives such as Cantonese merchants (including the compradors) and littoral populations flocked to the newly established ports to take advantage of the business opportunities in there. It was estimated that around 250 major compradors were operating on the Chinese coast in 1854; by 1870 the number had risen to at least 350, in line with an increase in the number of foreign firms from 250 in 1854 to 550 in 1870.[6]

In particular, the compradors achieved remarkable success in late nineteenth-century Hong Kong. In the early 1870s, most foreign firms with a base in Hong Kong employed compradors. The *China Directory for the Year of 1874*, a trade guidebook for businessmen in Hong Kong, had a one-page list of the principal compradors. A principal comprador was usually the head of the Chinese staff in each company. This list included nearly 70 names of the principal compradors serving different foreign organisations. A principal comprador could have multiple duties. He could act as a cashier, banker, broker and supervisor of all the Chinese staff, as well as an information agent and business partner for the foreign firms.[7] According to the list, a great diversity of multi-national companies employed the compradors. Examples of them were Chartered Mercantile Bank of India, London and China (hereafter called as the Mercantile Bank), Comptori d'Escompte De Paris, Great Northern Telegraph Company, Hongkong Club, Lane Crawford & Co., and the Hongkong and Shanghai Banking Corporation.[8] A photo of the compradors (Figure I.1), estimated to be taken in the 1860 also indicates their economic success during that time. It is abundantly clear that the compradors formed an essential economic group in late nineteenth-century Hong Kong.

Figure I.1 Compradors in Hong Kong, 1860s
Courtesy of Wattis Fine Art

The career of Pedro Leung Hing Kee (alias Pang Ahim) symbolises the notable economic success of the compradors in nineteenth-century Hong Kong. Hing Kee was a commissariat comprador serving the British troops in Hong Kong and later became a well-to-do hotel owner in Hong Kong and Macau. In 1909, Warren W. Foster, an American judge for the City of New York, wrote his encounter with Hing Kee, then probably over 60 years old, on a ship travelling from Hong Kong to Canton (present-day Guangzhou). According to Foster's account, Hing Kee could speak French, Chinese, English and Portuguese. He started his career as a cabin boy on a French warship and later became a hotel owner in Macau. When Foster met Hing Kee, he already appeared to have sold his hotel in Macau to an English naval captain. Throughout the journey, Hing Kee and Foster talked about the issue of China – the opium smoking and child slavery. Foster later described Hing Kee as a 'guide, philosopher and friend' during his journey to Canton.[9]

By referring to the trading guidebooks and resources in company archives, it is possible to verify Foster's account and to know more about Hing Kee's hotel enterprises. In the 1870s and the 1880s, Hing Kee owned at least two hotels in Hong Kong, but seemed to move his business base to Macau in the 1890s. Hing Kee was one of the lessees of the Hongkong Hotel on 17 Queen's Road Central and of the Victoria Hotel on 51 Queen's Road and 22 Praya, in the 1870s and the 1880s respectively.[10] By 1893, Hing Kee also owned a hotel in Macau. The *Hong Kong Guide* of 1893 recorded that Hing Kee's hotel on the Praya Grande was one of the oldest in Macau.[11] Before 1907, he also became an owner of the Macao Hotel, on 65 Praya Grande. In 1903, Hing Kee relinquished his hotel business in Macau to William Farmer, a notable hotel owner and manager who had come to Hong Kong from Australia in the early 1890s.[12] Like Hing Kee, dozens of the compradors worked with the foreign houses, vigorously developing their own enterprises at the same time.

Earlier researchers on the colonial history of Hong Kong have generally regarded the compradors as a type of colonial elite cooperating with the British. Together with other Chinese elites, such as government servants, merchants, lawyers and doctors, the compradors were handling Chinese economic and public issues, maintaining the social order of the city.[13] As part of this role, the compradors mediated economic intercourse between foreign and Chinese businessmen and this underpinned the development of the Sino-foreign business culture in Hong Kong. They also used their accumulated wealth for charitable activities and to fund public associations.[14] For instance, the Hong Kong compradors had their own guild and sent representatives to the board of directors of the Tung Wah Hospital in the 1870s. The Tung Wah Hospital not only provided healthcare services to the Chinese public, but also functioned as a semi-official administrative ancillary of the colonial government for the purpose of the management of the Chinese community. The compradors provided $1,000 annually to the hospital from 1873 to 1896. Between 1869 and1871, the group of compradors had the largest number of representatives on the board, numbering five out of 13.[15] The compradors' notable contribution to the management of the Tung Wah Hospital suggests that they constituted a core group of Chinese intermediary elites in late nineteenth-century Hong Kong.

However, we still do not know how and why the compradors turned into indispensable intermediary elites in Hong Kong. What was the social and historical background of the first generation of compradors, who appeared in Hong Kong after the British occupation in 1841? How did the colonial government deal with them? What work did the compradors do in foreign firms with bases in Hong Kong? How did compradors evolve into entrepreneurs? And what was the overall impact of the formation of the group of compradors from the 1860s to the 1880s on the development of the political basis of Hong Kong society? This book aims to address these key questions throughout, exploring the individual lives of both well-known and lesser-known compradors. In doing so, an important aspect of economy and society of Hong Kong in its formative years will be highlighted.

Defining the compradors

To avoid conceptual confusion, in this monograph, 'comprador' simply means a Chinese middleman employed by a foreign organisation or individuals in nineteenth- and twentieth-century China. I also used the concept of the 'comprador system' in order to refer to an employment system in which Chinese staff were led by compradors in foreign organisations. It should be noted that the term 'comprador' does not include other social and economic intermediaries. This research particularly focuses on Chinese middlemen who worked in foreign companies under the designation of 'comprador' at least once in their careers, since the compradors in most cases also acted as merchants, investors and traders. These compradors' multifaceted economic and social activities are laid out in the successive chapters. However, in this monograph, the term 'comprador' does not include Chinese merchants, traders and 'shroffs' (currency examiners and exchangers), who did not work under the occupational title of 'comprador'. These other socio-economic middlemen are not the main consideration of this book. It is important to clarify and limit the definition of the comprador. This is mainly because the term has often been figuratively used both inside and outside academia, a practice which has become an impediment to our comprehension of the socio-economic reality of modern China.

The definition of the term comprador has been amorphous, multiple and flexible from the 1840s to the present. An anonymous Japanese researcher of the Shanghai Branch of the East Asia Research Institute (Tōa Kenkyūjo), an imperial Japanese research organisation, pointed out the fuzziness of the concept of 'comprador' in his report regarding economic influences of Shanghai compradors in the 1930s. The author of the report stated that 'comprador' is one of the unclear and opaque terms and concepts frequently used to explain the Chinese economy and society at that time. Despite the popularity of the terms and the concepts such as 'comprador' and 'national bourgeoisie', most researchers and intellectuals did not have a clear-cut definition of 'comprador'. He further stressed that scholars had a tendency to use the term in an incoherent manner, as both a noun and an adjective. This inconsistent use of the term entailed 'shallow interpretation' of the compradors' actual functions in Chinese economy between the nineteenth and twentieth centuries.[16]

The Japanese author of the report continued to state that the definition of the term varied over time, place and company.[17] Indeed, the meaning of the comprador kept changing over the course of time. The Chinese term, *maiban*, had existed in the Chinese vocabulary since the Ming dynasty (1368–1644). In Ming period, *maiban* was used as a verb referring to purchasing provisions for the government or local official institutions.[18] In the Ming period, the term was also a noun representing 'a group of official purveyors'. By the middle of the eighteenth century, the meaning of *maiban* included the licensed suppliers of provisions to the foreigners in China. In this period, for the translation of *maiban*, Europeans in Asia began to use the term comprador, which was originally a Portuguese word meaning 'purchaser'.[19] At the outset of the nineteenth century, a provision supplier to foreign visitors to Canton was called a comprador. During that period, Canton was the only officially open port for Western traders in China.[20] After the First Opium War between 1839 and 1841, the term came to mean a Chinese middleman serving a foreign official or private organisation. Meanwhile, Chinese provision suppliers were still called 'compradors' or 'ship compradors'.

More importantly, in the early twentieth century, Chinese nationalist and communist intellectuals formulated abstractive concepts of 'comprador'. The communists and nationalists' concepts of the 'comprador class' or 'comprador bourgeoisie' referred to Chinese collaborators serving foreign imperialists who hindered China's economic development.[21] The modern comprador system perhaps ended in Hong Kong in 1960 when the job title of the last comprador of the Hongkong and Shanghai Banking Corporation, Peter Lee, was updated to 'Chinese manager' from 'comprador'.[22] Nevertheless, in Hong Kong, 'comprador shops' continued to open and sell daily necessities, liquors and food in the 1960s and the 1970s.[23] By this token, the term 'comprador' included a great diversity of meanings.

Scholars of modern China have paid much attention to the compradors since the 1910s, for the purpose of analysing the causes of China's economic problems in late Qing China and the early Republican period (1912–1949). These preceding works shed light on the compradors' economic functions in Chinese economy. At the same time, these works also formulated concepts such as the 'comprador system', the 'comprador bourgeoisie' and the 'comprador class'. Pao Kuang Yung's article, 'The Comprador: His Position in the Foreign Trade of China', which appeared in the English *Economic Journal* in 1911, is the one of the earliest pieces of research on the compradors. This was translated into Chinese by Gan Zuolin in 1919.[24] Pao can be identified as a student at the University of Birmingham who wrote a dissertation titled 'The Public Accounts and Statistical Returns of English Railways' for his Master of Commerce degree in 1912. Before that, Pao had obtained a Bachelor of Commerce in 1911.[25] After completing his period of study in Britain and returning to China, Pao started working in Zhongfu Bank in 1925 in Tianjin, and later became a manager of branch covering Shanghai and Tianjin, and then a vice chairman of the bank.[26] According to Pao, who was part of the Chinese foreign-educated nationalist elite in the 1910s, the compradors, who had dealt with foreign trade since the period of the Canton System, became an obstacle to the development of free trade and direct intercourse with foreigners in the early twentieth century. In his view, were it not for the compradors, 'the natural growth of the Chinese nation' would have happened much faster.[27]

Pao's analysis of the compradors as impediments to China's economic growth was widely shared among Chinese and foreign intellectuals in early twentieth-century China. These intellectuals and researchers into Chinese society produced the number of writings discussing the 'comprador system' from 1920 onwards. Among them, Sha Weikai's book published in Shanghai in 1927 comprehensively explained what the 'comprador system' was to general readers.[28] It introduced the brief functions of different types of compradors working in banks, steamship companies and insurance companies. More importantly, in his book, Sha discussed the advantages and disadvantages of the comprador system for the Chinese nation in the ongoing 'Commercial War' (*shangzhan*), which had involved the expansion of national markets across Asia from the early nineteenth century. Sha's conclusion was that the problem of the comprador system overwhelmed the benefits. From Sha's viewpoint, the compradors' lack of enthusiasm for the anti-Japanese and anti-British boycotts reduced the effectiveness of these movements, and their domination of the market damaged the interests of small private merchants. In the last part of the book, it was predicted that with the increase in the number of Chinese learning English and with direct communication between foreign and Chinese merchants, the comprador system would eventually disappear.[29]

During the same period, Japanese scholars conducted an investigation into the 'comprador system' in order to help Japanese economic interests as they attempted to penetrate Chinese markets.[30] One well-crafted works on the comprador system which summed up the Japanese scholars' findings before the end of Sino-Japanese War was Negishi Tadashi's monograph *Baiben seido no kenkyū* (A Study on the Comprador System), published in 1948.[31] Using available Japanese sources in the first half of the twentieth century, Negishi delved into the comprador system at great length and suggested that compradors were in the vein of Chinese traditional hawkers – '*yahang* (licensed brokers)' – who had been the officially permitted middlemen and commission agents for foreign trade since the Ming period. They even served Chinese merchants from different regions. In one case, Hubei merchants conducted their trade through the licensed brokers in Canton in a manner that was similar that of the foreign merchants in Canton until the end of the First Opium War.[32] The system of licensed brokers was applied to dealings with European foreign merchants in Canton and, after the Opium War, the fundamental functions of *yahang* were taken over by the compradors.

Another group of intellectuals focusing on the compradors in the 1920s was the communist activists who were keen to discuss the issue of the 'comprador class'. After the May Thirtieth Incident of 1926, Qu Qiubai, a leader of the communist party and Chen Duxiu, a political activist and founder of the magazine *Xin Qingnian* (New Youth), produced articles explaining the different degree of patriotism and political attitudes of the Shanghai merchant communities by using the categories 'national bourgeoisie' and 'comprador bourgeoisie'.[33] In like manner, in March 1926, Mao Zedong, who was a young founding member of the

Communist Party of China, described the class of compradors as supporters of the imperialists as well as of the warlords, bureaucrats and landlords.[34] It was perceived that the leading figures of the Shanghai Chamber of Commerce were less aggressive towards nationalist movements than were the self-employed merchants of associations with native ties. According to Chen and Qu, compradors needed to defend their economic profits from businesses with foreigners and, therefore, they were more conciliatory towards political activities which pursued the national interest.[35] This kind of discourse on the 'comprador class' was further strengthened after the establishment of the People's Republic of China (PRC) in 1949.

In September 1956, Mao Zedong, the chairman of the Communist Party, gave a speech known as '*Women dang de yixie lishi jingyan*' (Some Historical Experiences of Our Party), at a meeting with representatives of Latin American Communist parties, and in this speech the compradors were referred as 'the running dogs of the western imperialists'.[36] Furthermore, between 1957 and 1964 in Chinese academia, there came to be imagined a framework delineating a 'comprador class'.[37] Huang Yifeng and Wang Jingyu's works were representative of these academic analyses emphasising the issue of the 'comprador class'. They described the compradors as a newly emerged class which benefited from their employment relationship with foreigners.[38] Thereafter, until the 1980s, the Chinese notion of the comprador and 'comprador class' had negative political connotations.

These nationalists and communist ideas of 'the comprador system', 'comprador bourgeoisie' and 'comprador class' were mainly directed at well-to-do Chinese merchants who had moderate and ambiguous attitudes towards the anti-imperialist movements.[39] These categories of 'comprador' and 'national bourgeoisies' did, however, by no means capture the complexity of the treaty port societies and the lives of individual compradors in the Republican period. Nonetheless, this reductive discourse, portraying the compradors as a class of the bourgeoisie who were conciliatory to the foreign imperialists, became dominant in China.

Academic historians in the United States began a revaluation on the compradors between the 1970s and the 1980s.[40] Influenced by John King Fairbank's works on Sino-Western economic, political and cultural intercourse in the nineteenth century, Hao Yen-ping produced *The Comprador in Nineteenth Century China,* a comprehensive monograph on the comprador system published in 1970. This book established the foundation on which further research would be based. By using trade reports, English and Chinese newspapers, and the writings of Chinese intellectuals, Hao illustrated a wide variety of the functions fulfilled by the compradors, from supervising the Chinese house stewards in foreign firms to managing modern Western-style enterprises themselves. In addition to their economic functions, Hao shed light on the lifestyles of the compradors, which involved a mixture of Western and Chinese cultures, including playing political roles such as managing the associations with native ties and finding funding for charitable activities. Many were engaged in intellectual activities; an example is Zheng Guanying's work on the reformation of China in response to the increasing foreign influence. In his monograph, Hao argues that the comprador was a 'bridge between the East and the West', a figure whose absorption of Western ideas and technologies was by no means bounded by Chinese traditional values.[41] Hao's analysis on the compradors – key players in the development of Sino-foreign commerce in China – entailed the production of more research on the compradors' economic and non-economic activities from less-biased viewpoints.

Recent scholars have also assessed the problems with the comprador system without relying on concepts like 'comprador bourgeoisie' and 'comprador class'. In one case, Motono Eiichi shows how the rise of English-speaking Chinese intermediaries, including the compradors, dismantled the traditional economic order of China. By reviewing many court cases between compradors and foreign companies like Jardine, Matheson & Co. from the 1880s to the 1910s, he discusses the compradors' abusive usages of their privileges to conduct trade in the treaty ports under British laws. For example, by registering companies in Hong Kong, these Chinese merchants were able to avoid paying the *lijin*, the tax to the Qing officials, and this systematic tax evasion possibly damaged the fiscal base of the Qing Dynasty.[42] Motono overall highlighted the disadvantages of the comprador system. In like manner, Jerry L. S. Wang also estimated that trade in China was less profitable for British merchants than it should have been, precisely because they had to employ compradors.[43]

Researchers have paid less attention to the compradors in twentieth-century China, while there have been an extensive number of works on the compradors in the Chinese treaty ports in the nineteenth century. A few scholars have explored the history of the twentieth-century compradors, and they have usually emphasised the transitions in the comprador system for the purpose of addressing the question of how the compradors declined and disappeared in the twentieth century. Chan Kai Yiu, in particular, examined the causes behind this fall in the course of analysing the Kailan Mining Administration's policies on the employment of Chinese middlemen, as well as by examining comprador contractual documents.[44] Other scholars have also investigated the process of the abolition of the comprador systems in different companies. Yamafuji Ryutaro investigated the abolition of the comprador system by Mitsui Bussan, a Japanese trading firm, while Howard Cox, Huang Biao and Stuart Metcalfe examined the case of Butterfield & Swire.[45] Overall, this research on the twentieth-century compradors suggests each foreign company had varied and different approaches towards the reformation of the comprador systems throughout the twentieth century.

From the beginning of the twentieth century, scholars have struggled to answer a simple question: who were the compradors in modern China? One of the main impediments to addressing this question is the flexibility and multiplicity of the definitions of 'comprador'. Arthur Waldron stresses how the concept of *junfa* (warlord) was produced to fit an interpretation of violence, or, to put it more directly, 'imperialism' and 'militarism' in the twentieth century.[46] In a similar manner, the concept of 'comprador' came to be one type of notions shared widely among intellectuals and scholars for the interpretation of China's economic and social reality. However, these figurative concepts of 'comprador' oversimplify the causes of the rise and fall of Chinese intermediaries cooperating with foreigners during the late nineteenth and the first half of the twentieth century. As such, rather than producing a clear-cut, single definition of the comprador, my research attempts to shed light on the uniqueness and the commonality of the comprador system in Hong Kong in order to stress the diversity of the compradors in modern China. For that purpose, this research also draws on theories of the history of the British Empire, coupled with the concept of the 'comprador system' used in modern Chinese historiography.

Intermediaries in the British Empire

To study the local middlemen in Hong Kong, it might be pertinent to draw on theories used in the historiography of the British Empire. Scholars of the British imperial history have long discussed the issue of 'collaborators' and 'indigenous elites'. Ronald Robinson highlighted the significance of the 'indigenous collaborator' who streamlined the expansion of European imperialism in Africa, Asia and Oceania.[47] According to Robinson, rather than expanding the actual territories of their empires, imperial policymakers put more emphasis on the informal expansion of economic, diplomatic and militaristic influential areas of empires. This is known as the concept of an 'informal empire'.[48] Local intermediaries participated in the management of these informal territories of the empires, coupled with the imperial settlers and administrators. The local intermediaries took new areas of processional opportunities created by the colonists or imperialists in order to raise or maintain their social status and economic profits.[49] After they improved their social position in indigenous society and increased their influence on colonial politics, they could also become an obstacle to the mass mobilisation of the native populace opposing colonial rule because they always aimed to protect their interests. However, Robinson stresses, connecting the activities of the nationalistic and collaborative elites to the project of European imperialism were a necessary condition for decolonisation.[50]

In one case, in Anglo-Egyptian Sudan, from the late nineteenth to the early twentieth century, anti-Mahdist 'Notables', including Khatmia Muslim, orthodox Muslim ulama and anti-Mahdist Sheikhs, and local elites, were employed for the effective administration of the colony and to prevent a mass uprising of the Mahdists. These mediators accumulated wealth and improved their position in society through collaboration with European settlers; many of them had an English education and some of them had received a higher education in the metropole From the 1930s to the 1950s, after years of division between the neo-Mahdists and the Khatmia, who were in the colonial administration in several levels, in 1956 both factions eventually agreed to work for the independence of the country.[51] The case of Sudan has many similarities with China. This can clearly be seen in the activities of the compradors, who had an English-language education, attempted to improve their social positions, and participated in the administration of the colony and the treaty ports.

Following Robinson's argument over the local collaborators, in 1986, Jürgen Osterhammel suggested that, in terms of the coastal areas of China after 1842, these 'indigenous collaborations' could be exemplified by the comprador system, which consisted of the comprador merchants, other institutions (such as Chinese-style companies built on foreign capital and native banks cooperating with foreign banks), and Chinese workers providing a variety of services to foreigners in relation to the rule of the colony and the administration of the foreign settlements.[52] Robinson and Osterhammel's arguments mainly focused on the economic functions of the middlemen; however, their approach can be used to analyse the intermediaries' social and cultural roles and their involvement in local and national politics. In effect, this research utilises the concept of the local mediators in the historiography of the British Empire in order to elucidate the process of the emergence of the compradors and their roles in the formulation of Sino-foreign business culture in Hong Kong.

Themes of the book

This book has five main themes: 1) compradors before the end of the First Opium War; 2) compradors in the administrative institutions in the colonial government; 3) compradors in foreign firms; 4) compradors' entrepreneurship and 5) the compradors' social and political activities. In addition to the five main chapters addressing these themes, a conclusive chapter provides an overarching argument for this research, a perspective analysis of the uniqueness and universality of compradors in Hong Kong, and discusses the legacies of the compradors in Hong Kong today. The main five chapters chronologically trace the rise of the Hong Kong compradors. These begin with the description of the dismantling of the old comprador system in Canton in the 1830s and end with the consolidation of the new comprador system in Hong Kong in the 1880s.

The first chapter describes the general functions of the compradors under the Canton System before and during the First Opium War. This is for the contextualisation of the first generation of compradors in Hong Kong, some of whom began work in Canton and moved to Hong Kong after 1841. Under the Canton System, the main function of the compradors was supplying foreign visitors to Canton with provisions. The provision suppliers had to obtain a license from the local Qing officials to work as compradors.[53] The main focus of this chapter is the licensed comprador system and its dissolution. Using the records of American and British merchants and officials preserved in the state-level archives and the published memoirs of the foreign visitors to Canton and Macau, this chapter overall illustrates the process of the privatisation of the licensed comprador system.

It should be noted that the term 'privatisation' is used to refer to the deregulation of the comprador system in the Qing state. As a result of this, private individuals were able to style themselves as compradors without obtaining an official licence issued by the Qing government. This was because the state licensing system for the employment of the compradors was dismantled between the 1830s and the end of the First Opium War. However, this did not mean the disappearance of the compradors working for the state, since there were a certain number of compradors working for the colonial government in addition to foreign private firms during the 1840s and the 1850s. Hence, in this research, the privatisation of the comprador system simply means the abolition of the official licensing system of the compradors and the opening up of job opportunities allowing private individual actors to work as compradors.

The second chapter focuses on the early compradors who served government institutions and colonial officials. It also portrays the expansion and reduction of their functions from the 1840s through the 1850s. When establishing the colony, many Chinese compradors were employed in government institutions such as the Treasury, Commissariat, Post Office and Police Office. This in turn provides information on the variety of functions of the government compradors in different institutions. Consulting the official reports of the colonial government held in the National Archives in London, and reports of the court cases related to the government compradors that appeared in Hong Kong newspapers, the second chapter delves into the duties of the government compradors and their involvement in the corruption of the colonial government, as well as examining possible factors causing the decline of the government compradors by 1860.

The third chapter discusses the emergence of the company compradors and their dual functions in foreign firms as internal intermediaries and external business partners. From the late 1860s on, the rise of Chinese comprador merchants came to be clear in Hong Kong. Most foreign companies and organisations employed compradors during that period, including Swire; Jardine; the Hongkong and Shanghai Banking Corporation; Lane, Crawford & Co.; and smaller foreign organisations and clubs.[54] Thus, by examining the business correspondence and records kept in the company archives, in particular the Jardine Matheson Archive in Cambridge (UK) and the Heard Collection in Baker Library in Boston (USA), this chapter addresses the questions of how compradors came to have jurisdiction over Chinese matters, and how they increased their importance in these companies.

The fourth chapter throws lights on the compradors' roles as independent merchants and entrepreneurs, and their conducting of Sino-foreign business, from the 1860s to the 1880s. By acquiring information on Chinese and foreign markets through their work for foreign employers, compradors became involved in many industries, including steam-shipping and the sugar refining business. Many also managed pawn shops and real estate. The diversification and internationalisation of compradors' economic activities is the main subject under consideration in this chapter. In this part, I also underline compradors' competitive and collaborative relationships with foreign merchants. The trade reports listed above, as well as the business correspondence in Jardine's archives, trader guidebooks, commercial reports and newspapers, are compiled and analysed to clarify the compradors' relationship with their foreign employers.

The main theme of the fifth chapter is the compradors' non-economic activities from the 1860s to the 1880s. Coordinating the interests of the Chinese community, the Qing and the British colonial government, the compradors were integrated into the class of Chinese elites in Hong Kong in this period. To shed light on the compradors' public activities, I draw on the minutes of meetings and annual reports of public institutions held in the museum of Tung Wah Group of Hospitals and the museum of Po Leung Kuk (The Society for the Protection of Women and Children).[55] This chapter also discusses the marginal position of the compradors between the Qing and the British governments, as well as the compradors' struggle to stabilise their social positions.

The five chapters together stress the compradors' contribution to the establishment of Hong Kong as a trade and financial centre in Asia and a politically semi-autonomous entity. The historical context of the attributes of contemporary Hong Kong society can be traced by exploring the activities of compradors, who were also part of the group of early settlers. Compradors served the colonial government and British firms, managed their own enterprises and participated in the administration of Hong Kong. Studying the compradors is methodologically challenging. The quantity of records written by the compradors themselves is limited. Contemporary records on the compradors were scattered and partial, yet it is possible to piece together their lives by utilising Chinese, English and Japanese sources held in company and national archives, coupled with printed sources such as newspapers, diaries and trade reports. In doing so, I attempt to reconstruct the history of early colonial Hong Kong from the viewpoint of the compradors.

Notes

1 SCMP, 6 January 1991.
2 Carroll, *Edge of Empires*, 33.
3 Hao, *Comprador*, 1–2.
4 Bickers, *Scramble for China*, 84–85.
5 Hu, 'Xiangshan maiban', 42.
6 Jardine, Matheson & Co., Jardines and Ewo., 48; *Chronicle and Directory for China, Japan and Philippines (1870)*, 221 cited in Hao, *Comprador*, 102.
7 Hao, *Comprador*, 64–65; Smith, *Chinese Christians*, 155–156; 'Comprador Question', *China Mail*, 19 June 1871, 3; *Daily Press*, 8 March 1867.
8 *China Directory* 1874, 47; See Table 3.1; The Mercantile Bank had different names throughout the nineteenth century. In 1853, it was known as the Mercantile Bank of Bombay as well as the Mercantile Bank of India, London and China. In 1858, it was called the Chartered Mercantile Bank of India, London and China. Then in 1893, it was known as the Mercantile Bank of India.
9 Foster, 'Things Chinese', 121–122.
10 JMA: C37/7, Letters re Hongkong Fire Insurance Co. Ltd, General Manager to Dorabjee & Hing Kee (Victoria Hotel), 12 March 1886, 311; *China Mail*, 5 June 1879, 3. *China Directory* 1874, 44; *Chronicle and Directory for China, Corea, Japan* 1889, 324.
11 Shepherd, *Hong Kong Guide 1893*, 132.
12 England, *Quest of Noel Croucher*, 26–27.
13 Smith, *Chinese Christians*, 120–127; Hui, 'Comprador Politics', 30–45; Tsang, *Modern History*, 58.
14 Carroll, *Edge of Empires*, 33–35.
15 Sinn, *Power and Charity*, 54, 74; TWM: *Zhengxinlu* 1933.
16 Toyo Bunko: Tōa Kenkyūjo Shanhai Shisho, *Shanghai ni okeru baiben.*
17 Ibid.
18 Iwai, *Chūgoku kinsei zaiseishi*, cited in Motono 'Baiben', 227.
19 Hao, *Comprador*, 45.

20 Hunter, *'Fan Kwae'*, 28–30.
21 Zhang, 'Jindai maiban', 111. Qu, 'Shanghai maibanjieji'.
22 Hao, *Comprador*, 59–63; Hongkong Shanghai Banking Corporation, Comprador File, HSBCS 0019/0001, HSBC Archives, London.
23 SCMP, 1 May 1971, advertisement; SCMP, 21 April 1960, advertisement.
24 Xie, 'Maiban yanjiu', 391–412; Bao, 'Lun yanghang maiban'.
25 *Birmingham University Calendar, 1911–1912*, 644; *Birmingham University Calendar, 1912–1913*, 733.
26 Pao, 'Shouzhou sunjia', 127, 132.
27 Pao, 'Comprador', 637.
28 Sha, *Zhongguo maibanzhi.*
29 Ibid., 1–2, 42–44.
30 Xie, 'maiban yanjiu'.
31 Negishi, *Baiben seido.*
32 Hao, *Comprador*, 2.
33 Zhang, 'Jindai maiban', 111. van de Ven, 'Emergence of Text Centered Party', 21–23; Qu, 'Shanghai maiban jieji'.
34 Mao, 'Analysis of Classes', 13–22.
35 Yeh, *Alienated Academy*, 80; Clifford, *Shanghai*, 20, 29–30, 53–55.
36 Mao, Kau, and Leung, eds, *Writings of Mao*, Vol. 2, 136.
37 Zhang, 'Jindai maiban', 111.
38 Ibid., 111; Wang, *Tangtingshu yanjiu.*

Huang Yifeng was one of the top-officials in the East China Regional-Administration in Shanghai but he was once expelled from the party due to his involvement into the suppression of a student's criticism of him in 1953 in the campaign against 'bureaucratism'. Walker, *China Under Communism*, 81.
39 Yeh, *Alienated Academy*, 80–81.
40 Fairbank, *Trade and Diplomacy*; Liu, *Anglo-American Steamship*; Cohen, *Discovering History*, 9–12.
41 Hao, *Comprador*, 201–206, 223.
42 Motono, *Dentō Chūgoku.*
43 Motono, 'Study of Legal Status'; Wang, 'Profitability of Anglo-Chinese Trade', 39–65.
44 Hao, *Comprador*, 61–63; Chan, 'Turning Point', 52–53; Chan, 'Jindai zhongguo maiban', 347–358.
45 Yamafuji, 'Mitsui Bussan' (2009); Cox, Biao and Metcalfe, 'Compradors, Firm Architecture', 15–34.
46 Arthur, 'The Warlord'.
47 Robinson, 'Non-European Foundations', 118–119.
48 Ibid., 117–140.
49 Ibid., 120–121.
50 Ibid., 121–122, 137, 139.
51 Ibid., 135–137.
52 Osterhammel, 'Semi-Colonialism', 305–306.
53 Van Dyke, *Canton Trade*, 51.
54 Bickers, *Britain in China*, 173. *China Directory 1874*, 47.
55 Sinn, 'Materials for Historical Research', 195–223.

1 The licensed compradors in Canton

Hong Kong's comprador system had been incubated in Canton in the 1830s. The licensed compradors and provision purveyors operating in the Pearl River Delta were the predecessors of the compradors that appeared in Hong Kong after the British occupation in 1841. During that period, all compradors were required to obtain a license from Qing officials to transact business with foreign merchants in Canton. Licensed compradors were generally divided into two types: ship compradors (*chuan maiban*) and house compradors (*yiguan maiban*). Within the framework of the Canton System, the licensed compradors' principal functions were providing provisions and assisting in the commercial activities of foreign traders. The local Qing officials were responsible for regulating and defining the works of the compradors.

Nevertheless, there was a rapid growth of unlicensed provision suppliers to the foreigners during the 1830s.[1] The licensed comprador system started dissolving in this period when markets formed for smuggling opium and other illegal articles in the Pearl River Delta.[2] The formation of smuggling markets outside Canton also created new areas of commercial opportunities for the local Chinese populace. In this vein, the great number of littoral populations participated in the business of selling provisions to the British during the First Opium War.[3] After the end of the war, the oligopoly of the licensed compradors came to an end, and the foreigners were able to employ any local provision suppliers who were willing to work with them as compradors. The comprador system was gradually privatised before and during the First Opium War.

The Canton trade

Different types of compradors already existed in the Pearl River Delta, especially in Canton in the 1830s, before the establishment of Hong Kong and the emergence of the comprador merchants in the late nineteenth century. Canton, a city located on the southern coastline of China, had flourished as a centre of trade since the Qing government proclaimed in 1759 that it would be the only port officially open to foreign trade in China.[4] This system of trade, known as the Canton or Cohong (*gonghang*) System, prospered until the First Opium War ended it. Canton had the third largest population, following Beijing and Hangzhou, in the sixteenth and seventeenth century, and the estimated population of the city in the early nineteenth century was about one million.[5] Under this system, only local Chinese people who were officially licensed by the Qing authorities were allowed to conduct trade with foreigners. The licensed compradors were one category of local workers who were allowed to engage in business with the foreign traders. Chinese workers licensed for foreign business were divided into four types: hong merchants (*hangshang*), also called security merchants (*baoshang*); linguists (*tongshi*); compradors and river pilots (*yinshuiren*). These four kinds of intermediaries were responsible for delivering the Qing's officials' messages, orders and instructions to the foreigners in Canton.[6]

The hong merchants were the main Chinese traders, and the Cohong was the association of the officially licensed hong merchants. Therefore, Canton's trade system was also described as the Cohong System. The linguists mainly acted as translators and interpreters between Chinese authorities and foreigners, and were further responsible for the account keeping of import and export duties for foreign vessels. The general functions of the compradors were providing provisions and bookkeeping for foreign residents. The river pilots were navigators for foreign ships travelling through the complicated Pearl River near Canton.[7]

In addition, hoppo (*hubu*), a revenue commissioner, played a key role 'to channel a portion of earnings of the port of Canton to the imperial Treasury'.[8] The hoppo was the responsible authority for foreign trade in Canton and supervised the four groups of Chinese officials. The hong merchants were responsible for the duties of the linguists to the Qing officials in Canton. In a similar manner, the linguists were responsible for the compradors' duties, and the compradors were responsible for their servants' duties.[9] By fragmenting the functions of the intermediaries and introducing supervisory responsibilities, the Qing government efficiently regulated the mediators' activities. If only one kind of intermediary had existed, it would have been able to abuse its authority and manipulate business between foreign and Chinese merchants.

The licensed intermediaries' other main function was the supervision of the foreign traders. In 1830, in his report to the Emperor, Li Hongbin, the Viceroy of Liangguang (Liangguang meant Guangdong and Guangxi provinces) outlined the duties of the hong merchants, linguists and compradors to conduct an immediate investigation of foreigners' involvement in the contraband and opium trade once it was discovered.[10] If foreigners broke the Qing's regulations, because of the failure of supervision, the Qing officials punished the compradors, hong merchants and linguists. In the 1830s, the compradors were accused several times because of their failure to prevent foreigners from bringing foreign women to Canton. John C. Whiteman, head of Whiteman & Co., arrived in Canton in 1830, and brought his wife to the city. The Qing government had prohibited the bringing of foreign women to Canton and ordered Whiteman to send her away from the city immediately. Although Whiteman was not punished, a security merchant, a linguist and compradors were arrested because they had not prevented Whiteman's action.[11] When a commander of a Danish vessel, Kierulf, brought his wife to Canton for a week in the spring of 1831, the Qing officials again warned the security merchants, linguists and compradors that they would be punished if a foreigner brought in a foreign woman again.[12] The punishment was severe, although sometimes the licensed intermediaries were pardoned. In May 1831, another hong merchant, a linguist and a comprador were charged with allowing a foreign woman into Canton. The punishment was beating by bamboo or wooden sticks, but this was commuted to a payment of silver to the Qing government and an assurance that they would not allow a foreigner to bring in a foreign woman again.[13]

For foreigners, the licensed intermediaries were cooperative ancillaries dealing with Chinese matters of business. At the same time, they were watchmen. By giving supervisory responsibilities to the licensed intermediaries, the Qing government attempted to prevent the intermediaries from establishing an excessive symbiotic relationship with foreigners. In that sense, the Canton System was designed to regulate both foreign traders and commercial intermediaries. Thus, during the Canton System, the compradors remained as only one type of officially approved intermediary and were not as influential as the nineteenth-century compradors in the world of the treaty ports.

The licensed compradors

Despite the regulation and the system designed to prevent licensed intermediaries' collusion with foreign traders, the compradors gradually expanded their areas of responsibility and established a close relationship with the foreigners in Canton, Macau and other commercial centres in the Pearl River Delta by 1830. As mentioned, the licensed compradors were divided into two groups: ship compradors, involved in the supply of provisions for foreign ships; and house compradors, also known as factory compradors, who stayed in foreign houses, took care of foreigners and supervised the factory accounts. The ship compradors were hired when a foreign ship arrived in Macau or around Panyu. The responsible person on the foreign ship was required to select a licensed ship comprador, and this ship comprador provided provisions to the ship thereafter. The Qing officials selected the ship compradors from local well-to-do figures who had a recommendation letter from the head of the family clan.[14]

Starting in 1831, the office of hoppo licensed ship compradors, and foreigners could recognise the compradors by the wooden licences they wore. Then the selected ship comprador accompanied the ship and provided provisions until it reached Whampoa (*Huangpu*), the main anchorage area in Canton for foreign ships.[15] The ship compradors provided a diverse range of commodities to foreign ships. In one case, a comprador, surnamed Fo, provided provisions including tea oil, beer, soda powder and pickled beef to Zhan Guchuan, who was likely a Chinese employee of Jardine, Matheson & Co in Whampoa around the 1830s.[16]

The ship compradors' work was usually supported by family members and sampans, as these were needed to handle the large amount of provisions required for the crew of a ship.[17] In general, the ship compradors charged engagement fees to each ship of between 50 and 200 Spanish dollars during the latter half of the 1830s.[18] Because the total cost to a foreign merchant, including cumshaw (a gift of money), pilotage, linguists and the comprador's fee, was between 2,300 and 2,500 Spanish dollars in the early 1830s, the fee for the ship compradors was not necessarily high for foreign traders.[19] Primarily, the ship compradors were provision purveyors, but they also dealt with problems that arose on the foreign ships, such as the burial of foreign sailors.[20]

Linguists and hong merchants also supported foreign traders in making business deals with ship compradors. In 1831, Howqua, a hong merchant conducting trade with the British East India Company (EIC), settled the issue of ship provisions from compradors for the Select Committee of the EIC.[21] Linguists dealt both with foreign ship owners and the ship compradors' payment of port charges at Whampoa. In 1831, four linguists required that managers of Jardine pay the debt incurred from their payment of port charges to the governor. The linguists had funded this debt on behalf of the ship compradors and the ship owners, and therefore required the payment of the total debt, which amounted to 14,397.5 dollars.[22] Linguists and hong merchants occasionally arranged ship compradors' service for the foreign traders. The four types of intermediaries were this way assisted the foreigners' works and daily lives in Canton an extensive manner.

A representative of the ship compradors was Boston Jack (also known as Bohsan Jak) who was well known among foreigners in Whampoa during the 1830s and 1840s.[23] According to William C. Hunter, an American merchant, 80 per cent of American vessels employed him in Whampoa. His account of visiting Boston in America made him popular. Hunter wrote:

> He had once made a passage to Boston as steward, and returned to Whampoa, via Cape Horn and the north-west coast of America, in a small schooner of about 200 tons called the 'Cossack,' on board of which was Mr Oliver H. Gordon as supercargo. 'Boston Jack' was very fond of relating his experiences on board of the 'Cossack,' particularly off the Horn, where, as he would say, 'too muchee strong gale; sea all same high masthead – no can see sky, no can see water,' meaning that in the turmoil of the elements one could see nothing.[24]

It was believed that an American colonel, Thomas Handasyd Perkins, invited Jack to visit Boston. Residing in Perkins' house, Jack received some education and converted to Christianity there.[25] This Jack's adventurous experience made him famous in the Chinese community as he was respectfully called a 'great gun'.[26] Although Boston Jack's case was exceptional, it suggests that some of the ship compradors established close ties with foreigners visiting Canton. It also signifies that the Qing officials' inability to properly regulate the collaboration of ship compradors with foreign merchants. Most Chinese were not permitted to go abroad during this period, but Boston Jack clearly did so without being punished.[27]

The house compradors also established close relationships with foreigners as they served foreign traders in factory houses in Canton and lived there on a long-term basis. House compradors had a variety of duties. In the main, a house comprador provided provisions, dealt with the accounting and treasury of the foreign house, and hired Chinese domestic staff.[28] The house comprador and his assistants checked financial transactions with the Chinese merchants and traders outside and inside the house. They kept the house's accounts and the private accounts of members of the house. The amount of the money dealt with by the house comprador was generally more than a million dollars, and was 'rarely under $50,000 to $200,000'.[29] During the trading off-season, from April to October, the house comprador kept the principal books of accounts and the letter books of business correspondence. Hunter states that the comprador's responsibility was huge, and that the compradors themselves were mostly reliable.

Given their responsibilities, the salary of a comprador was relatively small. In general, the annual salary was between $250 and $300. The salary of Hunter's comprador was $500 annually. However, it was possible for compradors to make extra money by examining the quality of coins and commissions from business transactions.[30] The house compradors dealt with the bulk of the transactions between foreign traders and the hong merchants. In 1822, a house comprador was the intermediary in the payment of over 61,000 dollars for broadcloth from a British trader to a hong merchant.[31] In 1828, foreign and Chinese traders also made payments of over 10,000 dollars through the intermediation of their house comprador.[32] By the end of the 1830s, the multiple duties of the house compradors went well beyond purveying provisions, and included the brokering of financial transactions between foreign and Chinese merchants.

The regulations on the compradors produced by the British India Company describe the duties of the house compradors. The 'Compradore Code' written on 18 February 1828 states:

1 On the 1st of each month, the comprador should deliver the money of that month to the dealer. The date should be recorded in Western years.
2 Compradors are not allowed to alter or repair houses in the provincial capital (Canton) and Macau belonging to the company without a handwritten letter of permission.
3 If compradors want to alter or repair the house, they have to make a contract before doing so.
4 The fee for the ships (fast boat) cannot be registered in the company account if there is not a handwritten invoice from the dealer (the one who orders the fast boat) and without the money.
5 Compradors should sort income separately and deliver the amount as asked, registering the amounts according to how the money has been used.

In this way, the EIC's compradors were responsible for the foreign houses' business transactions and accounting, as well as for making contracts with local ships. The 'Compradore Code' also listed three major categories of expenditure which the compradors were supposed to record: 'Charges on Merchandise (*maoyi shiwu shifei*)', 'Charges Extraordinary (*wuchang shifei*)', and 'Canton Factory Expenses (*shengcheng hangnei shiyongfei*)'. It further listed the detailed categories of expenses, including the hiring of Chinese staff, sailors and ships, and the purchasing of daily necessities, provisions and office stationery.[33] The comprador to the EIC supported the company's diverse range of business activities during the late 1820s. Between 1832 and 1833, a comprador to the EIC continued to deal with the company's general expenses and to mediate business transactions between the company and the hong merchants.[34]

Throughout the 1830s, several other house compradors supported the commercial activities of foreign companies in Canton by dealing with the Chinese side of business, and they maintained a symbiotic relationship with their principals. Ayou, who served the American Company Russell & Co. (*Qichang yanghang*), calculated credits and debits, recorded the expenses of Russell, staff, and business partners, and purchased necessary articles in 1831 and 1832.[35] Thomas Fox, a director of the Dutch company Fox, Rawson & Co., states that their house comprador Amow (Yamao), who was an honest person, worked for 4 years at his company.[36] The house compradors served their principals for more than a year, and they were responsible for the management of each foreign company house. Therefore, it was difficult for foreign traders to conduct trade and manage their lives without house compradors. By 1830, the house compradors had become indispensable business assistants for foreign traders in Canton.

In the early 1830s, the ship compradors working in Canton acted as provision purveyors, while the house compradors were already acting as commercial intermediaries between foreign and Chinese merchants. Many of them established cooperative relationships with foreign traders, as can be seen in the case of the ship comprador Boston Jack and house compradors who served foreign companies long term. During that period, various actors, including hong merchants, linguists, Qing officials and foreign principals, supervised the compradors' work, and they were also crucial commercial intermediaries for foreign traders. Therefore, under the Canton System, despite the importance of the licensed compradors, they were not the predominant commercial intermediaries. The basic functions of the licensed compradors in Canton were inherited by the ship compradors and company compradors that appeared in treaty ports and in Hong Kong after 1842. In Hong Kong, the ship compradors acted as provision purveyors and the company compradors acted as commercial intermediaries throughout the nineteenth century. The key functions of the Hong Kong compradors were formulated during the Canton trade period.

It should be noted that licensed compradors and other local Chinese traders were also operating in other areas of the South China Coast, in Macau in particular. Macau is a small peninsula located on the shore of the South China Sea, and is about 37 miles directly west of Hong Kong. Macau had been a Portuguese settlement since 1557, when the Qing government offered the peninsula as a reward for Portuguese support in the suppression of pirates. As described above, in addition to Whampoa, Macau was a place where licensed ship compradors and pilots were employed when a foreign ship arrived on its way to Canton.[37]

Furthermore, although only Portuguese were allowed to conduct trade in Macau, it was possible for other foreigners to be involved in trade there. For instance, Jardine's Portuguese agent B. Barretto operated in Macau for the company for a long time.[38] Jardine's other British staff needed to stay in Macau frequently throughout the 1820s and the 1830s, as they were not allowed to stay in Canton during the off-season.[39] These foreign merchants in Macau employed compradors, as they did in Canton. Bailing, the Viceroy of Lianggaugn from 1809 to 1811, noted that the Chinese government of Macau (*aomen tongzhi*) had previously issued a license to the compradors but recently the responsibility had been transferred to the Governor of Canton Customs (*yuehaiguandu*). Bailing also claimed that the compradors in Macau were engaged in the smuggling trade because the Governor of Canton Customs was based in Canton, far distant from Macau, and had difficulty supervising their activities.[40] In 1829, Harriet Low, an American visitor to Macau whose uncle's family conducted trade in China, wrote about her encounter with a comprador called Apew, who she described as a young and smart person speaking 'pretty good English' and filled with curiosity.[41] In addition to Canton, Macau was where the local Chinese worked with foreigners as a pilot, servant or comprador. More importantly, in Macau, the British and Portuguese had been involved in the opium and contraband trade since the 1820s, and the compradors were involved in this illegal trade too.[42]

The end of the licensed comprador system

The formation of the smuggling markets in the 1830s and during the First Opium War prompted the privatisation of the licensed comprador system. The illegal contraband markets outside of Canton, including at Lintin Island, Whampoa and Macau, and the number of foreign ships anchoring there, attracted unlicensed provision purveyors who were conventionally unable to obtain a license from the Qing officials to conduct business with foreigners. This led to the rise of unlicensed compradors outside Canton during the 1830s. Furthermore, during the First Opium War, a number of unlicensed compradors supplied provisions to foreign vessels, including battleships operating in the Pearl River Delta. The end of the First Opium War and the subsequent abolition of the Canton System dissolved the licensed comprador system.

i) Before the First Opium War

A number of foreign traders and local Chinese engaged in the contraband trade in the Pearl River Delta before the First Opium War. By the 1830s, Qing officials were gradually losing control of the foreign trade in Canton due to the increase in the number of ships visiting the port. Between 1819 and 1820, 80–84 foreign ships were trading in Canton, but this grew to more than 170 ships by 1833.[43] Along with the increase in the number of foreign vessels, the quantity of provisions the compradors were required to prepare sharply increased. Yet the Qing officials controlled and limited the number of compradors. The number of compradors did not increase in parallel with the number of foreign residents in Canton, and this caused inflation in the compradors' fee from the late eighteenth through to the early nineteenth century.[44] In the 1790s, an Irish traveller recorded that hiring a ship comprador generally cost more than 200 dollars.[45] In 1828, foreign traders were required to pay a ship comprador about 200 to 300 dollars.[46] This fee kept increasing until the early nineteenth century. Robert Forbes, an American trader, recalled that the fee for linguists and compradors for each ship totalled between 600 and 1,000 dollars in the early nineteenth century.[47] To reduce the cost of the ship comprador's fee, foreigners sometimes avoided employing compradors and obtained provisions from other Chinese intermediaries, including linguists.

By the beginning of the nineteenth century, the linguists had entered the provision market. Hoppomen (tidewaiters, who were Chinese officers on board foreign ships in order to oversee the loading and unloading of cargo), who could share in the profits, tolerated the linguists' activities. In the case of the American ship *Minerva* in 1809, the captain of the ship paid 200 Spanish dollars to a linguist and 20 Spanish dollars monthly to Samueal Bull, the hoppoman. If the ship stayed in Whampoa less than a month, the total cost of employing the linguist was less than employing a comprador, which could cost 280 Spanish dollars at that time.[48] The linguists' involvement in the provision trade indicates that the other licensed intermediaries had weakened the compradors' monopoly over the provision market around Canton by 1830.

By the later 1830s, the fee for a ship comprador seemed to have reduced and was fixed at 50 dollars.[49] The German missionary Carl Gutzlaff recorded that American ships had to pay a minimum of 50 dollars and other foreign ships paid about 216 dollars in a book published in 1838.[50] Yet the ship owners paid substantial port charges, including the fee for the linguist, various small charges and pilotage, which totalled nearly 5,000 dollars.[51] Moreover, the process of paying the port charges was not simple. For foreigners, it was not even certain whether the compradors' and linguists' fees were 'legal or illegal fees' and whether or not they were categorised as port fees.[52] The entire cost of the port charges was heavy and the process of the payment was complicated for foreign traders. To avoid this high cost and complicated process, many foreign traders engaged in smuggling trade outside Canton and hired unlicensed compradors there during the 1830s.

Besides hiring linguists as provision purveyors, it was also possible for foreign visitors to hire unlicensed compradors around Lintin Island (present-day Nei Lingding Island, Neilingdingdao), located in the Pearl River estuary, and near the west side of the Kowloon peninsula. Lintin harbour (Lingdingyang) became a centre for contraband and tax-free trade in the early nineteenth century. Smugglers there dealt in commodities such as opium, gold, silk, tea and porcelain.[53] The contraband markets around Hong Kong expanded in the 1830s. Eventually in the late 1830s the number of foreign ships anchoring at Lintin Island outstripped the number at Whampoa. In October 1837, the *Canton Press* recorded there were 18 ships in Whampoa while there were 25 ships at Lintin. In September 1838, the same newspaper recorded 36 ships in Whampoa and 42 in the area around Hong Kong.[54] The emergence of the smuggling market was also prompted by the abolition of the monopoly of the British EIC in 1833. The privatisation of the trade system had occurred on the British side in the early 1830s, and the rise of private foreign merchants such as Jardine and Dent contributed to the formulation of the smuggling market for opium.[55] The emergence of alternative trade markets maintained by the Chinese and foreign merchants outside Canton contributed to the emergence of unlicensed provision purveyors.

The Qing government had regulated the selection, appointment and duties of licensed ship compradors and other licensed intermediaries since the mid-eighteenth century. In general, Qing officials provided licences exclusively to local Chinese whose social and economic background was well-established. In one case, a higher-ranking Qing official instructed a Macau magistrate not to select certain kinds of people, for example 'boat-dwelling people (*danjia*)' and 'scoundrels (*wulai*)', as ship compradors.[56] The smuggling market provided business opportunities for those who were traditionally unable to become licensed intermediaries.

The Qing government attempted to restrict the activities of unlicensed compradors. In 1830, the Qing government ordered local civil and military officials to prevent pilots and compradors from provisioning foreign ships engaging in the smuggling trade around Lintin harbour, and to prevent any danjia's boat from approaching foreign ships.[57] In March 1835, an edict issued by the hoppo's office warned that hiring unlicensed private compradors and pilots was not permitted. It writes:

> Lately there have been banditti about the coast aiding pilots and defrauding them by lying and then absconding. Moreover, there is a class of vagabonds who assume the name and employment of compradors, and who are connected with a set of rascals who defeat [possibly misspelling of 'deceive'] the captains of the officers by fictitious names.[58]

In this manner, people conventionally excluded from the licensed comprador system, especially those who belonged to the boat-dwelling community, had become alternative provision purveyors for foreigners by the mid-1830s.

The licensed compradors were also involved in this contraband trade in Whampoa, Lintin harbour and Macau. In 1820, a junior comprador was fined 1,200 Spanish dollars because of his attempt to smuggle Chinese labourers abroad the ship *Bridgewater* at Whampoa.[59] In 1803, a Macau comprador supported the smuggling of opium for 20 dollars per chest while paying a connivance fee of 15 dollars to Qing officials.[60] Whether licensed or not, a portion of the compradors were involved in illegal trade in collusion with foreign and Chinese merchants. As seen above, the Canton System of trade was undermined by the increase in foreign trade, including contraband trade, in which numerous local Chinese were involved. Subsequently, the dismantling of the Canton System and the rise of the private compradors progressed still further during the disturbances of the war period.

ii) During the First Opium War

The Qing government's strict suppression of opium smuggling and its successive diplomatic disputes and military confrontations led to the dissolution of the

Canton System and the licensed comprador system at the end of the 1830s. Primarily, the licensed compradors found it difficult to continue their normal business with foreigners following the diplomatic dispute over the opium trade between the British and Chinese government that started in Canton in 1839. The Chinese staffs in foreign trading houses and ships were frequently ordered to leave their duties by the Qing authorities. If the compradors did not follow this order, they risked being severely punished. After the arrival of the imperial commissioner Lin Zexu, who started the anti-opium campaign in Canton, many compradors working for foreigners without permission from the government were arrested. Some former compradors found new work in the Qing government. On the other hand, a number of compradors continued to serve foreigners. The emergence of private compradors was further observed during the First Opium War. This can be seen in the active role of the Chinese provision purveyors, and specifically those serving British expeditions. After the war, these provision purveyors were rewarded with land in Hong Kong by the British, and some of them became influential brokers, merchants and compradors there.

The increase in the quantity of imported opium led to disputes between the British and Chinese government. The volume of opium imported from regions of British India such as Bengal and Malwa had consistently increased since 1820. For the British, the opium trade brought revenue that covered the trade deficit. However, for the Chinese, it caused a drain of silver from China. A more serious issue was the worsening of corruption among officials in Canton who were involved in the smuggling of opium.[61] To solve this problem, Lin Zexu, well known for his successful suppression of the opium trade in Hubei and Hunan, was dispatched to Canton.[62] In March 1839, Lin arrived at Canton as High Commissioner (*qinchai dachen*) and thereafter carried out an anti-opium campaign while ordering foreign merchants to stop importing opium.[63] By August, it is estimated that over 1,700 people had been arrested, and that 39,845 catties of opium and 70,279 opium pipes had been confiscated.[64] Furthermore, in June 1839, backed by the Emperor's approval, Lin ordered the destruction of the confiscated opium chests.[65] Tensions between the British and Chinese became fierce, because Lin's strict policy on the opium trade was also applied to the foreign merchants in Canton. Lin arrested Howqua and Mowqua, wealthy hong merchants, because of their intimate collaboration with foreigners and also attempted to arrest Lancelot Dent, a notable merchant in the opium trade.[66] On 7 July 1839, tension in Canton was exacerbated when a Chinese villager was killed by drunken foreign mariners in Kowloon in Hong Kong. However, Charles Elliot, the Plenipotentiary and Chief Superintendent of British Trade in China, was reluctant to hand the perpetrators over to Chinese officials, and the possibility of military conflict increased.[67] Successive diplomatic disputes in Canton eventually resulted in naval confrontations and caused the series of battles later called the First Opium War.

The Qing authorities were able to apply pressure on foreigners in Canton by removing compradors, and these measures were carried out several times during the early nineteenth century. In 1839, Lin ordered Chinese compradors and servants of British merchants in Canton and Macau to quit their work and stop supplying provisions to foreigners, following an adjudication on the case in the 13th year of the Jiaqing period (1808).[68] Lin's policy, which stopped the provisioning of foreigners, resembled the tactics his predecessors had used to control the activities of foreign merchants in Canton. In 1808, Guangdong and Guangxi Governor General Wu Xiongguang ordered Chinese servants working with the British in Canton to stop work and prohibited the sale of food to foreigners. Wu carried out this measure to repress the aggression towards Macau by British Rear Admiral William O'Brien Drury.[69] Three months after the closure of trade and the prohibition on procuring provisions, Drury's troops were required to withdraw from Macau.[70] The Qing government's measure to stop the procuring of provisions was effective in solving the diplomatic issues with foreigners in Canton in the early 1800s. However, it was not effective in the late 1830s as the dispute over the opium trade continued and eventually resulted in a severe military confrontation. In part, this was because foreigners were able to obtain provisions from unlicensed provision purveyors even though the licensed compradors had ceased their service.

Despite the severe punishments meted out by the Qing government, some compradors continued to work with foreigners in the war period. In June 1839, a comprador on board a ship anchoring in Hong Kong was seized, and the Qing officials detained the other Chinese officers of the ship. The seized comprador was Huang Tianhua, a private comprador to Jardine's ship *Carnatic*. He was arrested because of his substantial involvement in the opium trade with the local Chinese and foreigners. In 1823, Huang Tianhua was had recommended to work with a Dutch ship, *Fanbachen*, for 7 years, and he learnt foreign languages until he resigned. In 1834, Huang Chaye, who worked for British ships as unlicensed comprador, began supporting Huang Tianhua's profitable business. Huang Tianhua and Huang Cheye rented a ship from a woman from the boat-dwelling community, hired pilots, purchased meat and vegetables, and sold them to British ships. In 1835, Huang Cheye recommended Huang Tianhua to American ships, and in 1838 he also recommended Huang as a comprador on a country ship, a type of local ship used by the British EIC, called *Litu*. The *Litu* carried opium, and Huang mediated the smuggling of opium between foreign and Chinese merchants several times, earning 12 dollars per month.[71]

Another unlicensed comprador captured by Lin Zexu was Wu Yaping, who lived in Macau and understood foreign languages. In 1838, Wu was employed by a foreigner known as '*Tuchanfu*' and received 5 dollars per month for providing provisions and boat transport services for foreigners going to hulk ships for the smuggling trade. In the summer of 1839, the British were expelled from Macau, and providing assistance to them was prohibited. However, Wu still worked for Tuchanfu on a salary of 8 dollars per month and provided provisions until he was arrested by soldiers in Macau.[72] In early 1840, when Lin destroyed some local ships assisting foreigners, large comprador ships were burnt together with more than 20 local ships carrying opium and provisions.[73] The provision suppliers arrested or attacked by Lin were mostly pilots, compradors, the various Chinese workers who conducted business with foreigners in Macau and those who were previously involved in the opium trade and provisioning in the Pearl River Delta.[74] These cases indicate that a number of unlicensed compradors provided provisions to foreigners during the First Opium War.

Furthermore, some compradors accompanied the British expedition to China. It was recorded that Chinese soldiers in Dinghai captured Bu Dingbang, a comprador to the British forces.[75] In Hong Kong, when the British ship *Louisa* was wrecked due to a typhoon on the island of Kowloon, a Chinese who styled himself as a comprador rescued the crew of the ship, including Admiral Bremer and Captain Elliot. The comprador provided basic medical care, brought them to a house, provided refreshment, and sent them back to Canton by small Chinese boat. The comprador received a reward of 3,000 dollars.[76]

Loo Aqui (alias Lu Yajin), a boatman, provided provisions to the British ships in Hong Kong during the war period.[77] On 1 October 1841, the captain of the British warship, the HMS (Her Majesty's Ship) *Nemesis,* decided to take a Chinese boy, Afah, on board when they attacked Chusan. Afah's father, a military man, died in the battle, and Afah lost contact with his mother and relatives. Thereafter he travelled together with crew of the *Nemesis.* He learnt basic English for communication, and few months later, he became a provision purveyor, bringing fresh food and medical supplies which were required by the sick and injured soldiers of the fleet. Eventually, Afah went on *Nemesis*' expedition to Nanking (Nanjing), Canton and then to England.[78]

Another provision purveyor to the British was Kwok Acheong. Kwok was from the boat-dwelling community in Canton, and when Nemesis attacked the Bogue Forts in 1841, he was on the ship working as a pilot. As a reward for his collaboration, Kwok received land in Hong Kong after the war and later became a comprador to the P&O Steamship Company there.[79] Tam Achoy (Tan Yacai), a native of Kaiping, was also a collaborator with the British fleet. He was formerly a supervisor in the Government Dockyard at Singapore before he came to Hong Kong with the British expedition. Thereafter, he became a contractor and helped to construct many new buildings in the colony.[80] In this fashion, the First Opium War benefited some compradors operating in South China.

Like Kwok and Tam, many Chinese collaborators received land grants from the colonial government as a reward for their support of British military operations. Loo Aqui (see above), also known as Lo-aking and See-mun King ('gentleman' King), was one of them.[81] Like Kwok, Tam and Lo, a number of local Chinese were reported to be serving British ships in Hong Kong during the war period. After the British fleet anchored at Hong Kong, hundreds of private compradors' boats gathered there. In 1839, The *Chinese Repository* reported:

> . . . [A]t Tseenshatsuy [sic] (or Hongkong), there are daily upwards of 100 compradors' boats, and several shops for the sale of rice, wine, and miscellaneous articles, opened near the seashore for supplying the foreign shipping with provisions: it is in accordance with the regulations that all such be now rigidly prohibited; and forasmuch as we now send our cruizors [sic], that they take up Tseenshatsuy, and stop and seize all the comprador's boats that come from every creek and inlet to sell provisions to the ships . . .[82]

In this manner, a number of private compradors operated around Hong Kong before the end of the First Opium War in 1842. On 25 January 1841, when a British naval force seized Hong Kong, numerous local Chinese began moving there. One clear reason for this was the existing local demand for work opportunities with foreigners. Some of these local Chinese migrants worked as suppliers of provisions to the foreigners there.[83]

It should be noted there was a famous former comprador working for the Qing government during the First Opium War. In the north-eastern province of Shandong, Qishan employed several interpreters, including Bao Peng (formerly Bao Yacong), a former unlicensed comprador in Canton. Bao Peng served the Americans and British, and acted as a supplier of opium to the wealthy of Canton before he moved to Shandong to avoid arrest by Qing officials. In 1829, he worked for an American merchant, but the merchant left Canton and he lost the job. In 1836, Bao Peng's uncle started working for Dent as a licensed comprador. However, due to the uncle's sickness, Bao Peng took over his cousin's work without obtaining a license for himself. His salary was 60 dollars per year, with an additional income of 200 or 300 dollars. In 1837 and 1838, Bao Peng was involved in the opium trade together with a linguist from Xiangshan, a long-term acquaintance. Bao apparently received commissions from the trade. After Lin's arrival in Canton and the start of his campaign against the unlicensed compradors, Bao Peng left the city and moved north, staying in a house owned by Zhao Ziyong in Shandong province. There, Qishan discovered the usefulness of Bao Peng's ability in foreign languages and employed him as an adviser.[84] However, both British and Chinese observers and officials were not positive about Bao Peng. Wei Yuan, a Chinese scholar who analysed the effects of Western foreign powers on China, sarcastically called Bao Peng the former 'pet boy of the traitor Dent'. Qing officials in the Law Department (Xingbu) also doubted how far they could trust Bao Peng because of his former cooperation with foreign traders.[85] A British lieutenant wrote that: 'He professed much regard for the English . . . but, like all his countrymen, he was a most intolerable liar.'[86] Bao Peng became involved in the diplomatic negotiation between China and Britain, and his former employers such as Dent were surprised to encounter him as a government authority.[87] The case of Bao Peng is emblematic of the duality of the compradors who worked with both Qing and foreign authorities as commercial and political intermediaries, as well as Chinese citizens' general critical view of them.

For the local Chinese engaging in trade, both the British and Chinese governments were potential employers. When the opium trade ended in the late 1830s, the participants in this trade – including transporters and suppliers – started working in a defence militia opposing the British that was organised by Lin Zexu in accordance with his strategy of 'fighting traitors with traitors, poison with poison'.[88] When this militia was disbanded, they turned into provision suppliers for the British. A Cantonese writer wrote: 'Without their [the local collaborators'] help, the British would not have known anything – this was how Charles Elliot found out how slack the defences leading up to Canton were.'[89] In many places, British drew on local Chinese people who offered services to them. In late

November 1840 when Elliot returned to South China and stopped the British fleet on the Pearl River estuary, local Chinese residents sold provisions to them. An English lieutenant noted: 'What a most extraordinary nation this is! . . . They will trade with you at one spot, while you are fighting, killing, and destroying them at another!'[90] A number of local Chinese vigorously participated in the provisions trade during the war. For them, the arrival of the British troops meant the appearance of new employers. As such, after the occupation of Hong Kong in 1841, a number of unlicensed compradors or provision suppliers appeared in Hong Kong, as they found business opportunities with the foreigners there.

The old compradors and Hong Kong

The end of the First Opium War in 1842 led to the abolition of the Canton System and the end of the Qing government's strict regulation of the foreign trade. In theory, this enabled foreign merchants to conduct direct trade with Chinese merchants. However, the private compradors emerged as influential intermediaries for foreign traders. Furthermore, these compradors established a successor to the Canton System known as 'the comprador system'. Various types of Chinese functionary had mediated between Chinese and the foreigners during the Canton System days. Why did compradors become predominant and not another type of licensed Chinese intermediary, such as the linguists, hong merchants or pilots? The answer may lie in the importance of providing provisions, in particular food and water, to foreigners in China. Without such basic supplies, foreign traders were unable to survive and conduct trade, and therefore foreigners hired compradors. However, it was still possible to call them simply 'purveyors' and not 'compradors'. In 1844 and 1848, Morrison described the later career of former compradors for Americans after the end of the First Opium War. A comprador to American ships, likely to be Boston Jack, established a company with a branch in Macau. Meanwhile, other compradors were serving the English, some of them styling themselves 'purveyors'.[91]

Although some old compradors attempted to change their job titles during the war, in many cases, provision purveyors were hired under the title of 'comprador'. Foreign merchants wished to continue hiring someone who could be responsible for hiring Chinese staff, bookkeeping and checking the value of Chinese silver in addition to procuring provisions. For the Chinese collaborators, it was convenient to call themselves compradors because the term could encompass a variety of work for the foreigners, while job titles such as 'linguist', 'purveyor' or 'pilot' were too specific. Because of the effectiveness of the licensed comprador system in Canton for Sino-foreign trade, the comprador system survived after 1842. More importantly, the end of the First Opium War and the collapse of the Canton System completed the process of the privatisation of the comprador system. Thereafter, the number of compradors increased, as anyone could become a comprador. However, the duties of the compradors were no longer regulated by the Qing authorities, and therefore foreign institutions and individuals were required to redefine the comprador system independently after 1842.

It is possible to trace the later careers of some of the notable well-to-do compradors. After the First Opium War, Boston Jack remained in Canton and began conducting his own trade. He owned a store selling a variety of commodities.[92] In the 1850s, he worked with foreign firms such as Thomas Hunt & Co. and Jardine, Matheson & Co.[93] In 1851, Gilman Currier in Boston asked Jack to provide a list of articles that would sell well in southern China. Currier also asked Jack to sell articles he sent to Hong Kong, including candles, soaps, brandy and chocolate.[94] On 3 November 1853, the *China Mail* reported the death of Boston Jack; it was estimated that he left an estate worth half a million dollars.[95]

In Whampoa, a number of ship compradors like Boston Jack continued to operate. Archibald R. Ridgway, a doctor in Hong Kong, describes the view of a Whampoa village where Boston Jack and other compradors lived.

> The village of Whampoa is a few hundred yards above Orange Grove and is situated at a little distance above the river and surrounded by a wall. The suburb in which the compradors, &c, live, is a long street running along the bank, close to the water's edge; indeed one side of it is built on piles in the water. These latter houses are principally occupied by timber merchants and boat builders; and one of them, the last in the row, and much larger than any of the others, is the store of Boston Jack who has a most extensive and miscellaneous collection of everything connected with shipping and is as I have already said the comprador of the American vessels.[96]

The purpose of Ridgway's trip to the village was to visit a house of the ship comprador Jimmy Appo. According to Ridgway, 'Jimmy' was a common first name for compradors in Whampoa.[97] For the ship compradors, having an English-style name became common.

After the war, some of the former Canton compradors moved to Hong Kong. In 1848, Benjamin Ball, an American ship's doctor, encountered a Chinese man called Ayou in Hong Kong who had been a comprador in Canton. On 31 August 1848, Ball visited a Chinese shop and met Ayou, a Chinese man who spoke English fluently, and who had been in Boston for 2 years. Before that, he was a comprador for Cushing in Canton. When Cushing returned to Boston, Ayou followed his principal. However, 2 years later, he decided to return to China. In 1848, Ayou ran his own business and owned a large alum establishment. According to Ayou, '[A] Chinaman who speak [sic] both English and Chinese can make "plenty money" in China.'[98] The children of other old compradors also became compradors in the treaty ports and in the colony. For instance, it was believed that the father of Wei Akwong, a well-known comprador merchant in late nineteenth-century Hong Kong, was a comprador to Benjamin Chew Wilocks and Oliver H. Gordon in Canton during the 1820s and the 1830s.[99] Of the provision purveyors during the First Opium War, Loo Aqui, Tam Achoy and Kwok Acheong stayed in Hong Kong after the war and established themselves as influential merchants. Lo grew in wealth through service to the British expedition and received land grants from the British in the Lower Bazaar near Victoria.[100] Tam became a well-known landowner and emigration broker in Hong Kong.[101] In this way, the First Opium War provided new opportunities for some local Chinese from the Pearl River Delta, the boat-dwelling community and overseas Chinese in South Asia, in addition to the former compradors in Canton. For them, the formal cession of Hong Kong and the opening of the treaty ports in 1842 provided further commercial opportunities. By that time, the privatisation of the licensed comprador system had been completed.

Conclusion

First and foremost, the prototype of the comprador system in nineteenth-century Hong Kong was the licensed comprador system existing in Canton prior to the First Opium War. The fundamental functions of the house compradors and ship compradors were inherited by the company compradors and the ship compradors, respectively, after the war. The demise of Canton System was mainly the result of the formation of the smuggling markets in the Pearl River Delta throughout the 1830s. The social confusion caused by the First Opium War accelerated this trend. The absence of Qing political authority in the Pearl River Delta led to the participation of local Chinese in the provision trade with foreigners. In this way, the number of private compradors surged during the war period. When the British occupied Hong Kong in 1841, these local provision suppliers came to Hong Kong to seek further business opportunities with the British fleet, foreign companies and other foreign traders. The local Chinese who made their livelihood by working with foreigners and by selling provisions often called themselves 'compradors' subsequently.

Compradors might have disappeared after the First Opium War. Yet foreign companies continued the practice of employing them for their trade in China even after the opening of the treaty ports and the development of the colony of Hong Kong. The new comprador system in the treaty port world inherited the basic structure of the old licensed comprador system. The new emerging comprador system contrasted sharply with the licensed comprador system in that functions of the compradors became more amorphous and unregulated by any kinds of political or economic authority. From 1842 onwards, the Qing officials no longer defined the functions of the compradors. In this manner, the old comprador system was privatised. Yet, in the case of Hong Kong, a portion of the compradors continued working as intermediaries serving government officials. The British colonial government in Hong Kong employed multiple compradors from the 1840s through the 1850s, and this is the main theme of next chapter.

Notes

1 Hao, *Comprador*, 44–48; Van Dyke, 'Compradors and the Provision Trade', Chapter Four in Van Dyke, *Canton Trade*, 51–75.
2 Murakami, *Umi no kindai Chūgoku,* 93–94; *Chinese Repository*, Vol. 6, 'Memorial on the Condition of Kwangtung' (April 1838), 603–605.

3 Bingham, *Narrative*, 187, 284, 358; for the littoral population's cooperation with the British, see Luk, *Opium War*.
4 Carroll, *Edge of Empires*, 20.
5 Garrett, *Heavens*, 13; *Chinese Repository*, Vol. 2 (1833), 307–308.
6 TNA: FO 1048/31/40, Order from viceroy to hong merchants, 5 June 1831; FO 1048/31/37, Order from Nan-hai magistrate, acting under instructions, to hong merchants, 20 May 1831.
7 Le Pichon, *China Trade,* 14–15.
8 Ibid., 14–15; Morse, selected by Tuck, *Britain and China*, Vol. 4, 115, 137.
9 Hao, *Comprador*, 46.
10 YPZZ, Vol. 1, Lihongbin deng zoucheng DG10/6/17, 69.
11 TNA: FO 1048/30/83, Order from viceroy to Nan-hai magistrate (1830). The country merchant Whiteman brought a foreign woman into the Factories and was living in Puankhequa's hong. The security merchant, linguist and compradors concerned are to be put in chains, and Whiteman is to be ordered to send the woman away immediately; Morse, Selected by Patrick Tuck, *Britain and China*, 263.
12 TNA: FO 1048/31/40, Order from viceroy to hong merchants, 5 June 1831; British Parliamentary Papers (BPP), *Papers Relating to China*, Vol. 39, General Correspondence, Dispatches and Reports Relating to the Rules, Regulations, and Other Aspects of the Trade between Great Britain and China, 1831–99, 97–98 (81–82).
13 TNA: FO 1048/31/37, Order from Nan-hai magistrate, 20 May 1831.
14 Van Dyke, *Canton Trade*, 51; Hunter, *'Fan kwae'*, 62–63; *Chinese Repository*, Vol. 3, April 1835, 582.
15 TNA: FO 1048/22/47, Howqua to Select Committee, 1822; Hao, *Comprador*, 46; Williams, *Chinese Commercial Guide*, 5th edn, 153.
16 JMA: H1/96, receipts and a note from Fo to Zhan Guchuan, ca. 1837.
17 Van Dyke, *Canton Trade*, 56.
18 Gützlaff, revised by Reed, *China Opened*, Vol. 2, 85.
19 Phipps, *Practical Treatise*, 143; *Chinese Repository*, Vol. 2, November 1833, 301–303.
20 Wood, *Sketches of China*, 51.
21 TNA: FO 1048/22/47, Howqua to Select Committee, 8 August 1822.
22 TNA: FO 1048/31/14, Linguists to Jardine, 14 January 1831.
23 Van Dyke, *Canton Trade*, 71–72; Wood, *Sketches of China*, 7.
24 Hunter, '*Fan kwa*e', 62–63.
25 State Street Trust Company, *Other Merchants*, 7.
26 Hunter, '*Fan kwa*e', 62–63.
27 Yun, *Coolie Speaks*, 65.
28 Medhurst, *China; Its State*, 284–285; Negishi, *Baiben Seido*, 65.
29 Hunter, *'Fan kwae',* 33.
30 Ibid., 32–34.
31 TNA: FO 1048/22/11, Urmston to Howqua, 6 May 1822; FO 1048/22/15 Howqua to Urmston, May 1822.
32 TNA: FO 1048/28/43, Plowden to Howqua, 23 August 1828; FO 1048/28/17, Letter from Howqua to Plowden, 17 May 1828.
33 TNA: FO 1048/28/3, Company instructions to the comprador, 18 February 1828; Morse, *Chronicles*, Vol. 3, 53.
34 India Office Records, British Library (London): G/12/249,1832–1833, China and Japan: Canton Factory Consultations, 26, entry of 5 September 1832; 53, entry of 17 September 1832; and 57, 24 September 1832.
35 Baker Library, Harvard: Forbes Family Business Papers, v. E-3 Ayou Comprador waste book, 1832.

36 TNA: FO 1048/33/63, Petition to viceroy from Fox, complaining that his comprador was seized by runners who released him only after he had paid them $80, 2 November 1833.
37 Morse, *Chronicles of East India Company*, Vol. 3, 235–236, 355.
38 Hao, *Commercial Revolution*, 15.
39 See Pichon, *China Trade and Empire*, for instance, 85–86, 97–99, and 121.
40 Huang, *Aomenshi gangya*, 116.
41 Hao, Macau History and Society, 62.
42 Hao, *Commercial Revolution*, 15; Greenberg, *British Trade*, especially Chapter 6.
43 Gibson, *Otter Skins*, 313–314.
44 Van Dyke, *Canton Trade*, 57–58.
45 Dobell, *Travels in Kamtchatka*, Vol. 2, 132–133.
46 Blunt, *Merchant's and Shipmaster's Assistant*, 388; *Asiatic Journal*, Vol. 25, 49.
47 Forbes *Remarks on China*, 15–16.
48 Phillips Library, Peabody Essex Museum, Salem: Benjamin Shreve Papers, 'Ship Minerva account book 1809', cited in Van Dyke, *Canton Trade*, 68–69.
49 *Canton Press*, Vol. 4, 17 November 1838, 'Whampoa Port Charges. &c.'
50 Gützlaff and Reed, *China Opened*, Vol. 2, 91.
51 *Canton Press*, Vol. 4, 17 November 1838, 'Whampoa Port Charges'; Gützlaff and Reed, *China Opened*, Vol. 2, 90–91.
52 *Canton Press*, Vol. 2, 10 June 1837, 'Charges on Rice-Laden Ships.'
53 Murakami, *Umi no kindai Chūgoku*, 90; Morrison, *Chinese Commercial Guide*, 1834, 28–29.
54 *Canton Press*, Vol. 3, 7 October 1837, Shipping at Whampoa and at Lintin; Vol. 4, 29 September 1838, Shipping at Whampoa and at Hong Kong.
55 Fairbank, *Trade and Diplomacy*, 78–79.
56 TNA: FO 1048/31/1, Reprimand from viceroy to sub-prefect for Macau, January 1831.
57 TNA: FO 1048/30/61, Proclamation at Macau, 1830; *Canton Press*, Vol. 1, 21 November 1835, 'Jardine Steamers'.
58 *Canton Register*, Vol. 8, 24 March 1835, 48.
59 Van Dyke, *Americans and Macao*, 60.
60 Van Dyke, *Canton Trade*, 127.
61 Fairbank, *Trade and Diplomacy*, 74–78; Fay, *Opium War*, 42–43.
62 Fairbank, *Trade and Diplomacy*, 80.
63 Waley, *Opium War*, 246–247.
64 Chang, *Commissioner Lin*, 129.
65 Hillemann, *Asian Empire*, 101.
66 Beeching, *Chinese Opium Wars*, 78.
67 Waley, *Opium War*, 55, 76.
68 YPZZ, Vol. 1, Lin Zexu's report, DG13/7/24, 671–672; *Chinese Repository*, Vol. 8, August 1839, 216–220.
69 Sirr, *China and Chinese*, Vol. 2, 272.
70 Davis, *Chinese: General Description*, Vol. 1, 67–69.
71 YPZZ, Vol. 1, Lin Zexu'r report, Year of Daoguang 19 (1839)/10/16, 725–729; *Chinese Repository*, Vol. 7 or 8, 112.
72 YPZZ, Vol. 1, Lin's memorial on the arrests of local Chinese supporting British ships, DG19/12/4, 756–757.
73 YPZZ, Vol. 2, Lin's memorial on the burning of local ships to stop them from assisting foreigners, DG20/2/4, 28.
74 YPZZ, Vol. 1, Lin's memorial on the arrests of local Chinese supporting British ships, DG19/12/4, 753–758.
75 Hanes and Sanello, *Opium Wars*, 94; Hao, *Comprador*, 194–195.
76 *Monthly Chronicle of Events*, Vol. 2, 555–556.

77 *Chouban yiwushimo*, Daoguang vol. 37, 33b and 52, 3b–4a and 58, 40b–43a Deng Yasu, Ho Asek (He Yasu, Shi Yusheng were also listed with Lo's name; Norton-Kyshe, *History of Laws*, Vol. 1, 265.
78 Hall and Bernard, *Nemesis in* China, 3rd edn, xi–xiv.
79 Holdsworth and Munn (eds), *Dictionary of Hong Kong Biography*, 233–234.
80 Munn, *Anglo-China*, 74; Smith, *Chinese Christians*, 124–125.
81 Munn, *Anglo-China*, 75; TNA: CO 129/27, Caine's observations, 25 February 1848, 286–7; Tarrant, *Hong Kong: Part 1*, 16–17.
82 *Chinese Repository*, Vol. 8, August 1839, 'Art V Proclamation from the high imperial commissioner concerning the murder of Lin Weihe', 215; Tseenshatsuy means Tsim Sha Tsui (Jianshazui).
83 Carroll, *Concise History*, 1.
84 YPZZ, Vol. 4, Ruiqinwang renshou's report on Bao Peng, DG21 (1841)/7/26, 55–57; *Chouban yiwu shimo*: DG29, 13b–15a, DG, Vol. 30, 28b–29a; Waley, *Opium War*, 241–242. Bao Peng's uncle Bao Renguan was Dent's comprador in 1838, but he became sick and Bao Peng took over his position.
85 Wei and Parker, *Chinese Account*, 23; YPZZ, Vol. 3, DG21/4/20, Xingbu's report on Qishan's statement, 473–474, 476.
86 Bingham, *Narrative*, Vol. 1, 249.
87 Bingham, *Narrative*, Vol. 2, 40–41.
88 Bingham, *Narrative* Vol. 1, 388; Mao, *Tianchao de bengkui*, 134.
89 Liang, *Yifen wenji*, 51, translated by Lovell, *Opium War*, 127.
90 Bingham, *Narrative*, Vol. 1, 408, 410, 413.
91 Morrison, *Chinese Commercial Guide* (1848), 125 (edited by Sammuel Wells Willliams).
92 JMA: Business letters (America), B6/2/am410, Gilman Currier to Boston Jack, 10 February 1851.
93 JMA: A8/26/11, Account of Boston Jack, April 1854–December 1855.
94 JMA: B6/2/am410, Business letters (America), B6/2/am410, Gilman Currier to Boston Jack, 10 February 1851.
95 *China Mail*, 3 November 1853, 178.
96 Ridgway, 'Letters from Hong Kong', 369.
97 Ibid., 311–312.
98 Ball, 'Diary of a Hong Kong Doctor' in Barbara-Sue White (ed.), *Hong Kong*, 45.
99 Smith, *Chinese Christians*, 62–69.
100 TNA: Caine's observations, 25 February 1848, CO 129/27, 286–287; Tarrant, *Hong Kong: Part 1*, 16–17; Munn, *Anglo-China*, 75.
101 Munn, *Anglo-China*, 74; Smith, *Chinese Christians*, 124–125.

2 The compradors of the colonial government

The government compradors acted as oligopolistic communication channels between the colonial government and the local Chinese community in Hong Kong between the 1840s and the 1850s. Each colonial government organisation hired compradors on a contract basis. Meanwhile, individual colonial officials also privately employed house compradors, who occasionally supported their employers' services to the colonial government. These functions differed from those of the company compradors, because the government compradors possessed the authority to intervene directly in the lives of the Chinese residents in Hong Kong.

Due to their opaque employment status, the house compradors were particularly susceptible to corruption in the colonial government. It was not hard for them to engage in this, since their activities were merely overseen by a principal. There seemed almost no institutional check on the house compradors' work. It was worse if the foreign employer himself was corrupt – then nothing could hinder the comprador's malfeasance. As Christopher Munn stresses, the corruption of colonial officials, from low to high-ranking, was one of the most serious social issues in Hong Kong in the first two decades of the colony.[1] The symbiotic relationship between the colonial officials and the compradors in many corruption cases is one of the main focuses of this chapter.

The government comprador system was relatively short-lived, in part because of their recurrent involvement in malpractice. At the onset of the 1860s, the significance of the government compradors was already overshadowed by the rise of the alternative socio-economic intermediary elites in Hong Kong, including the company compradors. The reformation of the employment system for Chinese staff in the colonial government was another factor reducing the number of the compradors working within colonial officialdom.

The government comprador system

Before moving to an exploration of the government compradors, this section briefly sketches the core structure of the colonial government in order to clarify the duties of the compradors serving high-ranking officials and colonial organisations. The structure of the colonial government and duties of the compradors steadily evolved throughout the nineteenth century. At the beginning, in 1841, the colonial government consisted of institutions run by the Governor, the Chief Magistrate and the Harbour-Master. The General Post Office and the jail were established in the same year.[2] William Caine, the first Chief Magistrate, was responsible for both the police and the jail from April 1841.[3] William Pedder was appointed Harbour-Master in August 1841.[4] *The Chinese Repository* recorded that the Land Officer and Surveyor had been appointed by February 1842.[5] The Colonial Treasurer and the Chief Justice were appointed in 1842 and 1843, respectively. In 1844, the Attorney General and Register General's offices were created.[6] In addition, British troops had been housed in Hong Kong ever since the First Opium War. In 1846, the colonial government included the offices of the Colonial Surgeon and the Surveyor General.[7]

These were the major official organisations established in Hong Kong by the middle of the 1840s. Thereafter, additional organisations and branches were set up as required, but the main institutions remained the same. In 1876, the authorities in the colonial government were the Governor, the Colonial Secretary, the Colonial Treasurer, the Auditor General, the Surveyor General, the Chief Magistrate, the Harbour-Master and the Register General. The Supreme Court was established by this time.[8] These organisations of the colonial government employed both foreign and Chinese staff, including compradors. Specifically, records are available on the compradors serving the commissariat in the British Army and Navy, the Treasury and the Post Office. Details of the compradors in these institutions are explored below to shed light on how the Chinese intermediaries supported the establishment of these core institutions and the management system for them.

i) Compradors working in official institutions

As explained in the first chapter, the compradors' primary function was supplying provisions, and that remained true for the government compradors. The British Navy employed provision purveyors during the First Opium War, and the commissariat department of the colonial government hired compradors after 1841. However, there were also compradors who supported the colonial government's Chinese portion of administrative works and who were deeply involved in the public work of the colonial government, rather than simply providing provisions to the colonial officials. Multiple receipts from the colonial accounts preserved in CO129/5 suggest that in the early 1840s several compradors were responsible for business transactions between the colonial officials and the Chinese external service providers, including merchants, contractors and carpenters.[9] A treasury comprador was an economic and politically influential figure in the Chinese community based on his position as an agent of the colonial government. Post Office compradors supported the establishment of the network of the British postal service in Hong Kong and Shanghai. The compradors supported the establishment and consolidation of the British official institutions and their services in Hong Kong in its formative years.

A certain number of unlicensed compradors procured provisions for British expeditions during the disturbances of the First Opium War. One of them was Bu

Dingbang, also known as Poon Neen or Poo Ting Poon, who served the British commissariat as a comprador. He served the commissariat as early as 1840 and accompanied the British expedition to the eastern coast of China. However, he was arrested by Qing officials at Zhoushan when he went inland to purchase bullocks for the British troops. He was sent to Ningbo in Zhejiang province and executed there.[10] The commissariat hired several local compradors and provision purveyors like Bu Dingbang during the war period and it continued to do so after 1842.

Although the *Hong Kong Blue Book* providing census records of Hong Kong, did not formally record the employment of commissariat compradors, it is certain that the British troops continue to employ compradors. In the late 1840s, *The China Mail* reported a court case in which an army commissariat comprador was involved. In July 1849, 12 bakers who were employed by the comprador to the army commissariat were prosecuted for manslaughter.[11] At the select committee on the mortality of troops in China, held on 4 June 1866, a Royal Engineer responded to questions about the comprador system of the colonial government of Hong Kong by stating, 'it is used to a certain degree in the Commissariat.'[12] Since the beginning of the colony, compradors worked for the commissariat of the British troops in Hong Kong.

The incident of manslaughter and its court case in 1849 revealed the government compradors' influential power, which could affect the daily lives of the Chinese citizens. On 21 June 1849, a Chinese man died after a quarrel between more than 10 coolies hired by the commissariat comprador and cooks of the 95th regiment. Cheong-ayee, a cook to the regiment, came to the commissariat to collect wood and claimed it was wet, which triggered the fighting. The comprador's employees were armed with 'billets of wood'; meanwhile, the regimental cooks were armed with 'bamboo'. Cheong-ayee went to the police to report the incident. When he returned to the scene of fighting with constables, they found one of his colleagues dead. The commissariat comprador employed a number of Chinese staff of rowdy character. Before the trial took place, two witnesses for the prosecution consulted Tepo (a semi-official Chinese elder nominated by the colonial government, *dibao*) of Canton Bazaar to ask whether they should try to extort several hundred dollars from the commissariat comprador if the comprador wanted them not to appear in court.[13] When the jury asked why the witnesses did not directly ask the comprador in court, they stated that they were 'afraid to speak to the comprador'.[14] Although the witnesses' attempt was not successful, this case suggests that the government compradors were to some extent recognised as influential figures by Chinese residents.

In addition to the commissariat, another indispensable department of the colonial government was the treasury office. It also employed a comprador named Chow Aaon (Cao Ya'an, alias Cho'On, Tsoo Aoan, Cho Yune-choong and Cho Wing-chow) in the 1840s and 1850s. He was one of the most influential and controversial compradors in the colonial government. His case shows how indispensable the compradors were for the colonial government and how they came to have excessive authority because of their deep involvement in the colonial government's financial work.

Chow served the colonial government from 1843 and 1857, but his career working with foreigners started much earlier than that. In 1834, he worked at the British office of the Superintendent of Trade in Macau, and subsequently moved to Hong Kong after the First Opium War. In 1843 and 1844, Chow worked as a comprador managing multiple business transactions between the colonial government and Chinese merchants and contractors.[15] In 1847, his annual salary was about $32 for his services to the General Department, which consisted of 'servants employed about the Government and Chief Superintendent's Office'.[16] The duty of the treasury comprador was to support the other staff in the office. Chow was responsible for eight other Chinese staff, including a shroff (currency-examiner and exchanger), a gardener, a messenger and a porter. He made about £20 extra annually from his work in the Chief Superintendent Establishment.[17] In addition to his work as a comprador, Chow was able to obtain an income from sideline businesses including the management of real estate and pawnshops.

Chow's position in the government was controversial. Charles May, a British police officer, claimed that Chow was 'a cunning, lying, well-informed Chinaman', who had yet managed to become indispensable to the government. Chow was notorious for his involvement in government extortion and corruption. In particular, he collaborated with other house compradors employed by officials working in the judicial and legal sector, which will be explored in the latter part of this chapter. After he retired from government in 1857, Chow was able to live on income from his sideline ventures without a pension.[18] Drawing on connections and information that he had obtained through his work in the colonial government, Chow succeeded in various businesses. He left a fortune valued at $50,000 when he died in Macau in 1874.[19] After Chow's retirement, there was no successor for his position. The *Blue Book* issued after 1857 did not record the appointment of a new treasury comprador. The treasury office therefore appears likely to have ceased hiring compradors after 1857. However, it is possible that Chinese clerks and shroffs continued to support the financial transaction of the colonial government.

Aside from Chow, the organisations of the colonial government employed various compradors who dealt with provision procuring and business transactions in the early 1840s. In 1843, the police establishment employed a comprador named Mok Shing (Mo Sheng or Mo Yasheng), whose main duties were providing provisions and assiting in a diverse range of activities for the foreign and Chinese staff of the police establishment. For instance, he received payment for the cost of providing food for prisoners, oil for the prison guardroom, large black books and baskets for prisoners of the colonial government.[20]

The troops also temporarily employed compradors. In July 1843, two office compradors, Ahow and Ayung, supported the British military personnel's supervision of ordnance, barrack-building for the troops, the repairing of barracks and the Engineer Department.[21] In 1843, another comprador, Achun (Yasong), worked for a postage and boat-hiring service to and from Canton.[22] In the same year, Achun also purchased furniture for the government house, such as carpets and shelves for records.[23] The colonial government began hiring compradors primarily for the construction of colonial institutions. Chinese contractors, carpenters and sellers of daily necessities provided a diverse range of service to the colonial government for the construction of the colony in the early 1840s.[24] Yet both Chinese workers and the colonial officials required intermediaries because of the barriers of language and the differences in business practices. Therefore, the colonial government employed compradors as a temporary emergency measure to complete the establishment of the institutions of the colonial government. However, the General Post Office (*Shuxinguan*) employed compradors much longer than other official organisations.

The Post Office was one of the rare institutions that constantly hired compradors throughout the nineteenth century. Unlike the compradors employed by the commissariat and the treasury, the duties of compradors in the Post Office were clarified and well-controlled by establishing a seniority-based wage and lifetime employment system. The General Post Office was established immediately after the British occupation of Hong Kong in 1841.[25] Thereafter, the Post Office continued to hire compradors. At least one comprador was employed at the Post Office from the 1840s to the 1860s.[26] The Post Report for 1865 recorded staff in the Post Office including the Postmaster General, his assistant, a chargetaker, sorters, a comprador, 10 coolies and 5 boatmen.[27] Of these, the comprador held the highest position.

Chun Mau Yung, a comprador who worked in the Post Office in Shanghai in 1912, had started working in the Post Office in Hong Kong in 1863 as messenger. He became a shroff in 1869 and a comprador in 1901. Claud Severn, Acting Administrator of Hong Kong, states that Chun Mau Yung was of 'excellent character' and worked 'in a most exemplary manner'.[28]

Details of his work are unknown, but Man Fook Tin (Meng Futian), a native of Panyu prefecture in Guangzhou, started working in the colonial government as early as 1861.[29] A decade later, in December 1871, he reached the highest position of the Chinese staff in the Post Office.[30] The organisation selected the compradors from its Chinese staff, making it possible to establish a trustworthy relationship between the foreign staff and the compradors there.

Governor George William Des Vœux's letter to Lord Nutsford dated 10 January 1890 concerning the payment of pension to a comprador, Ching Tsun, is a good example of the seniority-based wage and long-term employment system of the Post Office compradors. Ching Tsun climbed the ladder of the hierarchy of Chinese staff in the Post Office as Chun and Man did. According to des Vœux's letter, Ching Tsun entered the services of the Post Office on 1 December 1866 as a messenger. At that time, his salary was $72. In July 1864, he was promoted to postman with an annual income of $84, which increased to $96 in 1871. On 6 December 1871, he became a shroff, with a salary of $216, and finally became a comprador on 14 February 1876, with a salary of $360. Ching Tsun was recognised as a credible comprador by the authorities of the government. The Governor wrote that his predecessor introduced Ching Tsun as 'the most useful man in the Post Office' in 1875. Although the comprador's work was demanding, Ching Tsun was able to handle it and sometimes worked until late at night.

Surprisingly, Ching Tsun declined the offer of a salary increase to go along with an increase in his responsibilities (which he accepted). In 1890, at the age of 56, Ching Tsun retired from the government after serving the Post Office for 24 years.[31]

The cases of Chun, Man and Tsun also highlight the stability of the comprador system in the Post Office. The compradors there were likely to have had long careers before they reached the position of comprador. In the nineteenth century, colonial officials generally considered the Post Office compradors to be reliable. This is partly because the Post Office was able to internally select and employ a credible comprador from its staff, which may be one reason the Post Office employed compradors longer than other institutions. Moreover, for the establishment of an inter-regional postal network in China, it may have been necessary for the Post Office to employ compradors long term. The construction of the administrative buildings and their management system was completed quickly, while the construction of a postal service network in China required a much longer development. As Chun Mau Yung worked in both Hong Kong and Shanghai for nearly 49 years, the Post Office clearly needed intermediaries who supported the long-term and evolving project of constructing the Anglo-Chinese postal system.[32]

Overall, the colonial government depended on the work of the compradors for the establishment and management of fledging administrative organisations. Many of the compradors were responsible for obtaining provisions as well as supporting business deals between the official institutions and external Chinese workers and merchants. Being responsible for these key tasks, which were indispensable for the colonial government, some of the compradors, including the commissariat compradors and the treasury comprador, became economically and socially influential figures. The Post Office established its own unique and stable employment system for compradors. The government compradors therefore supported the establishment of the British colonial structure related to military activities, policing, finance administration and the formation of the postal network in Hong Kong. Furthermore, the personal compradors of the colonial officials were involved in the work of the colonial government by supporting their principals' duties.

ii) Relationship with colonial officials

In nineteenth-century Hong Kong, the majority of foreign officials employed a house comprador along with other Chinese staff, including cooks, houseboys, coolies and boatmen for their daily needs.[33] Chisholm Anstey, the Attorney General of Hong Kong, was famous for his efforts to eliminate the corruption in which some of the high-ranking officials and the compradors were involved. However, it was inevitable that even he employed a comprador. The *Times* correspondent G. Wingrove Cooke describes his travel to Macau with Anstey and his comprador in 1857.[34] Anstey's comprador, who was a native of Macau, guided, guarded and supported his principal during his stay there. These house compradors serving high-ranking officials established close relationships with their principals and occasionally supported their employers' duties in the colonial government. Furthermore, these house compradors and their employers were often both involved in corruption in the government. These types of compradors were not usually recorded in official documents, despite their involvement in their principals' works. Some reports on the court cases in which the compradors appeared are available, and these reports make it possible to illuminate their socio-economic activities from the 1840s to the 1850s. The following section examines the functions of the house compradors and their principals in well-known corruption cases in Hong Kong. However, it should be noted that there may be a greater number of ethical compradors who were not recorded in these documents on scandals.

One representative of the compradors in positions of authority who served colonial officials is Lo Een-teen (Luo Jiantian), alias Lo Yun Suey and Lo Chong. Lo was the comprador to William Caine, who was Chief Magistrate in the 1840s.[35] During this time, utilising Caine's authority, Lo and the treasury comprador Chow Aaon extorted bribes from Chinese leaseholders and franchise holders in the public markets of Hong Kong. After 1841, the government owned the public markets, which were located near the Upper and Lower Bazaars in the city of Victoria.[36] In 1844, Sir John Davis, the second Governor, resolved to sell the market franchise to the public to obtain revenue for the government. The short-term market franchise and the lease on the premises were granted to private individuals on a bidding basis. At the end of the 1840s, the stakeholders in the market area were mostly Chinese merchants.[37] Utilising their positions as government employees, the two extorted money from leaseholders and applicants for market franchises. In 1845, Lo demanded that Wei Aqui (Wei Yagui) pay an extra $150 per month on top of market rent to secure the renewal of his market licence. Wei Aqui agreed to pay the fee and prepaid the sum of $1,000 from July to August 1845.[38] However, Wei Aqui did not manage to complete the payment of cumshaw to Lo before his (Wei Aqui's) death, and about $1,300 was left unpaid. Therefore, Wei Aqui's younger brother, Wei Afoon (Wei Yakuan), an overseer of the Central Market, became responsible for paying the remaining cumshaw.[39] In June 1847, Wei Afoon made payments to Lo several times. On one occasion, Afoon made a payment of $200 to Lo in the comprador's room in Caine's house in June 1847.[40] Due to financial difficulties, Afoon sometimes had to reduce the amount of payment.

When Afoon refused to make a payment, Lo threatened to report it to his principal.[41] Whether Caine permitted Lo's extortion or not, it appears that Lo used Caine's authority to collect bribes from leaseholders in the market area. Chow Aaon was also involved in the collecting of money. In July 1847, Wei Afoon stated to William Tarrant, a member of staff in the Surveyor General's office and an energetic investigator of extortion, that he paid $100 monthly to Lo and Chow, who functioned as 'go-between' in the extortion system.[42] Collaborating with and drawing on the authority of his principal and the treasury comprador, Chow was able to extort bribes from Chinese property owners who required official support from the colonial government for their business.

Controlling communication between the colonial officials and local Chinese businessmen enabled the government compradors to increase their authority.

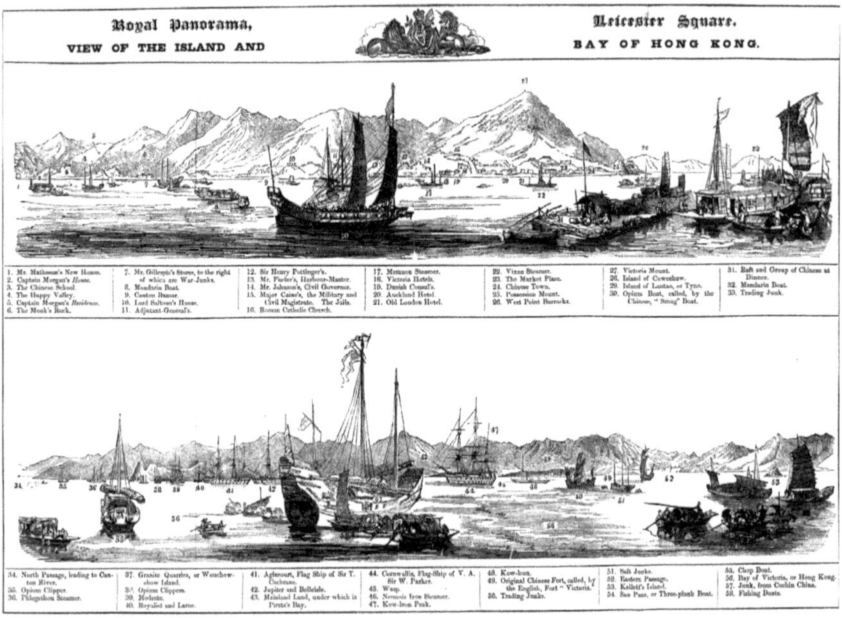

Figure 2.1 A picture of Hong Kong in 1844. Robert Burford, Description of a View of the Island and Bay of Hong Kong: Now Exhibiting at the Panorama, Leicester Square

(London: printed by J. Mitchell & Co., 1844). @P&O Heritage Collection www.poheritage.com

Another well-known extortion case relating to the market licensing system concerned Chow Aaon's collecting of bribes from Tam Choy in 1847. Tam Achoy was one of the monopolists of the market area of Hong Kong. When Tam Achoy applied for a market licence to Colonial Secretary Caine in March 1847, Chow supported the process of the application. Chow suggested that Tam pay a cumshaw to Caine to secure the lease at a lower rate. According to Tarrant's account at the extortion inquiry, Tam was required to pay $500.[43]

Tam did not pay the money following Tarrant's advice. Tarrant promised Tam that Cleverly, the Surveyor General, would grant a 10-year lease at a much lower price, less than $500 per annum. Therefore, Tam did not pay the bribe to Chow, but the outcome was not very successful. Tam was able to obtain only the shorter and more expensive 1-year lease for about $1,200 per annum.[44] Many of the new Chinese settlers in Hong Kong did not sufficiently understand the administrative system of the colonial government, and it was difficult for them to directly communicate with the colonial officials. Therefore, compradors like Chow and Lo were able to dominate and sometimes manipulate communications between British authorities and local Chinese businessmen.

It was not easy for newly dispatched colonial officials to supervise their house compradors because they did not have sufficient knowledge of the administration system and the accompanying extortion in the colonial government. Shay-Afoo, a comprador working for Attorney General Paul Ivy Sterling, extorted money from Chinese residents by pretending to be the comprador to the Chief Justice.[45] In 1844, Shay falsely arrested Sheang-ahoy and his cook Mok-aying in order to extort money from them. On 22 October, policemen arrested Sheang and Mok on charges of robbing a man at Sheang's shop in Aberdeen. The policemen ordered Sheang and Mok to come to see Shay to return the money to the robbed person. They went to Shay's house in Victoria, where the two were forced to sign a paper promising to return the stolen money. Shay styled himself the Chief Justice's comprador and threatened to beat Sheang if he did not sign the paper.

Sheang was also informed that he should go to the Supreme Court, not to William Caine, who was the Chief Magistrate at that time, if he had further enquiries. In the Supreme Court, Henry Sirr, the first barrister of Hong Kong, was defending Shay as counsel. A witness produced by Sirr described a different story. According to the witness, the shop owner and cook went to Shay's house of their own free will and offered to return the stolen money to avoid imprisonment. Shay offered to let them stay in his house so that they could avoid breaking the curfew, and so this was not a detention. Eventually, Shay was acquitted, while the other three policemen were sentenced to a month in jail.[46] This case reveals the existence of corruption within the judicial and police system in early Hong Kong, as Shay was able to collaborate with police officers to conduct his extortion.

Shay's employer, Paul Ivy Sterling, the Attorney General, had arrived in Hong Kong 3 months before the incident.[47] As a newcomer to Hong Kong, it may have been difficult for him to oversee and control his comprador's activities. On the other hand, Shay understood the system of corruption and extortion in the colonial government well. He recognised that the Chief Justice's comprador had the authority to make an arrest and the power to extort money from Chinese residents. Sterling might not have permitted his compradors to commit extortion, yet several colonial officials were certainly part of the extortion system.

The extortion and corruption system was underpinned by a mutually collaborative relationship between colonial officials and government compradors. While several officials were keen to investigate and reveal the extortion system maintained by colonial officials and their intermediaries, their efforts were hampered by other colonial officials' reluctance to combat corruption. For instance, Tarrant's investigation into market extortion did not greatly affect the later careers of the compradors and officials involved. Based on Tarrant's accusation in July 1847, Lo and Chow's extortion cases were investigated and enquiries held in the government. However, due to the absence of Lo Een-teen, who was reported to have left Hong Kong, the progress of the investigation was slow. Eventually Campbell, the acting Attorney General and a friend of Caine's, concluded that there were no legal grounds for the case. To make matters worse, Tarrant was sued for defaming Caine and discharged from his work in the government.[48] Lo escaped to Canton after the enquiry, but he returned to Hong Kong and worked for Caine as comprador again as early as in 1849. After his retirement, Lo even received a pension from Caine.[49] It seems Lo was still an influential

Chinese businessman in the late 1850s. Thomas Chisholm Anstey recorded that Lo ran several businesses in Hong Kong and Canton during that period.[50] Government compradors' commercial activities, corrupt or not, were often silently permitted, if not clearly supported, by their foreign principals.

For instance, in the mid-1850s, the collaborative relationship between a high-raking colonial official and his comprador in private commercial activities in Hong Kong drew public attention. The colonial official was Daniel Richard Caldwell, Register General and Protector of Chinese Inhabitants, and the comprador was Lai Sze Kai, a house comprador for Caldwell.[51] Lai Sze Kai was not involved in Caldwell's duties in the government; he was more involved in Caldwell's sideline businesses. Lai served Caldwell during the 1850s, but left his service in 1856 when Caldwell was appointed as Register General. Although Caldwell was known as an important intermediary between the foreign and Chinese community, he was frequently suspected and accused of connections with gang-related Chinese interests. In 1858, Anstey, the Attorney General, made accusations against Caldwell about his connections with Ma-chow Wong, a Chinese merchant who was arrested and charged with being in league with pirates. Anstey made 19 charges in total against Caldwell, one of which related to Lai's imprisonment for debt. Lai was suspected of making payment to obtain bail for Ma-chow Wong, and that constituted his debt. Lai Sze Kai was called to the witness stand in the enquiry led by the Governor Bowring in early June 1858. According to his testimony, Lai supported Caldwell and Ma-chow Wong's business in small coastal steamers between 1855 and 1856. During that period, Caldwell did not work for the government but ran a business protecting ships from pirates with Ma-chow Wong's collaboration. In 1858, after ceasing comprador service with Caldwell, Lai made his living by managing properties. He managed a shop with Low Ateem, a pharmacist and doctor who took care of Caldwell's children, and owned a shop on Stanley Street.[52] One of the witnesses stated that on the steamship, Lai provided shipping provisions to the crew, and therefore the witness recognised Lai as a ship comprador rather than house comprador.[53] That Lai could be regarded as either a ship or a house comprador suggests the demarcation line between the two types of the compradors had become blurred. Given the multiple services Lai provided to Caldwell, it is better to regard Lai as Caldwell's business partner and assistant.

Although Lai did not work for Caldwell as a comprador after Caldwell returned to the colonial government, Lai maintained a constructive business relationship with him. For instance, he collected rent on houses owned and managed by Caldwell and his wife, Mary Ayou Caldwell. He maintained a close relationship with them and collaborated in their property investment businesses. Working as comprador to Caldwell, Lai was able to establish extensive personal connections to conduct his property business. By 1858, Caldwell sold his four houses to Lum Ateen. Some of them were let to Lai for $50 per month, and Lai sublet the house for $57.[54]

Lai still had contacts with Caldwell's wife, Mary Ayou Caldwell. Lai introduced a Chinese house owner, Leong Atai, to Mrs Caldwell to arrange the sale of Leong's house. Lai and Caldwell maintained a trusting relationship after 1857. For instance, in February 1858, Lai went to see Caldwell to make a rent payment for Lum Ateen's lot. Lai asked Caldwell to provide a note to Lum so that Lai would be able to take money from the treasury. Caldwell suggested that Lai give the $50 rent to him directly, and that he would pay the money to Lum. Lai established partnerships with other Chinese intermediaries working around Caldwell. However, Lai's business was risky. He insisted that he was imprisoned for 6 or 7 days as a result of his partner's debt, rather than because he provided bail for Ma-Chow Wong in 1857.[55] It was beneficial for Lai to become a comprador to Caldwell in order to expand his business of property management. In return, Caldwell was able to conduct his own business because Lai was flexible and provided a variety of assistance in Caldwell's work.[56]

The symbiotic relationship between the colonial officials and the compradors can be further observed in the case of Ow A. Hoong and William Thomas Bridges, the Attorney Barrister. Ow A. Hoong was a comprador who worked with William Thomas Bridges for several years until early May 1858. Bridges was the Attorney Barrister and the Acting Attorney in the early 1850s, and the Acting Colonial Secretary in the late 1850s.[57] Ow supported Bridge's business with Chinese customers as well as his services to the colonial government. Bridges was known for his strong connections with the Chinese community, and this enabled him to make huge profits from various businesses in the colony, including in the opium trade and in land speculation.[58] In 1858, Bridges was suspected of receiving a bribe from an opium monopolist before the Opium Monopoly Ordinance was issued in March 1858.[59] Governor Bowring issued an ordinance on the opium monopoly in 1858 that granted an opium monopoly license to Chun Taikwong, a Christian convert, who had tendered a bid of $7,075 dollars.[60] Concerning this, the *Friend of China*, a local English newspaper, alleged that Bridges indirectly received the bribe as a retaining fee, and the issue came to public attention.[61] From the end of April, court cases were held to examine it.[62] During the inquiries, the mutually profitable relationship between Bridges and his comprador was highlighted.

According to the testimonials in the inquiries, Bridges' comprador supported his work in the colonial government and functioned as an intermediary between Bridges and his Chinese clients. In March 1858, Ow informed Bridges' Chinese client, Chun Taikwong, of the price of the retainer and collected $400 from him.[63] Before Chun was given the monopoly, he did not meet Bridges directly. Rather, the comprador mediated between them. Ow was sent to Chun to bring him to sign a bond at the government office. At the same time, he was also sent to Caldwell to bring Yeong Achew, who had been acquainted with Ow for 10 years, as surety.

Both Ow and Chun were familiar with Caldwell. Chun seems to have worked with Caldwell before 1858. He went to see Caldwell to confirm that his name was not on the list of the interpreters in the Supreme Court, because if he were on the list, he would not be able to obtain the monopoly. During the inquiries, Ow mentioned that he himself was interested in the grant of the opium monopoly and that he held one share out of 8 or 10 in a firm called 'Tai-Foong', which was one of the applicants. Ow stated that he stopped providing services to Bridges about

2 weeks before the commission on 17 May, and he insisted that thereafter he had not communicated with Bridges. After ceasing his service to Bridges, Ow stayed in Macau for a month from the middle of April. When Ow returned to Hong Kong in early May, Bridges discharged him due to his long absence.[64] However, as Ow had worked with Bridges for several years, this discharge seemed too sudden. It was possible that Ow acted as a collector of bribes on behalf of Bridges. The government compradors and the colonial officials who employed them formulated a mutually profitable extortion and corruption system in the 1840s and the 1850s.

It should be noted that the position of comprador itself was not necessarily profitable when compared with other Chinese staff positions in the colonial government, including interpreters, writers, coolies and police officers. Compradors' salaries were not as high as those of other Chinese staff. In 1845, the annual salary of the comprador in the Surveyor General's office was in the lowest grade in the office, and was likely to be less than £40, while middle-ranking class officials, such as clerk and bookkeeper in the office, obtained more than £200.[65] In the same year, different types of Chinese staff in the public sector obtained substantially greater incomes. Two Chinese clerks for the Colonial Surgeon were estimated to receive £52 and £39 individually.[66] The position of comprador itself was not lucrative, and this might have been because they were expected to receive commissions from mediating in business deals between foreign officials and Chinese merchants. However, it could also be one of the reasons for the government compradors' engagement in external businesses and corruption-related activities.

The case of Wong A-tong, who was the Chief Justice's comprador in the 1850s, demonstrates the kind of commercial activities the house compradors of colonial officials engaged in.[67] John Walter Hulme was the Chief Justice of Hong Kong from 1844 to 1860, and was believed to be Wong's employer.[68] In addition to his work for the Chief Justice, Wong conducted a business providing Chinese servants to European residents. By doing this, he could obtain 15 per cent to 20 per cent of the servants' salaries as a commission fee.[69] Wong also worked with other merchants and compradors in Hong Kong. In 1856, Wong mediated a trade of flour between Sing Long Hong, a Chinese firm, and Woochoon, a comprador.[70]

It was common for government compradors to manage external businesses. However, the cases of the compradors of Caldwell and Bridges indicate that collaborative external commercial activities of the compradors and their principals were sometimes related to corruption and extortion.

In the first two decades of the colony, the government compradors acted as indispensable official intermediaries and contributed to the construction of official institutions and the establishment of British public services. While the compradors were supporting the colonial officials' work, they established close ties with their foreign principals. The compradors' in-depth involvement in their official work gave them authority as the dominant communication conduits between the colonial government and the local Chinese residents. Both the compradors and the colonial officials were keen to make a profit from their work for the colonial government and their sideline businesses, and their symbiotic relationship created systematic corruption and extortion. Some British officials, especially Tarrant and Anstey, vigorously investigated this symbiotic, mutually profitable system involving some of the colonial officials and the government compradors from the late 1840s to the late 1850s. The devaluation of the credibility of the compradors hastened their decline in social significance during that period.

The decline of the government compradors

The government compradors became less significant by the end of the 1850s in Hong Kong society. After 1860, the number of records on government compradors in newspapers and official documents declined.[71] The social importance of the government compradors faded, and the term 'comprador' came to refer to 'the wealthy, influential and semi-independent manager-intermediaries' working in large foreign firms rather than the compradors in the public sector.[72] The main reasons for the decline of the government compradors were the reformation of the employment system of the colonial government, the government compradors' lack of social credibility as representatives of the Chinese community, and, related to that, the emergence of external mercantile intermediaries, especially the company compradors, by the late 1860s. It should be noted that analysis of the decline of the government compradors was methodologically challenging, as many colonial organisations did not formally record the employment of compradors, or recorded them in a different category, such as 'Chinese clerk'. Within the limited available primary sources, it is possible to determine these three main causes of the fall of the government comprador system, as explained in the following section.

Throughout the nineteenth century, the institutions of the colonial government gradually abolished the position of the comprador while appointing a greater variety and number of Chinese staff. This reflected the British officials' accumulation of knowledge about the Chinese community in Hong Kong and decades of working experience with them. By 1860, the colonial officials learnt what kind of Chinese workers were required for the smooth administration of the colony, and demand for compradors – flexible intermediaries providing a variety of services to the officials – decreased. The duties of the compradors were fragmented and were inherited by a variety of Chinese staff. In 1847, Governor John Francis Davis suggested to Earl Grey the abolition of the position of comprador and two chain-bearers in the Chief Magistrate's Department, because the 'provisions for the convicts were now obtained by contract'. Instead of employing the comprador, Davis was authorised to employ a Chinese shroff for £10 per month, which could be cheaper than employing a comprador.[73] As Davis stated, a number of external purveyors procured provisions for the prisoners in Victoria Gaol from the late 1840s. Their main duty was serving provisions to the jail on a yearly contract. Contract documents relating to the provision purveyors serving the jail demonstrate that multiple purveyors were employed at a time. In 1848, Lang Akhuw (Liang Qiu), Tang Atim (Tang Tian) and Tang Aming (Tang Ning) were suppliers of provisions to the jail. They brought provisions listed in the contract, for instance, 'wood, oil, lamp-wick and soap', for a year.[74] In this way, the work of the compradors was gradually taken over by other internal and external Chinese workers in the colonial government.

This trend of the reduction of compradors in the government continued at the end of the nineteenth century. In 1897, Governor William Robinson wrote to Joseph Chamberlain about the resignation of comprador Cheng-Chung, who worked in the Police Works Department. Chan Ashing, a former foreman in the Ordinance Store Department, was recommended as the comprador's successor. The Director of Public Works who had recommended Chan Ashin suggested that the new officer be called 'Head Store Keeper' rather than 'Comprador' because the latter title seemed a 'misnomer' for the position.[75] By 1897, the Police Works Department was able clarify what kinds of Chinese staff they needed, and so did not need to utilise the makeshift term 'comprador' any longer. In this manner, the positions of the compradors in the colonial government were dissolved, while different kinds of Chinese staff were employed, or sometimes the title of comprador was altered to a different title.[76] The reformation of the employment system of the staff of the colonial government also enabled the elimination of government compradors.

The Governor, Sir Hercules Robinson (1859–1865), led a reformation of the administrative system of the Chinese community, and this reduced the number of colonial officials who were employers of influential government compradors. In August 1860, Robinson organised a Civil Service Abuses Enquiry, which investigated the works of Caldwell again, and eventually led Caldwell's dismissal from government service.[77] Caine had already retired in 1859, and Bridges left the colony in 1861. The retirement of the early generation of colonial officials who maintained Anglo-Chinese extortion system caused the decline of the government compradors associated with them.[78] Moreover, Robinson introduced the Hong Kong Cadet Scheme, which aimed to produce colonial officials to act as mediators between the government and the Chinese populace. Under the scheme, young British administrative recruits studied Chinese languages and received administrative training before their dispatch to Hong Kong.[79] From 1862, the colonial government started employing the trained cadets, who were generally effective as interpreters and mediators and who had a degree of knowledge of the Chinese language, culture and society. One of their representatives was Cecil Clementi Smith, who was a student interpreter in Hong Kong in 1862 and later became Colonial Treasurer there.[80] In this way, the colonial government reduced dependence on Chinese intermediaries for communication with the local Chinese citizens in the early 1860s, and this led to the reduction of the number of compradors in the colonial government.

Another possible cause of the decline of the government compradors was their inability to secure social positions in Hong Kong. Everett Stonequist argues that the 'marginal man' who belongs to two opposing ethnicities and cultures is vulnerable to rejection and scorn from both sides. Those people in marginal positions, for instance Eurasians, constantly feel isolation and insecurity, and therefore are eager to engage in charitable work to obtain 'social recognition' and 'social approval'.[81] Late nineteenth-century company compradors recognised their vulnerability and therefore actively participated in public activities to strengthen their social status in Hong Kong. This will be explained in detail in the fifth chapter. However, government compradors were not greatly involved in public activities in the 1840s and the 1850s. During that period, the group of representative figures in the Chinese community did not include government compradors.

Chinese merchants, property owners and contractors (for example, Tam Achoy) took leading roles in the Chinese community through their involvement in public issues. However, influential government compradors like Chow Aaon and Lo Een-teen were not eager to participate in public activities in Hong Kong in the 1840s.[82] In addition, the recurrent scandals and the government compradors' involvement in extortion and corruption decreased their capability to function as intermediary elites advancing the interests of the Chinese community in Hong Kong.

Besides, the rise of the company compradors and other commercial and intellectual elites enabled the colonial government to outsource the role of the intermediaries streamlining communication between colonial officials and Chinese citizens. These intellectual and mercantile elites emerged during the late 1850s due to the influx of well-to-do Chinese merchants escaping from the devastation in South China caused by the Taiping Uprising.[83] The intermediary elites established multiple social associations and institutions for policing, administration, education and medical services, and they consolidated their social status. In 1872, the Tung Wah Hospital was formally established. It was recognised as a semi-official administrative institution of the Chinese community by the colonial government.[84] In this manner, the colonial government increased the number of credible British intermediaries and began drawing on external intermediary elites for the administration of the Chinese community during the 1860s, reducing the colonial government's reliance on internal Chinese intermediaries.

Government compradors after the 1860s

Although the government compradors became less significant in Hong Kong society, a small number of government compradors continued to work for colonial institutions in the 1860s and the 1870s. Working with company compradors, some of the government compradors advanced their commercial activities and their social credibility. For instance, guarantees of the Post Office compradors included notable company comprador names. In 1860, Fung Achew (Feng Daozhao) engaged at the Post Office as comprador and his surety was Ng Tuk hang (Wu Deheng), a comprador to Lindsay & Co.[85] The surety of Mang Fook Liu, a shroff at the Post Office in the 1870s, was Tsoi King Nam, a comprador to Jardine, Matheson & Co., who paid $1,000 for the security bond.[86] Security bonds from well-known company compradors increased the reliability of the Post Office compradors and other Chinese staff. This contributed to the maintenance of the stable comprador system at the Post Office in the latter half of the nineteenth century. For the government compradors, networking with company compradors was key to surviving the decline.

In the 1860s and the 1870s, Pedro Leung Hing Kee, a commissariat comprador, acted as a company comprador and was successful in the commercial world of

Hong Kong. Hing Kee, alias Pang Ahim and Pang A. Yim (Peng Yan), became more than a provision purveyor. He was a notable commissariat comprador in the 1870s. He was well known for running various private businesses in addition to taking a compradorship.[87] In the 1870s, Hing Kee was a well-to-do entrepreneur and property owner in Hong Kong. In February 1870, he owned 50 shares in Saigon & Straits S. S. Co. Ltd.[88] When Fletcher's Buildings on the Queen's Road East caught fire during the night of 12 March 1876, Hing Kee was using a portion of the building.[89] Hing Kee seemed to be responsible for the management of the godown (warehouse), but it is not certain whether he used the building for his own business purposes or for his service to the commissariat. Hing Kee invested heavily in property and land and succeeded in its management in the 1870s in the same manner as company compradors including Kwok Achoeng had.[90] The exceptional prosperity of Hing Kee as a government comprador was possible because he emulated the commercial activities of the company compradors.

Conclusion

During the period when administrative institutions were being established, from the 1840s to the 1850s, the colonial officials employed compradors who could deal with Chinese matters. During the first decade of the colony, it was hard for the colonial officials to determine what work was necessary for the administration of the Chinese community, and therefore they employed compradors who could flexibly conduct and expand their work to establish colonial organisations. An absence of clear and coherent policies for the employment of the intermediaries resulted in the concurrent existence of two types of government comprador. First, an official institution could employ a comprador. Second, an individual civil servant could personally employ a comprador. The functions of these compradors included providing provisions, overseeing Chinese staff, assisting their principals' duties in the colonial government, and assisting in the external commercial activities of their principals. Working opportunities in the colonial government provided the compradors with the knowledge and human network to run side businesses, such as in land and property investment. In this way, the government compradors emerged as official intermediaries between the colonial government and the Chinese society during the 1840s.

However, the colonial government gradually reduced its dependence on the compradors in the 1850s and the 1860s. A lack of a clear policy defining and supervising the government compradors' duties enabled the corrupt colonial officials and the government compradors to establish a symbiotic relationship. This unhealthy relationship between the compradors and their principals caught public attention and became a scandal in the 1850 and the 1860s. Eventually, the employment system for Chinese and foreign staff was reformed to reduce the problem. The government introduced a more effective employment system by educating and hiring British intermediaries. By allocating tasks previously performed by compradors to other positions, the colonial government reduced the number of compradors in its employ. In parallel, mercantile elites, including the company compradors, had formed a semi-official organisation and an alternative system for the administration of the Chinese community by the late 1860s. These mercantile and intellectual elites obtained broader public support than did the government compradors, whose credibility was often questioned because of their involvement in extortion and corruption, in collaboration with high-ranking colonial officials. In effect, the colonial government began to draw on external Chinese social organisations, such as Tung Wah Hospital, to bridge the gulf between the Chinese and British communities, instead of directly hiring Chinese intermediaries. In this way, the government compradors lost their oligopolistic status; their importance had declined by the late 1860s while the prosperity of the company compradors continued to rise.

Notes

1 Munn, *Anglo-China*, 325–328.
2 *Hongkong Government Gazette*: Nos 1 and 2, 1 and 15 May 1841, containing official notices of the government and population of the island, 286–287. In September 1841, the *Chinese Repository* gave notice that T.G. Fitz Gibbon was appointed as a clerk in charge of the Post Office. *Chinese Repository*, Vol. 10, from January to December 1841, 528.
3 Endacott, *Biographical Sketch-book*, 60.
4 *Chinese Repository*, Vol. 10 (1841), 479.
5 *Chinese Repository*, Vol. 11 (1842), 'List of British Authorities in China' (February 1842), 114–115.
6 Ho, *Administrative History*, 48–49, 222.
7 BPP: Accounts and Papers, Estimates, & c. Miscellaneous Services: for the Year Ending 31 March 1846, 'Hong Kong and Ports in China', 405–406.
8 Jarman, *Hong Kong Annual Administration Report*, ed., Vol. 1, 'Colonial Estimates, Hong Kong, 1876', 472.
9 TNA: CO 129/5, Colonial Accounts, 14 June 1844, 404–516.
10 *Canton Press*, 24 July 1841; Smith, *Sense of History*, 47; Fay, *Opium War*, 226–227.
11 *China Mail*, 19 July 1849, 115.
12 BPP: *House of Commons and Command*, Vol. 15 (1866), 124.
13 In the early 1840s, the colonial government decided to let the village elders administer the Chinese population. For the detail of Tepo system in Hong Kong, see Ting, 'Native Chinese Peace Officers', 147–158.
14 *China Mail*, 19 July 1849.
15 TNA: CO129/5, Colonial Accounts, 14 June 1844, 398–403 includes the number of receipts signed by several compradors working for the colonial government including Aaon.
16 TNA: CO133/4, *Blue Book* (1847), 81.
17 Ibid.
18 Smith, *Chinese Christians*, 127–128.
19 BPP: *China*, Vol. 24, May to Bridges, 29 July 1856, 509; *Government Gazette*, 29 January 1876, 49.
20 TNA: CO129/5: Wages for persons working for the police establishment, July 1843, 427–428; Mok's receipt, 1 August 1843, 429 and September 1843, 497–499. Another person whose surname was Mok was working in the police establishment as clerk.
21 TNA: CO129/5, Special service under the order of Major General Lord Saltoun Commanding Ordnance, 1 August 1843, 468–469.

22 TNA: CO129/5, Her Britannic Majesty's Government of Hong Kong to Achun (Comprador), Hong Kong, 6 September 1843 (Macau), 492.
23 Ibid., 491.
24 For the Chinese builders and contractors, see Carroll, *Edge of Empires*, 23–28; Smith, *Chinese Christians*, 114–116.
25 *Chinese Repository*, Vol. 10, from January to December 1841, 528.
26 Royal Mail Archive, London: POST 4/15, Colonial and Foreign Allowance Book, Salaries and Allowances to Postmasters, Agents and Other Post Office Employees Overseas, 1844–1857 (microfilm). On 14 September 1846, 1 comprador and 4 coolies were working. During the 1840s to the 1850s, 1 comprador was constantly working in the Post Office.
27 Proud, *Postal History*, Vol. 1, 43.
28 TNA: CO 129/389, Pension of Mr Chun Mau Yung, 20 March 1912, 196–202.
29 TNA: CO133/30, *Blue Book*, 1873, 72–73.
30 HKPRO: HKRS149–2-628, Security Bond; CO 133/28, *Blue Books*, 1871, 76.
31 TNA: CO 129/244, Despatches, Pension to Mr Cin Tsun, Compradore in Post Office, 10 January 1890, 32–39.
32 TNA: CO 129/389, Pension of Mr Chun Mau Yung, 20 March 1912, 199; for the establishment of the British postal service in nineteenth-century China, see Bishop, Morton and Sayers, *Hong Kong and Treaty Ports*, 2nd edn.
33 George Wingrove Cooke noted his impression of the house compradors in Hong Kong in the late 1850s. For him, the most of the residents of the colony had a comprador who dealt with accounts and employment of Chinese staff. Cooke, *China and Lower Bengal*, 57.
34 Cooke, *China and Lower Bengal*, 67.
35 TNA: CO129/30, Gaskell to Bonham, 8 December 1849, 408.
36 Evans, 'The Origins of Hong Kong's Central Market', 150. Lower Bazaar was around the present-day Bonham Strand and Jervois Street. Upper Bazaar was around the area of today's Aberdeen Street and the east side of Hollywood Road, close to Kau U Fong and Gough Street. Ho (Johnson, trans.), *Challenges for Evolving City*, 44; also see Plate 2. Lower Bazzar was estimated to be in the area of Chinese Town (No. 24).
37 Evans, 'The Origins of Hong Kong's Central Market', 150–151.
38 Luk, 'Monopoly, Transaction and Extortion', 158. TNA: CO 129/20, Inquest by Campbell, 6 July 1847, 235–236.
39 The Central Market was located on the same site as the present Central Market on Des Voeux Road. Luk, 'Monopoly, Transaction, and Extotion', 143; TNA: FO233/186, Will of Wei Aqui, 32; CO129/5, Receipt for wages paid for persons employed in the government market places at Victoria, Hong Kong, July 1843, 413.
40 TNA: CO 129/20, Inquest by Campbell, 6 July 1847, 247–248.
41 TNA: CO 129/20, Inquest by Campbell, 6 July 1847, 237. Wei Afoon also stated, 'Lo-Een-Teen has told me that the money which I have paid him form the market was for Major Caine's use. He always said every time he talked to me'. 249.
42 Chow-aon's connection with Tam Achoy and Colonel Caine's comprador, TNA: CO129/20, Lo Een-teen. Tarrant to Cleverly (Acting Colonial Treasurer), 3 July 1847, 233–234.
43 TNA: CO 129/20, Inquest by Campbell, 6 July 1847, 244, 260–261.
44 Ibid. 260–261. Luk,'Monopoly, Transaction and Extortion', 156–157. In the inquiry, Tam also stated that when he visited Major Aldrich's office to make a contract, Aldrich's comprador, Lum Choong alias A-how, attempted to obtain a five per cent commission from the total amount of money Tam should receive, since 'all others paid the same' (261).
45 *Hongkong Register*, 24 December 1844, 215, cited in Munn, *Anglo-China*, 187–188.
46 Ibid.

47 Norton-Kyshe, *History of Laws*, Vol. 1, 56.
48 Anstey, *Crime and Government*, 40–46.
49 Luk, 'Monopoly, Transactions and Extortion', 166.
50 Anstey, *Crime and Government*, 40–46.
51 *Report of Commission*, 15; Endacott, *Biographical Sketch-book*, 97.
52 BPP, *House of Commons Paper*, Vol. 48 (1860), Hong Kong, Minutes of Meeting of a Commission, held at the Council Chamber, 27 May 1858, 92–195, List of charges, 88; *Report of Commission*, 15–16.
53 BPP, *House of Commons and Command*, Vol. 48, Hong Kong, Minutes of Meeting of a Commission, held at the Council Chamber, 27 May 1858, 171.
54 Report of Commission, 15.
55 Ibid., 15–16, 23, 25–26.
56 For a detailed explanation on the Caldwell affair, see Christopher Munn, 'Colonialism "in a Chinese atmosphere" '.
57 *Friend of China*, 27 October 1858, 342; Norton-Kyshe, *History of Laws*, Vol. 1, 551 and Vol. 2, 13.
58 Report of Commission, 66.
59 Endacott, *Biographical Sketch-Book*, 127.
60 TNA: CO129/67, Bowring to Labouchere, 23 March 1858, 303–306.
61 BPP, Accounts and papers of the House of Commons, Vol. 38 (1860), Hong Kong, 11.
62 *Hong Kong Register*, 30 March, 20 April, 4 May, and 11 May 1858, 55, 70, 78 and 84.
63 BPP, *Accounts and papers of the House of Commons*, Vol. 35 (1860), Hong Kong, 16–17.
64 Ibid., 23.
65 BPP, *House of Commons Papers*, Vol. 29, Accounts and Papers, Estimates, &c. Miscellaneous services: for the year ending 31 March 1846, 'Hong Kong and Ports in China', 20.
66 BPP, *House of Commons Papers*, Vol. 28, Accounts and Papers, Estimates, &c. Miscellaneous services: for the year ending 31 March 1846, 'Hong Kong and Ports in China', 19–20.
67 Munn, 'Hong Kong', 391.
68 Endacott, Biographical Sketch-book, 66.
69 *China Mail*, 11 December 1851, 198.
70 *China Mail*, 14 February 1856, 26.
71 The *Blue Books* issued form the 1840s to the 1880s suggest a general increase in the number of Chinese staff in the colonial government; however, no comprador was recorded from 1860 onwards except the comprador in the Post Office.
72 Munn, 'Hong Kong', 390.
73 TNA: CO 129/21, 23 September 1847, Resignation of Mr Fittock, 47–50.
74 HKPRO: HKRS77-1-4, Provisions Bond, May 1848–May 1849.
75 TNA: CO 129/278, William Robinson to Joseph Chamberlain, 18 December 1897, Comprador in Public Works Department, 458–461.
76 TNA: CO133/1–CO133/31, *Blue Books*, 1844–1874.
77 Endacott, *Biographical Sketch-book*, 98–99; Minutes of Inquiry.
78 Endacott, *Biographical Sketch-book*, 45–46, 128.
79 Ding, 'Lishi de zhuanzhe'.
80 Tsang, *Governing Hong Kong*, 21–22; *NCH*, 12 February 1916, Obituary of Cecil Clementi Smith, 407.
81 Stonequist, *Marginal Man*; Zheng and Wong, *Xianggang dalao,* 87–89.
82 Chan, *Making of Hong Kong*, 73; TNA: CO129/23, The Memorial of British and Other Inhabitants of Hong Kong, 222–227.
83 Carroll, *Edge of Empires*, 49–50.

84 Ding 'Lishi de zhuanzhe', 100–101.
85 HKPRO: HKRS149–2-248 Bond from the comprador to office – cancelled, 18 August 1860.
86 HKPRO: HKRS149–2-589, Bond: Mang Fook Liu, 30 November 1870.
87 *China Mail*, 5 June 1879, 3; *The China Directory* published in 1873 and 1874 recorded that Pang Fong Poo was a comprador to Commissariat in Hong Kong.
88 JMA: B7/15, Business letters: Hong Kong, Pang A Yim to the General Agent, Saigon & Straits S.S. Co. Ltd, 8th February 1870.
89 *Straits Times*, 25 March 1876, 4.
90 *Government Gazette*, 4 March 1882, 241. Hui, 'Comprador Politics', 37–38; Yuan, ed., *Xianggang Shilue*, 130.

3 The company compradors

A great diversity of compradors mediated business transactions between foreign and Chinese businessmen in mid-nineteenth century Hong Kong. There were compradors simply procuring daily necessities for foreign residents and ships, while there were also compradors managing shops selling provisions. In this milieu, between the 1840s and the 1860s, the compradors working for foreign companies and banks achieved recognisable commercial success and increased their economic importance in Hong Kong society. From the 1840s to the 1850s, the compradors working for the colonial institutions and officials emerged as essential intermediaries between the colonial government and the Chinese settlers. However, the government compradors had lost their indispensability by the middle of the 1860s while the company compradors emerged as socio-economic mediators. This chapter explains the general functions of the company compradors in the foreign houses, suggesting possible factors that transformed the commercial compradors into indispensable and able economic middlemen.

Compradors in the private sector

In outlining the rise of the company compradors, this section explains the general features and transitions of the comprador system in the Hong Kong private sector from the 1840s to the 1880s. Specifically, it focuses on the transformation of the population of compradors, the continuous importance of ship compradors as provision purveyors, and the social background of the company compradors. The population of compradors gradually increased throughout the nineteenth century, sharply increasing from the late 1860s to the early 1870s. As explained in Chapter 1, the early compradors were intermediaries or provision purveyors working with foreigners in the Pearl River Delta before the British occupation of Hong Kong in 1841. In addition, compradors emerged from the Christian community in China. Several notable compradors were formerly educated in missionary schools. Many foreign companies employed these Chinese graduates of Western schools as compradors. However, there were also individual compradors who were externally providing provisions to foreigners in the colony. Focusing on the emergence of the different types of compradors, the following sections highlight the complexity of the comprador system in the private sector in nineteenth-century Hong Kong.

Official census records highlight the shifts in the population of compradors in nineteenth-century Hong Kong, as the colonial government recorded the numbers and types of local Chinese shops from 1847. However, the accuracy of this census, which was conducted in the early period of the colony, is often questioned. The census usually merely investigated the foreign residential areas like Stanley and Victoria, neglecting Chinese residential areas such as villages in Kowloon and the communities of boat-dwelling people. Yet the information of the census is still useful for analysing the general transitions in the population of compradors from the 1840s to the 1880s. According to the census recorded in the *Blue Books* and the *Government Gazette*, the number of compradors increased overall from the 1840s to the 1880s. During the 1840s, the government did not determine how many compradors were operating in Hong Kong. Rather, the censuses recorded the number of shops, houses or occupational populations of Chinese residents. In 1847, only two comprador shops were recorded.[1] These two shops were Acow & Co. (*Anji*) on Queen's Road and Wing-woe at Taipingshan, as recorded in the *Hong Kong Almanack and Directory for 1846*.[2] Acow & Co. seemed to conduct its business in Canton in the 1850s; the company sold provisions to Thomas Hunt & Co. in 1856.[3] But it is highly probable that there were more than two compradors in 1847. The census in 1847 recorded only those compradors who had opened shops; however, there were compradors directly employed by foreign residents or companies during this period. Table 3.1 suggests, from 1852 to 1867, the population of compradors gradually increased from around 10 to 40, but it did not increase at a constant rate. From 1854 to 1864, the number of compradors fluctuated between 20 and 33.[4] The demand for compradors slowly increased throughout the decade. Then the number of compradors sharply rose between 1866 and 1870; the census recorded 43 compradors in 1866 but 76 in the 1870s. Thereafter, the total number of compradors kept increasing until it reached 95 in 1881. Compared to the population of other middle-class intermediaries, the number of compradors was not small. In 1876, the census recorded nine linguists, 40 shroffs and 77 compradors.[5] The compradors thus became a pivotal group of middlemen from the early 1870s onwards.

Table 3.1 Population of compradors[1]

1847	*1851*	*1852*	*1854*	*1855*	*1856*	*1857*	*1858*	*1859*	*1860*
2	6	10	22	27	20	23	30	26	33
1861	*1863*	*1864*	*1865*	*1866*	*1867*	*1870*	*1871*	*1876*	*1881*
28	26	33	37	43	39	76	76	77	95

[1] From *Blue Books* 1847–1871, *Government Gazette*, 1877, *Administrative Reports*, 1881. In 1847, two compradors' houses or shops in Stanley; in 1851, six shops of compradors in Victoria; in 1856 and 1857, a total of 20 and 23 compradors' houses in Victoria respectively. The data on 1857–1868 included both Victoria and villages.

The question is, why did the population of compradors rise sharply between the end of the1860s and the beginning of the 1870s? A possible explanation is the economic growth of Hong Kong during this period. By the 1870s, many foreign firms had opened offices in Hong Kong. The number of ships coming from and going to Hong Kong sharply increased from the late 1850s to the early 1860s. Between 1859 and 1860, the number of fishing junks increased from 2,000 to 2,500. From 1850 to 1860, the total number of ships arriving and leaving Hong Kong increased from 883 to 2,888.[6] In 1867, almost 20 per cent of goods imported to mainland China came from Hong Kong; by 1877, this had increased to about 36 per cent. Similarly, in 1867, approximately 14 per cent of the mainland's export goods were coming to Hong Kong; within a decade, this had increased to about 23 per cent.[7] In addition to that, a significant number of Chinese merchants and traders were operating in Hong Kong during this period. There was an influx of Chinese business elites to Hong Kong from South China due to the social confusion caused by the Taiping Uprising and the Second Opium War.[8] The Chinese population nearly doubled from around 40,000 to 75,500 between 1853 and 1858.[9] There were also a large number of Chinese firms engaging in business with foreign firms during this period.[10] In 1875 and 1881 respectively, there were 215 and 393 trading hongs (Chinese trading firms and merchants).[11] The demand for compradors to act as commercial intermediaries increased concurrently with the rise of Hong Kong as a trading centre.

Additional types of compradors were operating in Hong Kong in the nineteenth century aside from the commercial compradors who were working with foreign firms and banks. For example, individual residents employed compradors on their own. The main function of these compradors was to obtain provisions for individual foreign residents. Elizabeth McMullin Muter, the wife of British military personnel Lieutenant-Colonel Douglas Muter, noted the comprador's role as a provision purveyor when they stayed in Hong Kong in 1861. The comprador sought out food provisions, for instance, rice birds, Whampoa beef and Shanghai mutton, and brought them to Elizabeth's house upon her request.[12] In the 1860s, there were also compradors responsible for the domestic duties of foreign residences in Hong Kong.[13] However, while these two traditional types of compradors continued to work as house stewards and provision purveyors, company and bank compradors increased their importance in the commercial world of Hong Kong in the 1860s.

One of the most important duties of all compradors continued to be the provision of food to foreigners in nineteenth-century Hong Kong. During the 1840s, a few compradors opened shops selling provisions. One of the earliest comprador shops was the above-mentioned Acow & Co.[14] It should be noted that there were also multiple ship compradors working with foreigners as provision purveyors in Hong Kong from the 1840s. For instance, a ship comprador called A-tai had been serving foreign ships for about 20 years by 1859.[15] By the 1870s, however, the main duty of commercial compradors was no longer seen as supplying provisions.[16] This was possibly because, by this point, foreign firms were able to obtain daily necessities from external ship compradors whose main work was selling provisions to foreigners. For instance, Jardine, Matheson & Co. purchased provisions from an external comprador in the early 1870s. Shew Yuan (Shaoyuan), a comprador whose shop was in Central Market, provided groceries and food to Jardine each day.[17] Another provisions comprador, Tai Yune (Taiyuan), was recorded in Shaw Yuan's account book, which is preserved in the Jardine Matheson Archive. The comprador Tai Yune, whose store was located in Central Market, provided provisions such as beef, boiling fish, Bombay onions, coffee and rice to Jardine. Both Shaw Yuan and Tai Yune's stores were on the list of ship compradors and chandlers in the *China Directory* (1874). These ship compradors' shops seemed to be concentrated in two areas: Central Market and Endicott Lane. Shaw Yuan's store was at No. 2 Central Market, and Tai Yune's store was at No. 4. Fourteen ship compradors' and chandlers' shops were located in Central Market, out of 42 in total. Another 14 stores were on Endicott Lane.[18] The owners of their own shops, these ship compradors acted as external provision purveyors to foreign firms and ships. Jardine's practice of obtaining provisions from external compradors could already be observed in the 1850s, as Acow & Co. were trading with the firm in Canton.[19]

By the 1860s, these ship compradors had become the main providers of provisions to foreign ships, companies and possibly also other foreign residences. The official census conducted in the 1870s to the 1890s categorised compradors and ship compradors differently.[20] In the *China Directory* issued in 1874, 'Ship compradors and chandlers' were listed in addition to the list of principal compradors.[21] In 1879, another commercial guidebook listed 24 shops run by ship compradors.[22] Ship compradors inherited the function of old Canton compradors as provision purveyors, while 'compradors' adopted the function of commercial intermediaries. The population of ship compradors increased in a similar manner to that of compradors. In 1876, there were 67 ship compradors in Hong Kong and 77 compradors.[23] In 1881, there were 113 ship compradors and only 95 compradors.[24] Numerous advertisements and notifications related to the ship compradors appeared in contemporary newspapers. For instance, an advertisement for Cheap Jack & Co., 'Ship chandlers and ships' compradors', appeared in the *Daily Advertiser* on 6 October 1871.[25] In 1889, Wing Kee & Co. styled themselves as ship chandlers, coal merchants and compradors in an advertisement.[26]

In this manner, while ship compradors continued to function as provision suppliers, the new wave of compradors emerged as a distinct category of commercial intermediary. In the middle of the nineteenth century, these various compradors were ubiquitous in Hong Kong society. Many foreign firms had employed compradors since the 1840s. Concurrently, different types of compradors worked with foreign residents for different purposes. Of them, company and bank compradors became especially influential in the commercial world of Hong Kong by the 1880s. For the Chinese, being a merchant or taking a compradorship with a foreign company provided avenues towards wealth in late nineteenth-century Hong Kong. As such, the following section illuminates who the commercial compradors were, and how they became indispensable intermediaries and wealthy merchants by working with foreign companies in nineteenth-century Hong Kong.

The company compradors

The company compradors were crucial internal intermediaries for foreign firms in Hong Kong throughout the nineteenth century. In particular, the socio-economic success of 'head' compradors became evident in the early 1870s. The *China Directory*, published between 1872 and 1874, listed the principal compradors (also called 'chief' and 'head' compradors) holding the highest positions among Chinese staff in foreign institutions in Hong Kong. Table 3.2 shows the list of the principal compradors appearing in the *China Directory* in the edition of 1874. The nationalities of the foreign firms in which the head compradors were working were diverse; they included British, American, French, German and Indian firms. Examples of well-known head compradors were: Leung On serving Gibb, Livingston & Co.; Wei Akwong (Wei Guang) serving the Mercantile Bank; Mok Sze Yeung (Mo Shiyang) serving Augustine Heard & Co.; and Ng Kee serving Jardine, Matheson & Co.[27] This section examines the social background and the multiple roles of these commercial compradors. It also examines their relationship with the foreign firms and banks from the 1840s to the 1880s in order to explain the rise of the head compradors in the late nineteenth century.

The social backgrounds of the commercial compradors were highly diverse, yet it is clear that the majority of Hong Kong compradors came from Guangdong. In particular, many compradors' hometowns or villages were located in Xiangshan county. Sung Chin Tseung (Song Zhanxiang) moved to Hong Kong with his father, Shau U (Shou Yu), from Xiangshan prefecture in 1842 'to do business as a comprador'. Sung joined Turner and Co.'s office as a comprador in 1854 and served the firm for more than 30 years.[28] Mok Sze Yeung and Wei Akwong were also from Xiangshan country. Aside from Xiangshan, Panyu county and Nanhai county produced multiple compradors in Hong Kong and the treaty ports of China.[29] These Cantonese compradors served foreign firms in Shanghai and the other treaty ports and established a large business network in the late nineteenth century. For these Cantonese compradors, Hong Kong was a popular destination for migration.

Another feature of the early compradors was their Western educational background. Specifically, Christian schools provided a Western-style education, which enabled Chinese students to learn the English language – an important ability for a comprador. The case of Wei Akwong was representative, as many compradors emerged from missionary schools. The Revd E. C. Bridgman rescued Akwong from illness and starvation on the streets of Macau in the late 1830s. Akwong was later sent to Singapore, where he studied at the American Board School for Chinese until 1843.[30] Thereafter, he worked for Bridgman, and ultimately became a comprador to Bowra and Co. in 1851.[31] Another example is Fung Ming-shan (Feng Mingshan), who studied at St Paul's College before he became a comprador, first to Hogg & Co. and later for the Mercantile Bank in the late nineteenth century.[32] In addition to language skills, Chinese students were able to establish connections with foreigners in Hong Kong since many of them were Christian. Chinese graduates of Western-style schools thus had an advantage when becoming commercial compradors. Overall, it is possible to say that the early Hong Kong compradors already had work experience with foreigners before the foreign firms employed them.

Table 3.2 List of principal compradors, from the *China Directory* 1874

Armstrong, J. M.	Cheong Sing
Arnhold, Karberg & Co.	Chun Kum
Belilios, E. R.	Wong Hew Chün
Birley & Co.	Pow Choong Hung
Borneo Company, Ltd.	Hu Yook Shan
Bourjau & Co.	Ng Tsz Yin
Brandão & Co.	Choy Chip
Burd & Co., John	Chü Pew
Butterfield & Swire	Ng Ahip
Carlowitz & Co.	Leong Wah Ting
Chartered Bank of India, Australia and China	Yoong Leung
Chartered Mercantile Bank of India, London and China	Wai Akwong
Comptoird' Escompte De Paris	Yip Ayuen
Commissariat	Pang Fong Poo
Deetjen & Von Bergen	Lum King Wan
Ehlers & Co., Paul	Tam Tse Nem
Gaupp & Co., C. J.	Chew Ting Yü
Ghandy & Co.	Tam Lok Chee
Gibb, Livingston & Co.	Leong On
Gilman & Co.	Chop Achip
Great Northern Telegraph Company	Chü Kum Tong
Grün & Co.	Foong Kew Sun
Heard & Co.	Mok Sz Yeung
Hesse & Co.	Chew Choong Ngam
Hogg & Co.	Foong Ming-shan
Holliday, Wise & Co.	Lai Alun
Hongkong and China Gas Company	Choy Hung
Hongkong Fire Insurance	Choy Sing Nam
Hong Kong and Shanghai Banking Corporation	Lo Yew Kee
Jardine, Matheson & Co.	Ng Kee
Kirchner, Boger	Lo Tsz Tsung
Lammert, Atkinson & Co.	Yip Sing
Landstein & Co.	Cho Tai
Lanecrowford & Co.	Foong Cheong
Lapraik & Co.	Ng Sang
MacLean, G. F.	Ho Tsun Shan
McEwen & Co.	Chun Man Poo
McGregor & Co.	Wai Piu
Melchers & Co.	Wong Chew
Messageries Maritimes	Ng Fai
Meyer & Co.	Pow Kai Ming
Mody & Co.	Loo Pew
National Bank of India	Yoong Chew
Norton, Lyall & Co.	Foong Kam Chow
Olypahnt & Co.	Pow Chow
Oriental Bank Corporation	Foong Awui
P. M. S. S. Company	Poon Chim Hing
P. & O. S. N. Company	Wong Sü Tong
Pustau & Co.	Wong Sun
Raynal & Co.	Kan Hing Wan

continued . . .

Table 3.2 Continued

Reiss & Co.	Yip On
Remedios & Co., J. J. dos	Choy Aloy
Russell & Co.	Kwok Achun
Ruttenjee & Co., D.	Wong Seu Hing
Sander & Co.	Chow Chee Tin
Sassoon & Co.	Foong hing Yin
Sassoon & Sons & Co., D.	Loo Yam Shing
Schellhass & Co.	Poon Yuet Low
Siemssen & Co.	Wong Ayew
Smith, Archer & Co.	Wong Yook Chune
Turner & Co.	Sun Pang
Vogel, Hagedorn & Co.	Poo Kat
Wahee, Smith & Co.	Choy Tsz Mee
Walker, R.	Yoong Sew Poo
Walker & Co., R. S.	Pong Yun

The Imperial Chinese Maritime Customs Service (*Daqing huangjia haiguan zong shuiwusi*) was another institution that produced compradors.[33] In 1854, the Foreign Inspectorate of the maritime customs, an organisation of the Qing government largely managed by foreign officers, was established to assess tax from the import and export trade.[34] In the 1850s and the 1860s, two brothers, Tong Kingsing and Tong Mow-chee, worked in customs before they became compradors to Jardine, Matheson & Co. in Shanghai and Tianjin, respectively.[35] Robert Hotung, perhaps the most famous comprador in Hong Kong, worked in customs in Canton from 1878 to 1880 before he started working for Jardine, Matheson & Co. In customs, Hotung received a fairly high monthly salary of about 30 silver taels. However, recognising the limitations of further development in his position, Hotung left customs to pursue working opportunities in foreign firms.[36] The subsequent success of the Tong brothers as comprador merchants of Jardine could have inspired Hotung's decision to pursue a career as a commercial intermediary between foreign firms and Chinese merchants.

In addition, personal connections with other compradors and their families were important for becoming a comprador, since a new comprador was generally employed following introductions from other compradors or influential merchants. It was judged that having a recommendation letter from a well-to-do merchant or comprador was required for becoming a comprador during the 1840s and the 1850s. Financial guarantors were also required from the late 1850s onwards. In 1859, Mok Sze Yeung, a comprador serving Augustine Heard & Co. in Hong Kong guaranteed Tang Neng, who became the firm's Foochow comprador.[37] Wei Yuk (Wei Yu) – a son of Wei Akwong's – was secured by his family members when he made a new contract with the Mercantile Bank in 1893. His guarantors were Ng She Yook Hing, a widow of Wei Akwong, Wei Wah Song, Akwong's third son and an assistant comprador in Shanghai, and Wai Wah Leen, the fourth son. In terms of the security deposit, the contract document stated that a sum of less than $50,000 would be paid to the bank from Wei's family. At the same time, Wei Yuk's premises, inland lot No. 78A in Victoria, was listed as a security at the bank.[38] Due to the need for well-to-do referees and the large sum of money required for security, positions for compradors and other Chinese staff in a foreign firm were likely to be dominated by relatives of the head comprador, his countrymen and close friends.

Indeed, when a head comprador retired, his position was often taken over by his son, a relative or someone who had a close connection with him. After the death of Wei Akwong in 1878, his son Wei Yuk succeeded Akwong as the comprador of the Mercantile Bank.[39] Sze Yeung, the comprador to Augustine Heard & Co., was a surety of Ng Ahip, the chief comprador of Butterfield & Swire. Then Sze Yeung's second son, Mok Cho Chuen (Mo Zaoquan), became Swire's chief comprador when Ng Ahip died in 1889.[40] Some of the government compradors were part of the commercial compradors' business network. Tsoi Sing Nam (Cai Xingnan), Jardine's comprador and Hotung's elder sister's husband, was the surety of Mang Fook Tin, who was a comprador to the General Post Office in the 1870s.[41] Many of the members of Eurasian Ho family also became compradors, especially after the 1870s, by following the success of Robert Hotung and the Ho family's close ties with Jardine, Matheson & Co. Robert Hotung was chief comprador of Jardine, Matheson & Co. from 1883 to 1900. During the same period, Hotung's two brothers, Ho Fook and Ho Kam Tong (He Gantang), worked in Jardine as assistant compradors. In 1900, Ho Fook succeeded Hotung as chief comprador.[42] Adopting both foreign and Chinese languages, education and cultural practices in their public and domestic lives, members of Eurasian families and foreign-influenced Chinese families acquired sufficient abilities to act as effective intermediaries, and existing compradors often provided their children with Western-style education and working opportunities in foreign firms to train them to take over their comprador positions in the future.[43]

For those looking to become compradors in Hong Kong during the early nineteenth century, it was advantageous to have relatives or close friends working with foreign firms in the same village or town. This is because recommendations and guarantees from reliable compradors and well-to-do merchants were required to become a comprador in foreign firms. Additionally, in the late nineteenth century, a Western education and previous work experience in foreign institutions became further advantages when seeking a compradorship. In this manner, the existing community of compradors dominated the job market. It became increasingly difficult for newcomers to become compradors in the latter half of nineteenth century, which was the period when the second and third generations of Hong Kong compradors emerged.

The roles of the compradors in the foreign firms

As they fulfilled multiple functions, commercial compradors became important members of staff in foreign firms and banks in mid-nineteenth-century Hong Kong. Compradors mainly acted as cashiers, bankers, agents, heads of Chinese staff and traders. An article of *The China Mail* in 1871 explains the work of the compradors in a report of a court case in which compradors' ambiguous position in a foreign firm, Dreyer & Co., was examined. The court case is explored in greater detail in a later section of this chapter. The following is my summary of the article, which lays out the features and duties of the compradors:

1. A comprador was guaranteed by sureties, who were in general well-to-do merchants.
2. He acted as a cashier responsible for the dealing of monies, bullion and cash.
3. He acted as a banker for finding monies. A comprador bore financial responsibility for their employer, sometimes even making payments from their own account to cover their employer's financial deficit.
4. He was responsible for the conduct of his Chinese employees.
5. He was a broker between his employers and local merchants in the making of contracts, commercial dealings and transactions.
6. He received a fixed salary but he could obtain commissions from local buyers or sellers on every transaction between them and his employer.
7. He often conducted trade by himself. This would not affect his services as comprador or his relationship with his master, as his own trade was outside his service as a comprador.[44]

These general activities of the commercial compradors in the 1870s were distinct from those of ship compradors, who were provision suppliers. The commercial compradors had become internal members of staff in each firm by the 1870s. However, they were concurrently external merchants who worked with foreign companies. Therefore, the following section analyses compradors' various activities with foreign firms and their dual positions as employees of the company and independent merchants.

One of the most important duties of a commercial comprador was acting as a cashier and treasurer for individual foreign traders. A merchant of Jardine, Herbert Magniac, recorded his transactions with his comprador, Achook.[45] The records of the cashbook suggest that Achook carried a diverse range of business transactions for Magniac & Co. In October and November 1864, monthly expenditure was about $1795 and $1482, respectively. Most of the transactions were made by Magniac himself, as well as by Chinese workers and foreign individuals who were business partners of Magniac. However, the account book also records payments made to compradors employed by other foreigners and institutions, such as the Hong Kong Club.[46] This example demonstrates how the company compradors supported a wide range of business transactions for their principals.

In was not unusual for foreign staff of Jardine to work with cash compradors. Joseph Jardine, a partner in Jardine, Matheson & Co. from 1845 to 1860 also employed a cash comprador named Ahoy (Yakai), who dealt with many transactions on his behalf in 1857 and 1858. This comprador sometimes dealt with large sums of money. According to a memorandum of Joseph Jardine's account with Ahoy, during 1858, the comprador made payments to the total of $194.50

in January, $3,499.08 in February, and $910.89 in March. The sum of payments in February was large because Joseph Jardine ordered the comprador to make payments of about $1,000 and $2,000 then. Most of the payments covered daily expenses and several subscriptions to charitable institutions, including the Hong Kong Dispensary, the Hong Kong Club, and the Union Chapel Fund for Alterations and Repairs on Building.[47] The comprador did not merely support their principal's commercial activities, but also their benevolent activities.

Compradors also acted as cashiers for foreign banks and companies. David McLean, a manager at the Oriental Bank who worked in Shanghai and Hong Kong during the 1860s and 1870s, recorded transactions with his compradors in his business letters. For instance, on 26 May 1864, $73,610.35 was in the hands of their Hong Kong comprador, which was about 2.5 per cent of the cash in the bank in Hong Kong.[48] Table 3.3 shows McLean's calculation.

Multiple compradors' names appeared in the letters, and it was not always clear which comprador worked for which branch of the bank.[49] Of them, Awoy was likely to have been a comprador working in the area of Canton and Hong Kong. Other staff of Oriental Bank also had accounts with Awoy.[50] In the 1860s, compradors of the Oriental Bank supported and organised its money transactions.

For compradors' transactions of money, a cheque called a 'comprador's order' was often utilised.[51] For instance, Joseph Jardine issued such comprador's orders to make payments to other individuals or companies in 1857 and 1858.[52] It was common to make payments between companies using a comprador's order in Hong Kong by the 1860s. Dent & Co., for example, sent a comprador's order for $4,246.57 to Jardine, Matheson & Co. in October 1860.[53] The holder of an order would bring it to the comprador and obtain the cash.[54] From the 1840s to the 1880s, it was possible to observe the use of the comprador's order as a form of cheque in Hong Kong. Augustine Heard issued these comprador's orders in as early as 1844 in Canton. On 28 January 1887, H. U. Jefferies, a member of staff at David Sassoon & Co., sent a comprador order for $73.08 to the Hong Kong General Chamber of Commerce to cover the cost of a telegram.[55] These comprador's orders remained in use until the early twentieth century.

In addition, the compradors played a role as internal bankers for foreign firms. In particular, Augustine Heard & Co. often raised money through their compradors.

Table 3.3 McLean's calculation[1]

Lower Treasury	Clear	$1,055,000	
do	Chopped	1,370,000	
$2,425,000			
Upper do	Clear	50,000	
	Chopped	420,000	
470,000			
Notes of other Banks			17,000
In Hands of comprador			73,610.35
	In all		$2,935,610.85

1 SOAS: MS 380401, David McLean's letters, Vol. 1, 26 May 1864, 37.

Table 3.4 An account for Augustine Heard & Co. with the comprador, Hong Kong, 1871[1]

Month	*Cr. by comprador**	*Balance (Mexican dollars)*
January	$222,328.18	$606.40
February	201,432.75	5,524.95
March	154,397.86	267.45 [due comprador**]
April	101,813.68	23,897.87
May	49,492.49	3,994.09
June	24,763.81	10,522.15
July	111,541.72	14,486.98 [due comprador]
August	219,404.44	1,784.80
September	215,782.29	13,147.14 [due comprador]
October	309,657.05	3,806.57 [due comprador]
November	327,427.41	32,625.92 [due comprador]
December	157,574.35	15,251.37 [due comprador]

* payment made by comprador on behalf of the company
** 'due comprador' indicates an amount of money paid by the comprador to cover the excess of the account
1 Hao, *Comprador*, 40–41; Baker Library: Heard Collections II, Vol. 56, Cash Account.

When Augustine Heard was not able to borrow money from the Canton comprador in 1853, he borrowed it from the Hong Kong comprador. In his letter to John Heard, he stated, 'comprador [See Yong] has come out like a brick. I can count upon . . . certain $23,000.'[56] The company's cash account with the comprador recorded that the company constantly borrowed money from the Hong Kong comprador in 1871.[57] Table 3.4 demonstrates that Heard's comprador in Hong Kong filled the deficits in the company's account. In 1871, the comprador funded a total of $79,585.43 to cover the excess of the account, which was about 37 per cent of the total payments made by the comprador made on behalf of the company.[58] The compradors in Augustine, Heard & Co. supported Heard's financing of money to a great extent. Similarly, an assistant of Augustine Heard in Foochow, Robert Sedgwick, worked with a comprador who occasionally funded Sedgwick's account, in addition to dealing with various payments for daily expenses, as well as receiving deposits. In his account book with the comprador for 1870 and 1871, Sedgwick noted:

> I spoke to Mr Dixwell and received instructions to make an order for the compradore [sic] on the House to that account & thereby after to make another order for £24.88 making a total of tael 200, thus paying my debt to the compradore, having a balance of T 27.88 in my name. I now begin a new & clear account with the compradore.[59]

In this way, Heard's compradors in Hong Kong and in other treaty ports functioned as bankers to foreign staff and companies in the early 1870s.[60]

It seems that some compradors externally lent money to the foreign firms. In February 1853, Ng Tuck Hing, a comprador at Lindsay & Co., received a bill of exchange of about $16,544 from Rawle of Rawle, Drinker & Co. in Hong Kong. However, the payment was not made by the due date, 4 August. On 16 August, Ng Tuck Hing served a notice that he would be a creditor. Then Ng took the case to court and sued Rawle, Drinker & Co on 8 September. May, the sheriff, who was responsible for carrying out the execution, seized properties belonging Rawle, Drinker & Co. It was unclear whether Ng Tuck Hing lent $16,544 to Rawle & Co. on behalf of Lindsay & Co. or simply as an independent merchant.[61] Regardless, it is possible to say that the compradors acted as both internal and external bankers to the foreign firms and traders.

Another important duty of compradors was the supervision of Chinese staff in foreign firms. The head compradors ran a comprador office or comprador department called the 'pan-fang' (*banfang*) in each company. The head compradors were responsible for the supervision of the Chinese staff working in the office. In 1872, a total of 16 foreign staff members were working in the Hong Kong office of Jardine, Matheson & Co.[62] In this case, the head comprador also supervised other Chinese staff including assistant compradors, shroffs, servants and cooks. In a similar manner to Jardine, the compradors of Augustine Heard & Co. were responsible for overseeing Chinese staff such as the shroff, bookkeeper and godown men. The compradors were responsible for any misconduct among their staff. During the bread-poisoning incident in January 1857, hundreds of foreign residents in Hong Kong were affected after eating bread poisoned with arsenic. Although no one died, after the incident, Augustine Heard ensured the comprador employed a reliable cook by informing the comprador that he would be held responsible if foreign residents in the house were harmed by any failures on the part of the cook taken on by the comprador.[63] Therefore, a comprador would tend to employ a person close to him, such as a member of his family, clan or home village. In Augustine Heard & Co., the group of Chinese staff supervised by the compradors were sometimes called the 'comprador firm'.[64] The comprador's department functioned as a small Chinese firm, which was integrated with the foreign firm. The department consisted of workers who had personal connections with the comprador. In a sense, Chinese workers in the foreign firms were segregated from the foreign principals. For foreign principals, the compradors were intermediaries for the recruitment and management of the Chinese staff.

More importantly, the compradors acted as business assistants for the foreign principals looking to conduct trade in China. In 1860, a Hong Kong comprador to Augustine Heard & Co. advised John Heard that the price of peas and rice would fall.[65] In the case of Jardine, Matheson & Co., many of its compradors were engaged in work related to shipping, lading and warehousing. One of Jardine's compradors in Hong Kong, Choy Sing Nam, shipped 500 bags of Bengal rice worth about $1072 from Hong Kong to Shanghai in September 1867.[66] Ling Atow, a godown comprador, supported the company's management of the warehouses in Hong Kong. Ling's work included supplying goods to foreign customers, in addition to supervising Chinese staff handling cargoes.[67] In September 1885, G. C. Anderson complained to Ling about damage to some of the goods and requested the discharge of some staff that had handled them carelessly.[68] When Ling became the head godown comprador to Jardine, Matheson & Co. in 1894, his security bond described his main duties as 'supplying boats for cargo and coals, and to find all coolie labour required'.[69] While employed by Jardine as a comprador, Ling established personal contracts with Jardine for building work. For instance, in 1888 he made a contract for the repair of the Hong Kong Fire Insurance Company's engine house, a sugar boiler house at East Point and a magazine store for the Hong Kong Explosives Company.[70] Again, Ling's case suggests the duality of the status of compradors to their employers. The compradors were capable of being both business assistants and external contractors for the company.

The compradors also supported the firm's trade with Chinese merchants. When Swire was seeking premises for their new office, John Swire attempted to find a venue that would enable their comprador to conduct trade in China. He stated, 'We must have a position that cannot be challenged, and above all, a comprador, that is able to work efficiently, in both import and Country trade'.[71] After 1842, Augustine Heard & Co. was engaged in the tea trade, and their compradors acted as purchasers of teas from Chinese merchants.[72] Kim Hing, a Chinese merchant and a business partner of the Oriental Bank, was a friend of the bank's comprador during the early 1860s.[73] In June 1862, On Sing Chung, a Chinese merchant, contracted to purchase 331.77 piculs of camphor with Jardine via the comprador Ng Chuck.[74] Chinese merchants became the main customers as well as business partners of foreign firms and banks in Hong Kong in the mid-nineteenth century. In parallel, the work and importance of the commercial intermediaries increased. In 1880, *Xunhuan Ribao* (Universal Circulating Herald) printed a Chinese notification stating that Swire had started providing the services of a Chinese comprador for Chinese passengers on the 'Blue Funnel' Line (Alfred Holt & Co.).[75]

In addition to brokering trade between foreign and Chinese firms, the compradors promoted foreign firms to provide short-term loans, called 'chop loans', to native banks in Shanghai and other treaty ports during the late nineteenth century.[76] It is not clear whether chop loans were common in Hong Kong as was the case of Shanghai. However, it is certain that Hong Kong compradors were involved in the transactions between foreign firms and Chinese banks in the same period. From the 1870s onwards, a number of Chinese banks, called 'native banks' (in Chinese, *yinhao*), increased in Hong Kong. Stanley Kwan Shi-kuang (Guan Shiguang) (1925–2011), who was well known for his contribution to the creation of Hong Kong's Hang Seng Stock Index in 1969, recalled in his memoirs what he heard about the compradors from his father and other elderly people. Guan Jidong, his father, Guan Zhunzhou, his great-uncle, and Deng Zhiang, his maternal grandfather, were all involved in the business of Chinese banks. Deng's maternal grandfather and great-uncle established Chinese banks in Hong Kong. Deng Zhiang was a founder of *Tianfu yinhao*, and Guan Zhunzhou was a founder of *Yongda yinhao* and *Yongde yinhao*. Nevertheless, they did not understand much English. Therefore, they required intermediation services from the compradors. For them, it was necessary to work with compradors to conduct business in Hong Kong.[77]

In terms of the income of the compradors, they could earn both fixed salaries and commission charges, which were earned by intermediation services between

Chinese and foreign customers. They could also earn income from their external businesses.[78] Various scholars suggest that compradors earned more in commission than from their salaried work.[79] In 1866, the salary of a comprador to Augustine Heard & Co. was about 20 taels, while he received 1 to 5 per cent commissions from foreign employers.[80] Choy Sing Nam, a Jardine comprador, received $100 per month in 1878.[81] The income of the compradors increased from the 1870s to the 1880s. Ho Kai (He Qi), a Chinese barrister and physician, stated that the compradors earned as much as foreign staff in the 1890s.[82] Some of the commercial compradors accumulated significant wealth through their business intermediating between foreign and Chinese firms.

The pros and cons of the comprador system

As described above, the compradors often acted as business partners to the foreign principals, since most of the compradors also ran their own businesses. However, these dual positions sometimes caused controversy. The legal dispute between Dreyer & Co. and Leong A-ting (Yang Yading) in 1871 indicates the difficulty of distinguishing between the compradors' work for the foreign firms and their conduct in their personal businesses. Leong A-ting was a surety of Leong Akum (Liang Yagen), a comprador to Dreyer. A-ting was sued for the loss of trade caused by Akum's failure in the sale of several commodities including umbrellas, flannels and tablecloths. The total loss was estimated at $1,133.20. In court, it was examined whether Akum's conduct of trade (a total of $32,000) should be regarded as part of his work as a comprador or not. The decision was made in favour of the defendant, because the comprador merely acted as interpreter for the sale of products, and because Akum's conduct of trade with his principals was regarded as outside his duties as a comprador.[83] The decision of the court suggests that the compradors could take economic and legal advantage of their ambiguous positions. This was one of the risks for the foreign firms working with compradors.

The legal value of security bonds was also questionable. On 12 June 1864, A. F. Heard wrote about the problem of the guarantee system of compradors in his letter to John Heard in Hong Kong. Heard asked, 'How do you know who secures our comprador, See Young (Mok Sze Yeung), the man here? Who secures all the Branch Compradors? Where are the security chops? Are there any at all?'[84] In fact, the foreign firms sometimes encountered difficulties in obtaining securities. In 1879, when Swire's Hong Kong passenger comprador absconded with a debt of around $10,000 to $12,000, John Swire wrote, 'I have always had some fears of how far the law would enforce your rights against securities, and we shall see how you succeed in your action in this case'. However, the company seemed to fail to obtain any security money.[85] Foreign principals resorted to collecting information about their compradors' sureties on their own. In early 1864, David MacLean visited Whampoa and Canton to collect information about the family background of his compradors and the value of the premises that the compradors' sureties owned.[86] However, the foreign firms still encountered difficulties in obtaining securities from sureties. When the Hongkong and Shanghai Banking

Corporation's comprador, Lo Hok Pang, absconded with debts of almost $1.3 million to the bank in 1892, it was discovered that his guarantees were not enough to cover his debt.[87]

Recognising the risks of the comprador system, foreign observers recurrently described the compradors as a class or clan that hindered direct trade with Chinese merchants. Contemporary English newspapers discussed the issues of the comprador system throughout the nineteenth and twentieth centuries. In 1871, in a report of a comprador defrauding his principal, the *China Mail* discussed the difficulty of the abolishment of the comprador system:

> Some two or three years ago, a shoal of communications and articles (editorial and otherwise) appeared here and in Shanghai on the evils of the comprador system of doing business. At that time we were to instruct our merchants and their assistants in the Chinese language, and the Chinese comprador was to become a thing of history only. But now in 1871 the comprador is as healthy as ever and the system is as sound as it ever will be, *i.e.*, not until men are not men beyond the power of strong temptation.[88]

Concerns about reliance on compradors were widely shared in foreign communities in different treaty ports. Already in the first half of the 1860s, foreigners were aware of the compradors' excessive responsibility for financial matters in foreign companies. In January 1864, *The North China Herald* published a letter from a foreign resident of Hankow concerning the problems with the comprador system. The writer of the letter claimed that the compradors obtained extra income by becoming involved in credit transactions between foreign and Chinese merchants. He suggested measures, including decreasing the number of credit transactions and increasing cash transactions, to 'reduce them (compradors) to what they should be, simply shroffs'.[89]

Hong Kong newspapers soon began to publish articles related to the issue of the compradors which had originally been published in newspapers issued in Chinese treaty ports such as Shanghai and Amoy. In September 1879, an article titled 'John Comprador' claimed that the compradors controlled Chinese guilds. It also pointed out the compradors' dominance in the handling of foreign firms' financial matters. It wrote that 90 per cent of the foreign firms in port cities in China employed compradors, and therefore most of the financial affairs were controlled by the compradors 'in the most despotic manner'.[90] During the 1880s, the compradors' entrepreneurial activities were discussed in the newspapers. In 1883, an article in the *Hong Kong Daily Press* criticised the compradors' commercial activities by stating, 'The compradoric class estimated a great error when they decided upon becoming their [the compradors'] masters.'[91] In 1884, another article in *The Hong Kong Daily Press*, entitled 'The compradoric class and their recent loss', analysed the compradors' involvement in modern businesses such as steam-shipping and coal mining.[92] These articles included some exaggeration of the compradors' functions, an indication of the biased viewpoint; however, they represented the fear and suspicion among foreigners surrounding the rise of comprador merchants. They also revealed a dilemma in the foreign mercantile community regarding the employment of the compradors. It was necessary for foreign principals to employ a comprador for their economic activities in China; however, doing so also meant running the risk of fraud and creating new business competitors.

Despite the foreign principals' recognition of the risks of the comprador system, and despite their calls for the abolition of the system, it survived until the late twentieth century.[93] This was partly because of the difficulty in finding foreign personnel who could conduct trade directly with Chinese merchants. Even for the compradors, conducting business in the Chinese market was not an easy task. The contemporary Chinese newspaper *Xunhuan Ribao* includes advertisements pointing to the chief compradors' attempts to streamline business with the Chinese merchants. For instance, on 24 May 1880, Douglas Lapraik & Co.'s comprador, Ng Sang, alias Ng Ying-sang or Ng Chuk-shau (Wu Zhuxiu), published an advertisement advising Chinese business partners not to claim payment without a signed contract and direct contact with him or his office. It states:

> Dear Sirs,
>
> Only a face-to-face meeting and signed contract between you and me is valid regarding the purchase, guarantee, borrowing of silver taels, taking goods of each company on credit, and other business conducted under the name of this office and mine.
>
> If anyone tries to cheat by forwarding letters and stamps and claiming that some stores have my stocks to do business, it is in fact unreliable. If anyone behaves in such a manner, I have nothing to do with it. Besides, if there is any accident, it is the dealer's responsibility only, and it will be your store's own loss.
>
> I declare here, no more issues like this.
>
> Yours faithfully,
>
> Office of Douglas Lapraik & Co, Wu Zhuxiu.[94]

Birley & Co.'s comprador, Bao Zonghong, published a similar notification in the advertisement section of the newspaper.[95] Such statements indicate the depth of the challenge the compradors themselves faced in trying to streamline business with Chinese merchants in the ever-changing commercial environment of nineteenth-century China.

In the 1920s, William Frederick Spalding listed several possible reasons for the continued existence of the comprador system in China. Primarily, although the language barrier had lessened throughout the years of the foreign traders' experiences in China, there was still an 'impenetrable barrier' of social communication between Chinese merchants and foreigners. This made it difficult for foreigners to conduct direct trade with Chinese merchants. Furthermore, despite recognising the costs and risks of the comprador system, many of the foreign firms required their services.[96] Drawing on the compradors' business networks, foreign firms were able to conduct trade in China on a large scale. John Heard commented on Mok Sze Yeung in 1860, 'I have no doubt he is worth $50,000 at least, probably more. He does not speak fluent English, but being rich and one of the oldest compradors of the place, he has "large face" '.[97] Dual status of the compradors as external and internal business partners could bring both losses and profits to the foreign employers. Therefore, for foreign entrepreneurs, one key to commercial success in China was finding credible and effective compradors and establishing symbiotic relationships with them.[98] If a foreign trader could find a good comprador and establish a constructive relationship with him, it was possible to conduct a profitable business in China.

To sum up, despite its risks, the benefits that the comprador system offered were attractive, and therefore the foreign companies and banks in late nineteenth-century Hong Kong accepted the commercial compradors as essential intermediaries. The employment, management and duties of commercial compradors were gradually systematised from the 1840s to the 1880s, while the colonial government decreased the number of compradors in its institutions. The decline of the government compradors could be related to the rise of the mercantile and intellectual classes of Chinese. Individuals within these classes became leading figures in the Chinese community of Hong Kong and intermediary elites between the colonial government and the Chinese community from the 1860s onwards. This point is further discussed in Chapter 5, which considers the political functions of the compradors.

There are still many unknown areas regarding the works of compradors. Though this chapter has explored only cases of British or American firms, there were many other European firms that employed compradors in nineteenth-century Hong Kong. The functions of compradors in these European firms should be identified as well in order to analyse the diversity of commercial compradors in the nineteenth century; this could be accomplished by using archives in European countries such as Germany, Italy and France. This chapter has also highlighted trading firms and banks; again, however, the duties of compradors may have been different in companies such as department stores, watchmakers and insurance companies. Although I reviewed all the Chinese correspondence preserved in the P&O archive in my effort to explore Kwok Acheong's works for the steamship company, resources on P&O compradors were scarce, suggesting strongly that much of the compradors' activities lay outside their duties to their principals.

Conclusion

The compradors' Sino-foreign commercial networks and growing wealth enabled them to act as effective economic agents for foreign houses and financial institutions in Hong Kong from the 1840s to the 1880s. After the British occupation of Hong Kong in 1841, much of the local populations in the Pearl River Delta came to Hong Kong to take advantage of the business opportunities there. The local Chinese who were selling provisions sometimes styled themselves compradors. These early compradors' duties were limited to supplying provisions to the foreign traders and residents in Hong Kong. Nevertheless, aside from the provision-selling compradors, there was a gradual rise of the compradors mediating business between foreign traders and Chinese merchants in the 1840s and the 1850s. The company compradors filled the requirement for middlemen from both the foreign and Chinese mercantile communities. To penetrate the Chinese market, foreign houses depended on the compradors, while the Chinese merchants depended on the compradors to make commercial deals with their foreign counterparts.

By this token, the foreign firms developed a custom of hiring Chinese intermediaries within the framework of the comprador system between the late 1860s and the early 1870s. The company compradors were gradually integrated into the organisations of foreign firms in the course of the time. Principally, the compradors gained employment through the introduction of other well-to-do merchants and guarantees by sureties. In effect, when a foreign employer sought a new comprador to hire, one of the compradors' family, countrymen or friends generally filled the new position. The compradors had a variety of duties in the foreign firms. By the late 1860s, the duties of the company compradors included accounting, banking, the supervision of the Chinese staff, and assistance with their principals' businesses. In addition to a fixed salary, the compradors received commissions by mediating trade between their principals and Chinese merchants.

By the early 1880s, most of the major foreign firms had established a comprador department consisting of a head comprador (or a principal comprador), assistant compradors, a shroff and other Chinese staff. The head compradors usually conducted businesses in their own right. Therefore, the head compradors sometimes worked with foreign firms as business partners, thereby strengthening the comprador system as an apparatus for mediating trade and transactions between Chinese and foreign companies in Hong Kong. Despite the risks involved in employing compradors, who might be competitors in their business in China, the foreign firms chose to continue hiring compradors throughout the nineteenth century. This was the product of the lack of effective foreign personnel who could directly work with Chinese merchants and simultaneously act as intermediaries who understood both foreign and Chinese business customs. In this way, new company comprador system was eventually formulated in Hong Kong, two decades after the collapse of the old one in Canton. Based on their expertise in foreign business, these compradors vigorously conducted entrepreneurial businesses as independent merchants. Their competition and collaboration with the foreign firms is the main theme to be explored in the next chapter.

Notes

1 TNA: CO133/4, *Blue Book*, 1847.
2 *Hong Kong Almanack and Directory for 1846*, 34.
3 JMA: B7/2–5519,5540, 5549, Letters from Acow & Co., to Thomas Hunt & Co., February to March in 1856, Business letters: Canton.
4 TNA: CO133/4 to CO133/21, *Blue Book*, year 1847 to 1864.

5 *Government Gazette*, 1877, 24 February 1877, 85.
6 Eitel, *Europe in China*, 385; Yuan, *Xianggang shilue*, 114–115.
7 Feng, Rao and Law, *Enriching Lives*, 24.
8 Carroll, *Concise History*, 29–30.
9 Wright, *Twentieth Century Impressions*, 149.
10 *Treaty Ports of China and Japan* (1867), 18–19.
11 *Hong Kong Government Gazette, 1876*; *Administrative Reports, 1881.*
12 Muter, *Travels and Adventures*, 321–322.
13 *Ballou's Monthly Magazine*, Vol. 24, 262.
14 Zhang, *Xianggang yu jindai zhongguo*, 15.
15 BPP, *House of Commons and Command*, Vol. 48 (1860), 301.
16 *China Mail*, 19 June 1871, 3.
17 JMA: A7/255, Provisions account for Shewyun, July 1873–May 1875.
18 China Directory 1874.
19 JMA: B11, MS JM/B7/27, B7/2, Letters from Acow & Co.
20 *Blue Books 1847–1871*; *Government Gazette 1877*; *Administrative Reports, 1881.*
21 *China Directory* 1874, 12–14.
22 *Directory and Chronicle for China, Japan, Corea, Indo-China* (1879), 242–243.
23 *Government Gazette*, 1877, 24 February 1877, 85.
24 *Administrative Reports*, 1881.
25 *Daily Advertiser*, 6 October 1871, 4.
26 *Directory and Chronicle for China, Japan, Corea* (1889), 417.
27 *China Directory 1874*, 47.
28 HKPRO: HKRS 144–4-734, Will of Song Chiu Fung, 7 January 1882.
29 Lee, 'Shijiu shiji maiban', 65.
30 Smith, *Chinese Christians*, 146; Will of Wei Akwong, 3 October 1866 cited in Smith, *Sense of History*, 7.
31 Smith, *Chinese Christians*, 66, 135; *China Mail*, 23 September 1852, 154.
32 Smith, *Chinese Christians*, 126; *China Directory*, 1872, 1873.
33 Bickers, *Scramble for China*, 290.
34 van de Ven, *Breaking with Past*, 26–28.
35 Smith, *Chinese Christians*, 49–50.
36 Zheng and Wong, *Xianggang dalao*, 65–66.
37 Hao, *Comprador*, 156–158; Heard Family Business Records. Baker Library, Harvard Business School (Heard Collection II, Agreements, 1846–1861, Carton 9).
38 HSBC Archive, London: MB 1225, Deed of Covenant and Security (i.e. Comprador's Agreement) re faithful performance of duties as comprador to Hong Kong Branch – Mr Wei A Yuk and others to MBI, 5 July 1893; Smith, *Chinese Christians*, 69.
39 *China Directory 1872*; Smith, *Chinese Christians*, 67–68, 135.
40 Wright, *Twentieth Century Impressions*, 182; Holdsworth and Munn (eds), *Dictionary of Hong Kong Biography*, 325.
41 HKPRO: HKRS149–2-628, Security Bond.
42 Hao, *Comprador*, 232, 173; Zheng and Wong, *Xianggang dalao*, 110–111.
43 For instance, Wei Akwong's son Wei Yuk studied at the Government Central School (later Queen's College) and travelled to England and Scotland for further study. *Hong Kong Daily Press*, Obituary of Wei Yuk, 17 December 1921.
44 *China Mail*, 19 June 1871, 3.
45 In the 1860s, Jardine, Matheson & Co. had a cash comprador, Achook, who was likely to be identified with Ng Chook (Wu Zhu).
46 JMA: A7/325, Comprador's cash book (Achook), October 1864–December 1866; Chan, *Making of Hong Kong*, 58.
47 JMA: A8/102/4, Memorandam of Joseph Jardine, December 1857–June 1858.

48 SOAS: David McLean's letters, Vol. 1, 24 October 1862, 2 and 14 February 1863, 6 and 16 May 1863, 12 and 26 May 1864, 37, *et passim*.
49 SOAS: MS 380401, David McLean's letters, Vols 1–3; *China Directory 1874*. The names that appeared in his letter were Awoy, Akoy, Ahun (Shanghai), Agun, Akau, and Aheen (identified with Fung Heen in Shanghai).
50 SOAS: MS 380401, David McLean's letters, Vol. 1, 27 January 1864, 25–26 and 9–17 June 1864, 42–44 and Vol. 2, 1 September 1864, 10, *et passim*.
51 Baker Library: Heard Collection II, Carton 1, Comprador's order, Augustine Heard & Co., Hong Kong.
52 JMA: Memos ordering the comprador to make payments are preserved in A8/102/4, Memoranda of Joseph Jardine, December 1857–June 1858.
53 JMA: Dent & Co. (Hong Kong) to Jardine, Matheson & Co. (Hong Kong), 3 October 1860, cited in Hao, 259, n. 30. 'We beg to hand you enclosed a cheque on our Comprador for $4,246.57 being balance at credit of our account with the ship "Witch of the Seas." '
54 Hao, *Comprador*, 72.
55 *Hong Kong General Chamber of Commerce, Report for the Year, 1887* (Hong Kong, Noronha & Co., 1888).
56 Baker Library: Heard Collection I, FM-4–1. A.F. Heard (Hong Kong) to John Heard, 28 February 1863.
57 Table 3.2, Hao, *Comprado*r, 40–41; Baker Library: Heard Collection II, Vol. 56, Cash Account.
58 $79,585.43 was the comprador's total funding. $2,095,616.03 is the total payment made by the comprador in the year 1871.
59 JMA: A7/637, Account book of Robert Sedgwick, 1870–1871.
60 Baker Library: Heard Collection I, HM-28–3, George B. Dixwell (Shanghai)'s letter, 20 February 1863.
61 *China Mail*, 19 January 1854, 10.
62 JMA: A2/44, *Journal* 1871–2, 546; Ishi. 'Jūkyū seiki kōhan', 357–482.
63 Baker Library: Heard Collection I, Box GQ-1 and GQ-2, Folder GQ-2–1, Various Articles by Augustine Heard Jr. Transcribed by Robert M. Gray. http://ee.stanford.edu/~gray/poisoningah.pdf, accessed 1 November 2016, 7–9; Carroll, *Concise History*, 26.
64 Lockwood, *Augustine Heard*, 41.
65 Baker Library: Heard Collection I, HM-6, John Heard (Hong Kong) to A.F. Heard, 8 October 1860; Hao, *Comprador*, 74.
66 JMA: A6/18, Invoices of the Hong Kong Office, February 1867–February 1868, 230.
67 JMA: B7/15/13403–13453, B11/1/3091–3105, Business letters, Hong Kong.
68 JMA: B11/1/S22, Ling Atow's letter, 29 September 1885.
69 JMA: C25/1, Letters re agreements and contracts, 1887–1903, 26.
70 JMA: C25/1, 1, 14–15, 18–19.
71 SOAS: John Swire & Sons Collection, Box1173 JSSI 1/1 1869, Liverpool, 20 September 1869, from JSS to Mr Lang Esq as partner in Butterfield and Swire Hong Kong, 8–10.
72 Lockwood, *Augustine Heard and Company*, 39.
73 SOAS: MS 380401, David McLean's letters, 23 December 1863, 24.
74 JMA: B7/15/7369, On Sing Chung to Jardine, 11 June 1862, Hong Kong.
75 XHRB, Year of Guangxu 6/5/18, 5 July 1880.
76 Hao, *Comprador*, 115.
77 Guan, *Qishi nian lai*, 14–15, 23; Hisasue, 'Honkon doru kessaiken', 38.
78 Smith, 'Compradores of the Hong Kong Bank'.
79 Wang 'Qingdai maiban shouru', 298–307.
80 Hao, *Comprador*, 90–91.
81 JMA: A8/131/1/10, Memo of office expenses and wages Hong Kong, 28 February 1878.

82 Bourne, *Report of Mission*, 144.
83 *China Mail*, 17 June 1871, 5.
84 Baker Library: Heard Collection I, FM-5–1, John Heard, A. Heard, Jr. from A.F. Heard, 1864.
85 SOAS: Swire Collection, JSSI 1/3 BOX 1174 A, Letters to Hong Kong and Shanghai. JSS to Lang Mackintosh, London, 26 May 1879, 238. JSS to Lang Mackintosh, London 13 August 1879, 243.
86 SOAS: David McLean's Letters, Vol. 1, 27 January 1864, 25–26. 'Adam Scott's Compradore, who knows all about Akoy, Yuen Chong, Awoy & Ahun's family told me that Akoy & Yuen Chong have property in Whampoa worth about $50,000 each & that Ahun himself has houses & land worth $20,000 but Awoy tells me Ahun has not more than $3000 to $5000 worth. The Consul at Canton promised to ask the Chinese officials to look after Akoy, Yuen Chong & Ahun's property & see that none of it is made away with until we can lodge a claim with him against the sureties.'
87 King, *History of Hongkong and Shanghai Banking Corporation*, Vol. 1, 515–516.
88 *China Mail*, 6 January 1871, 3.
89 Supplement to the NCH, 8 January 1864.
90 *China Mail*, 9 September 1879 (extract from the *Amoy Gazette*), 3.
91 *Hong Kong Daily Press*, 18 October 1883 (extract from *Shanghai Mercury*).
92 *Hong Kong Daily Press*, 18 January 1884 (extract from *Shanghai Mercury*).
93 *China Mail*, 19 June 1871, 3.
94 XHRB, 24 May 1880, GX6/4/17.
95 XHRB, 19 June 1880, GX6/5/12 and 19 June 1880, GX 6/5/12.

Dear Sirs:

Because we have numerous business partners working with our company, if anyone borrows silver cash and goods etc., please send the document to our office to sign for your company, which is the only certification. Otherwise, it is the dealer's responsibility and our accountant's office has nothing to do with it. If any other method is used, it is your companies own loss and you will not be paid by our accountant's office.

24 April

Sincerely,

Office of Birley & Company, Bao Zonghong

96 Spalding, *Eastern Exchange*, 402–404.
97 Hao, *Comprador*, 155.
98 Bickers, *Scramble for China*, 289.

4 Compradors' commercial activities

This chapter introduces four essential characteristics of the Hong Kong compradors' enterprises: modern entrepreneurship, international commercial activities, diversification of business and the formation of informal commercial ties. These four attributions were part and parcel of the commercial activities of the Hong Kong compradors from the 1880s onwards. The majority of prominent compradors were keen to carry out Sino-foreign joint ventures, based on their ties with foreign principals. The compradors' management of steam-shipping and sugar refining companies serves as a good example of their approach to entrepreneurships from the 1860s to the 1880s. The second feature of the Hong Kong compradors' commercial activities was their international business operations. The compradors' markets for their business were not necessarily limited to Hong Kong. The international social backgrounds of the Hong Kong compradors underpinned the expansion of their business markets to China, Australia, America, Japan and countries in Southeast Asia. Thirdly, almost all of the compradors used a diverse range of Chinese and Western styles of businesses to diversify investment risks. The fourth feature was the social ties between the compradors serving different companies, which were strengthened through marriage and collaborative joint ventures. These entrepreneurial, international, multilateral and collaborative commercial activities of the compradors became a model for successful businesses in Hong Kong by the end of the nineteenth century.

Yet the compradors' dual roles as internal staff of the foreign houses and as external entrepreneurs posed a problem for their foreign principals. The compradors, in other words, could be competitors to their employers. Working as internal mediators for foreign companies, compradors were able to acquire the information as well as financial and human resources they needed to give their own businesses an advantage. Hence, the second half of this chapter focuses on the dilemmas of the foreign principals and discusses why they were not able to abolish the comprador system during the nineteenth century.

Entrepreneurship

Connections with the foreign and Chinese mercantile communities enabled the compradors to carry out entrepreneurial business in Hong Kong during the late nineteenth century. Many of the compradors learnt their business through their work with foreign companies as intermediaries. They applied this knowledge in starting similar businesses in their own right. The case of Kwok Acheong is an example of a comprador who turned into a competitor of his principals. Kwok was a comprador to P&O and a well-known owner of steamships from the 1860s to the 1870s in Hong Kong. Scholars such as Kwang-Ching Liu have studied the steam-shipping enterprise in modern China and the compradors' involvement in it.[1] Most existing research examines the compradors' and Chinese merchants' contributions to the organisation of the semi-official enterprise, the China Merchants' Steam Navigation Company, or the modernisation of the Chinese shipping industry in the late Qing period. These studies mainly focus on the case of Shanghai, paying less attention to the rise of the Chinese shipping enterprise in Hong Kong during the same period. However, the Hong Kong compradors and merchants' contributions to the management of the Chinese steam-shipping business should not be ignored, since Hong Kong was an important trade entrepôt connecting China with Asian and Pacific countries. Furthermore, the management style of the steam-shipping business in Hong Kong was different from that of the comprador merchants in Shanghai and other treaty ports in China: Kwok independently operated steamships registered as British in Hong Kong, while the comprador merchants in Chinese treaty ports established a company supported by the Qing government during the 1870s. While Kwok did operate the steam-shipping business on his own, multiple Chinese merchants and compradors in Hong Kong and other port cities either formally or informally supported his business. As such, this section specifically explores how Kwok carried out a modern business based in Hong Kong before moving on to an analysis of the supporting factors that enabled him to conduct this large-scale, inter-regional shipping business. The following briefly summarises his career in the shipping industry before beginning the discussion.

As shown in previous chapters, Kwok was initially a pilot on the HMS *Nemesis* during the First Opium War and later became a comprador for British battleships. Soon after that, he was employed as a comprador in the P&O Company. While serving P&O, he started his own steam-shipping business. Table 4.1 lists the names of Kwok's ships, their sizes, operating years, nationality and the names of the captains. In the 1860s, Kwok managed approximately five river steamers operating in the Pearl River. In the 1870s, he owned large steamships connecting Hong Kong and Shanghai as well as other ports in Southeast Asia.[2] Records of Kwok's company no longer exist, and it is difficult to find details regarding the routes, passengers and cargoes of his ships. However, reports on the loss of his two ships, the *Mirage* and the *Bombay*, provide hints enabling us to understand what his ships carried and where they operated.

In late June 1871, *The China Mail* reported that the *Mirage*, registered as a British ship, was wrecked near Hailing Island (Hailingdao), located to the southeast of Hong Kong, due to a severe storm. The ship was on her way to Hong Kong from Bangkok. The cargoes of the ship included rice, copper, ivory, bird's nests and spices, the total value of which was estimated to be between $70,000 and $80,000.

The value of the ship itself was estimated to be $10,000. The master of the Mirage, Mr J. W. Finch, his family, and about 20 Malay crew and 60 Chinese passengers were on board.[3] The reports reveal that one line of Kwok's steamers ran between Hong Kong and Southeast Asia, and while Kwok's customers mainly were Chinese, the staff of his steamers were not necessarily Chinese. Kwok's ships also operated between Hong Kong and Shanghai.

In 1880, another of his ships, the *Bombay,* was burnt off Wusong near Shanghai. According to reports of the incident, the ship operated between Hong Kong and Swatow, and later between Hong Kong and Shanghai. Her cargoes were mostly secured by companies in north and south China, such as the Marine Insurance Company, Yangtsze Insurance Association and Canton Insurance Office.[4] The Bombay's route ran between Hong Kong and port cities in coastal areas of China, and the owners of her cargoes were traders operating in these areas. Her passengers included Cantonese migrant workers or merchants travelling to Shanghai. Thus, another line of Kwok's ships connected southern and northern China. Kwok's ships carried a large amount of trade commodities, as well as a number of Chinese passengers. His main customers were likely to be Chinese and overseas Chinese merchants and emigrant workers operating in China and Southeast Asia. Kwok was merely one independent commercial comprador of many. Nevertheless, his large-scale entrepreneurial business offered fierce competition to foreign and Chinese rivals.

Kwok's success was partly because he was able to access technological, financial and human resources from both foreign and Chinese mercantile communities in Hong Kong and Shanghai. The foreign entrepreneurs in Hong Kong underpinned Kwok's steam-shipping business enterprise. Surprisingly, P&O supported Kwok's personal steam-shipping business. First, in 1854, Kwok took over part of P&O's shipwright and engineering department.[5] Then, in 1859, P&O sold its steamer, Sir Jamsetjee Jeejebhoy, to him.[6] On 25 January 1878, the company sold another ship, the Bombay, to Kwok for approximately £5,726.[7] Other foreign firms also sold steamers to Kwok. On 1 October 1878, *The Daily Press* reported that he was planning to purchase the Olympia, a German steamer, for approximately $80,000 or $90,000. It is highly possible that Kwok purchased old ships from P&O and other foreign companies. On 10 June 1874, an article appeared in the *Xunhuan Ribao* which cast doubt on the quality of Kwok's new steamship and the advertisement surrounding the steamer. The article stated:

> It is advertised that Kwok Acheong's new steamer is strong and fast enough to ride the wind and break the waves. So it can get you to any of your destinations. In contrast, an English newspaper remarked, this new steamer was an old ship model, and therefore, the aforementioned description shows a fallacy that does not fully reveal the steamer's actual performance.[8]

Nonetheless, by purchasing steamships from P&O and others, Kwok gradually expanded his shipping enterprise from the 1850s to the 1870s. By the time he died in 1880, he was a powerful and wealthy figure in the society of Hong Kong, and the owner of more than ten steamers.[9] Directors of P&O seemed not to regard Kwok's external conduct in the shipping business as a problem since they continued to hire him as a comprador until 1872 or 1873.[10] For P&O, Kwok was a close business partner who took over an unnecessary part of the company and revitalised it for Chinese customers. Kwok managed to differentiate his business from that of his employer. Kwok's principal customers were Chinese traders in port cities in China and other regions in Asia. P&O provided mail and shipping services globally, and their main customers were foreign traders.[11] P&O provided services to the traders operating in areas within the British Empire, while Kwok provided services to the Chinese merchants and workers who were coming and going between Chinese migrant communities in China and Southeast Asia.

Aside from technological support from P&O, Kwok's steamship enterprise was underpinned by foreign human resources. Kwok hired foreign captains to run his steamers; at least three of his ships' commanders were foreigners.[12] On 17 September 1875, Kwok asked managers of *The Hong Kong Times, Daily Advertiser and Shipping Gazette* to publish a notice stating that he was not responsible for any debts contracted by a foreign captain who was under his employment.[13] Kwok's employment of foreign captains was not unusual for the period. Other Chinese owners of steamers staffed their ships with foreign commanders and crews in the late nineteenth century as well. The China Merchants' Steam Navigation Company's ships, the *Ocean* and the *Fusing*, were commanded by Captain Brown and Robert Morton Andrews, respectively.[14] Hiring foreign captains and officers, Kwok and other compradors reduced the time needed to set up a Chinese workforce to run steamers.

In addition to P&O, Kwok drew on services from foreign bank insurance companies to a great extent. For instance, he was one of the first clients of the Hongkong and Shanghai Banking Corporation. On 23 December 1865, he opened an account with a cheque for $30,000. In May 1870, Kwok and another Chinese merchant, Tsoo Wing Yong, borrowed $20,000 from the bank for their business.[15] A letter from Kwok to a foreign insurance firm suggests that he attempted to utilise insurance services to secure his steamers. In December 1879, an agent of the Canton Insurance Office, Jardine's insurance company, wrote to Kwok that they were unable to insure Kwok's ship *Bombay*.[16] Later, Kwok found other British and Chinese insurance companies willing to secure the ship. When the Bombay was wrecked in December 1880, *The North China Herald* reported that it was insured by the On Tai Insurance Company (*Antai baoxian gongsi*) for $40,000 and an insurance company in England for $60,000.[17] Clearly, Kwok worked with foreign companies to expand his steam-shipping venture. Kwok's advantage in this particular area was his ability to conduct direct business with foreign firms in Hong Kong, as he both understood Pidgin English and had a knowledge of how to conduct a steam-shipping business in China as a comprador to P&O. Therefore, he was able to rely on technological and financial services from Western companies for the management of his shipping company.

In terms of marketing, Kwok drew on Chinese merchants. In 1869, *The Government Gazette* pointed out that Kwok successfully operated river steamers on the Pearl River regularly, thanks to support from Chinese merchants.[18] It is uncertain how Kwok collaborated with Chinese merchants in Hong Kong. However, it is probable that he was able to draw on the Chinese merchants' commercial network, which covered Southeast Asia. Aside from Kwok, Yuen Fat Hong (*Yuanfa hang*), a large Chinese trading firm managed by Ko Mun Wa (Gao Manhua), was involved in the steam-shipping business in Southeast Asia and East Asia. Yuen Fat Hong, which mainly traded in rice, had branches in Bangkok, Singapore and Japan and provided agency services for several steam-shipping companies.[19] After coming to Hong Kong during the 1870s, Ko primarily worked for the Scottish Oriental Steamship Company, which operated lines between Hong Kong and Bangkok.[20] It was not clear whether Kwok worked with Ko; however, it is possible that Kwok was able to draw on the inter-regional network of the Chinese merchants for his steam-shipping business, as a number of Chinese and overseas merchants carried commerce between Hong Kong and Bangkok during the period.

Kwok invested in other foreign shipping businesses together with other Chinese merchants in Hong Kong and other treaty ports during the 1860s and the 1870s. In 1865, Kwok was one of the Chinese shareholders of the Hong Kong, Canton and Macao Steamboat Co. when it was established by Augustine Heard & Co. and Douglas Lapraik with initial capital of $750,000. The other Chinese shareholders were Lee Sing and Sin Tak Fan, the former a wealthy Chinese merchant and the latter a Eurasian solicitor.[21] Kwok was also a shareholder in the Union Steam Navigation Co., which was formed in Shanghai by Glover & Co., a British firm. Many of its shareholders were Chinese merchants, including Kwok Acheong, Tong Kingsing (Jardine's comprador), Zheng Guanying (Dent, Beale & Co.'s clerk), Li Songyun (the company's comprador) and Sinchong (Hongkong and Shanghai Banking Corporation's comprador at Hankow).[22] Kwok was involved in the shipping business in Shanghai at the time of his investment in these foreign companies. Since his son was a comprador to P&O in Shanghai, Kwok might have been able to obtain market intelligence about Shanghai and participate in the shipping business there.[23] It should also be noted that Kwok was in Shanghai during the 1850s for a period of a few months. In 1852, Xu Run recorded that a Cantonese called Guo Ganzhang, another name for Kwok Acheong, established a dock to repair ships somewhere not far from Hongqiao. Xu Run wrote, 'At first I heard that the collection of capital was not easy, yet after establishing the business, he earned huge profits.'[24] Kwok's connection with the Shanghai market thus enabled him to run steamers between Shanghai and Hong Kong. There were a certain number of Chinese merchants who were keen to be involved in the steam-shipping business as well, and they functioned as information providers and marketing agents in Shanghai and other port cities in China.

Being a shareholder and director of foreign firms, Kwok obtained internal marketing information about these companies in order to avoid direct competition with them. Kwok was a director of the Hong Kong, Canton and Macao Steamboat Co. in 1867 and received $12,000 when he retired from the board of the company as a subsidy for the withdrawal of his four vessels from the Pearl River. At the meeting of the company, on 20 January 1869, George Heard remarked, 'if the subsidy stopped, [Kwok's Pearl River business] might prove a formidable opposition'.[25] The company still tried to pay the subsidy in the early 1870s. On 20 July 1875, at the meeting of directors and shareholders of the company, directors attempted to make a decision to pay a subsidy to Kwok of about $2,400 per month. However, it was cancelled due to opposition from the shareholders.[26] As a director of the Hong Kong, Canton and Macao Steamboat Co., Kwok established a mutually productive relationship with other foreign directors and shareholders. They sometimes negotiated with each other to avoid overlapping their business activities. However, this would not bring benefits to customers of the ships, such as merchants and passengers, as free competition was evidently hindered. The directors of the Hong Kong, Canton and Macao Steamboat Co. agreed to increase the rates of fares for the Chinese passengers on the Canton route soon after they were assured of Kwok's withdrawal from the Pearl River.[27]

Overall, Western technologies, knowledge of foreign business, and access to the Chinese marketing network enabled Kwok to expand his steam-shipping enterprise in China and Southeast Asia. Kwok's involvement in the management of other Sino-foreign shipping ventures in Shanghai and Hong Kong provided him with knowledge about how potential competitors ran their businesses and allowed him to establish a mutually productive relationship with them. Scholars have emphasised the competition among the foreign and Chinese merchants in the steam-shipping enterprise.[28] However, Kwok Acheong's company and Canton and Macao Steamboat Co.'s formal agreement to avoid competition is representative of the symbiosis between the foreign and Chinese merchants during the late nineteenth century. The mutual dependence between the comprador merchants and foreign businessmen is discussed in the fourth section of this chapter.

The successive generation of Hong Kong compradors embarked on shipping ventures much like those of Kwok from the 1880s onwards. Aside from Kwok, however, there were not many Hong Kong compradors who were engaged in the steam-shipping business during the 1860s and 1870s. Within a few years of Kwok's death in 1880, the name of his company, Kwok Acheong & Sons, disappeared from the list of owners of ships in English newspapers. Kwok's sons inherited his properties and premises only to lose their fortunes during the economic crisis of the 1880s. By the mid-1880s, Kwok's steam-shipping company had ceased operating. However, from the 1890s onwards, young compradors embarked on new steam-shipping business ventures in Hong Kong. One of these individuals was Wong Kam Fuk (Huang Jinfu), a comprador to the Hongkong and Kowloon Wharf and Godown, Co. He graduated from Queen's College and, after working in an insurance firm, joined the Wharf Company as a comprador in either 1889 or 1890. Thereafter, the Wong family dominated the position of comprador in the Hongkong and Kowloon Wharf and Godown, Co. until the mid-twentieth century.[29] Besides his work as a comprador, Wong Kam Fuk managed a Chinese company running steamships to the West River (*Xijiang*).[30] Robert Hotung managed steam-shipping companies in addition to his many other businesses. In 1931, he was the chairman of the Hong Kong, Canton and Macao Steamboat Co.,

Ltd. and Indo-China Steam Navigation Co., Ltd, as well as a director of the Hong Kong and Whampoa Dock Co., Ltd.[31] Woo Hay-tong, a clerk and later the Chinese shipping comprador of Butterfield, Swire & Co., was known as a millionaire ship owner in the early 1830s.[32] After Kwok's death on 13 May 1880, *The Daily Press* reported on his funeral procession in Hong Kong. The editor estimated the cost of the funeral ceremony at $5,000 and stated that 'such an enormous procession was never seen in Hong Kong before.'[33] Kwok Acheong turned into one of the most influential comprador merchants by 1880, and the system of the shipping business, which was formulated under Kwok and other commercial actors, was inherited by the next generation of Hong Kong compradors and Chinese merchants. In addition to Kwok's steam-shipping, other compradors carried out different entrepreneurial modern ventures in Hong Kong from the 1860s to the 1880s. In particular, a number of compradors invested in the sugar refining business; this is the focus of the following section.

International enterprises

The second feature of the Hong Kong compradors' commercial activities was their international character, as observed in Kwok Acheong's steamship business between China and Southeast Asia and his collaboration with foreign businessmen. This section first examines the compradors' involvement in the sugar refining and other modern businesses in Hong Kong during the late nineteenth century since this enables an understanding of how the compradors worked with Western entrepreneurs and Chinese merchants. Foreign entrepreneurs, Chinese merchants and compradors played pivotal roles in the formation of the sugar refining business in Hong Kong during this century. Their market was not limited to China, but included other foreign countries such as Australia. In one case, in January 1871, Francis Binns Sams and Victor Kresser, directors in the Wahee, Smith & Co., a sugar refining company in Hong Kong, appointed W. M. Shepheard Hart as their agent in Melbourne.[34] In the course of the development of the sugar refining enterprise in nineteenth-century Hong Kong, several companies were established. Though many collapsed, some of them survived and prospered; compradors were involved throughout.

The early compradors participated in the formation of one of the oldest sugar refining companies in Hong Kong. Table 4.2 lists the names of five main sugar refining companies in the latter half of the nineteenth century, their operating periods, and the names of the major compradors who were involved in the management of these companies. The Wahee, Smith & Co. was the first company to carry out a sugar refining business in Hong Kong. Compradors and foreign and Chinese merchants contributed to its establishment. The sugar company primarily carried out its business in Shanghai during the first half of the 1860s. Wong Wahee, alias Wong Yam-ting, William McGregor Smith, Dahlbeck, and Tong Kingsing were early directors of the company. Smith held the largest share, 16,000 taels, while Kingsing held 3,000 taels.[35] Wahee was a merchant whose family background was connected to the compradors. He was the son of Wong Yook (Huang

Yu) who was a trader as well as a shop and property owner in Hong Kong. Wong Yook once purchased an estate from Kwok Acheong in 1866. According to the will of Wong Yook, dated 12 January 1876, Kwok Acheong was one of his witnesses. Two of Wahee's brothers, Wong Shu-tong (Huang Shutang), alias Wong Ka-yau (Huang Jiayou), and Wong Wing-kwan, alias Wong Achai, were also compradors.[36] His family background was one of the reasons he worked with Tong Kingsing, a well-known comprador merchant in Shanghai. In addition to Tong Kingsing, Tong Mow-chee, Kingsing's elder brother, later became a director of the company. The Tong brothers performed key administrative roles in the company from the mid-1860s to the 1870s.[37] Until the end of December 1869, Tong Mow-chee held a position of high responsibility in the company.[38] The company expanded its business in Hong Kong to construct a sugar depot for sales of refined sugar, golden syrup and molasses. Then, in 1869, a sugar refinery was also established at No. 25 Wellington Street in the East Point of Hong Kong.[39]

Nevertheless, the management of the Sino-foreign company was not smooth. Although foreign directors collaborated with Chinese merchants in the operation of the company, they did not sufficiently understand how the Chinese staff carried out business. Similarly, the Chinese merchants were not very engaged in the foreign side of business. In Wahee, Smith & Co., foreign staff mainly dealt with foreign matters, such as the purchase of machines from England, while the Chinese staff were responsible for Chinese matters, including the purchase of raw sugar from southern China.[40] A court case in 1869 underlined this division between the foreign and Chinese staff of Wahee, Smith & Co. In May of that year, the company sued its business partner, Lum Tak Kee, due to the low quality of raw sugar he had supplied. According to the contract between Wahee, Smith & Co. and Lum Tak Kee, '*Lau T'ong*' was supposed to be supplied from 'the sugar-growing districts' in China. The Chinese characters making up *Lau T'ong*'s can be read as *Liutang*. This could mean *tangjiang* (syrup) in the current Chinese language. Lum Tak Kee did supply more than 8,000 piculs of raw sugar; however, it turned out that the quality of the raw sugar was lower than the quality that the directors of the company had expected. Raw sugar was expected to produce at least 80 per cent refined sugar; Lum Tak Kee's sugar produced less than 57 per cent. Therefore, Wahee, Smith & Co. claimed that Lum Tak Kee should cover the loss to the company, a total of $14,558.39. After 4 days of examination in the court, it was discovered that *Lau T'ong* did not necessarily mean raw sugar, but in fact meant 'juice sugar', or mould and drained sugar, which was utilised to produce refined sugar in China. *Lau T'ong*'s productivity was usually less than 70 per cent. Therefore, the defendant was regarded as having fulfilled the contract. Losing the grounds for their claim, Wahee, Smith & Co. lost the case.[41] The foreign directors' lack of knowledge about traditional Chinese sugar refining customs and the quality of Chinese raw sugar caused this misunderstanding and legal dispute.

Another cause of conflict was the inefficiency of the communication between the Chinese and foreign staff of Wahee, Smith & Co. On 27 May 1869, a partner of Wahee Smith & Co., Tong Mow-chee, a purchaser of the raw sugar, appeared in court as a witness. His statement highlighted the differences in the concept of raw sugar among the foreign versus the Chinese staff in the company. Mow-chee stated that the company usually only produced 40 to 60 per cent refined sugar from the raw sugar. He purchased 10,000 piculs of *Lau T'ong* from a planter in Tangkoon, near the Bogue. Mow-chee stated that the Tungkoon (Dongguan) sugar produced 50 to 60 per cent refined sugar. Mow-chee also purchased 400 or 500 piculs of raw sugar produced in 'the celebrated district of Hop-noy' from Lum Tak Kee. For Mow-chee, the quality of Lum Tak Kee's sugar was similar to that of the Tungkoon sugar.[42] However, Mow-chee did not understand what *Lau T'ong* meant and also simply regarded it as raw sugar. Therefore, the foreign staff considered that Mow-chee had purchased raw sugar. Furthermore, although Mow-chee understood that the productivity of Chinese raw sugar was less than 60 per cent, the foreign staff thought it should be higher than that. To put it simply, there were two misunderstandings. The first was the misunderstanding of the quality of raw sugar between the foreign and Chinese staff in the company, and the other was the misunderstanding of the meaning of *Lau T'ong* between Lum Tak Kee and the company. Evidently, the foreign and Chinese directors did not communicate enough to conduct their business, since the difference of opinion between Chinese and foreign staff was not resolved before the court case started. In court, Smith, one of the directors, clearly stated that he was not involved in making a contract with Lum Tuk Kee. In the case of Wahee, Smith & Co., the foreign staff were reluctant to participate in the Chinese side of the business. Similarly, the Chinese director was not keen to be involved in the foreign affairs. Wahee did not appear in court at all, possibly because he did not speak English, he was away from Hong Kong, or because it was outside his business responsibilities. Despite the comprador merchants' participation in the business of the sugar company, it was still not easy to operate a Sino-foreign enterprise in late nineteenth-century Hong Kong.[43]

Although there were inefficiencies, Chinese merchants, foreign businessmen and the compradors continued collaborating in the management of sugar refining companies. After Tong Mow-chee left the company, Wahee, Smith & Co. employed a comprador called Choa Chee Bee, alias Choy Tsz Mee (Cai Ziwei), as early as 1872.[44] Choa Chee Bee was a Malay Chinese merchant who had come to Hong Kong from Malacca to seek business opportunities. His ancestors were Fujian merchants who had moved to Malacca and became successful landowners and traders there.[45] When Jardine took over Wahee, Smith & Co.'s business and established the China Sugar Refinery Co. during the 1870s, Jardine employed Choa Chee Bee as a comprador in his sugar refining business. Choa Chee Bee was also independently engaged in the sugar trade between Java, Hong Kong and China.[46] After the death of Choa Chee Bee in 1901, his nephew, Choa Leep-chee (Cai Lizhi), succeeded his position as comprador.[47] Wahee, Smith & Co. was a Sino-foreign company, and it was not impossible for the company to conduct direct trade with Chinese merchants. However, it still employed Choa as a comprador.

The compradors conducted other modern businesses that were also international and inter-regional. Kwok Acheong and other Chinese merchants established the On Tai Insurance Company in 1877 and Chinese Insurance Co. (*huashang baoan gongsi*) to cover the marine risks of Chinese merchants' steamship business in the Pacific Ocean and the China Seas.[48] The company was established with an investment of 400,000 taels from Chinese merchants and compradors. The company mainly insured cargo ship traffic between 'Australia, California, Manila, Singapore, Saigon, Penang, and all the treaty ports of China and Japan'.[49] *Xunhuan Ribao*, a Chinese newspaper that was established by several comprador merchants, had agencies in various port cities, including Canton, Macau, Yokohama, Kobe, Nagasaki, Saigon, San Francisco and Singapore.[50] The Hong Kong compradors conducted businesses connecting port cities in China, Japan, the United States, Australia and countries in Southeast Asia.

Some of the compradors themselves had previous experience living and working abroad. For instance, Tong Mow-chee had been in California and Choa Chee Bee came from Malacca. Fung Tang (Feng Deng) moved to California in 1857. He returned to Hong Kong in the early 1870s and became a comprador to the Oriental Bank and later to the New Oriental Bank, as well as a secretary to the Chinese Insurance Co. Before becoming a comprador in Hong Kong, Fung Tang was already an established merchant in California. In 1870, he had $6,000 in assets, according to the census of San Francisco. In Hong Kong, he operated the Gold Mountain firm and other firms conducting trade between China and California.[51] Wei Akwong, a comprador to the Mercantile Bank in Hong Kong during the 1870s, studied in Singapore in his youth.[52] The Hong Kong compradors' international background reflected the migration of Chinese workers to Australia and the United States triggered by the Gold Rush. The Gold Rush had turned Hong Kong into 'a large-scale entrepôt of people' by the 1880s.[53] The overseas network of the Chinese in Asian, American and Pacific countries enabled the compradors in Hong Kong to conduct international and inter-regional trade.

It should be noted that the business associates of compradors and Chinese merchants were not necessarily Western businessmen. Hing Kee, a commissariat comprador as well as a director of several hotels in Hong Kong and Macau, worked with a Parsee merchant named Dorabjee for a long time in addition to other Western entrepreneurs. In 1886, Dorabjee and Hing Kee were owners of the Victoria Hotel; this is evidenced by a notification issued in March of that year from the Hong Kong Fire Insurance Company informing Dorabjee and Hing Kee that the company would cover damage done to the shop window on 51 Queens Road.[54] Dorabjee Nawrojee Mithaiwala was a well-known Indian Parsee entrepreneur in nineteenth-century Hong Kong. It appears that the two – Dorabjee and Hing Kee – collaborated in their business over a long period of time. Dorabjee and Hing Kee were the lessees of Hong Kong Hotel on Queen's Road in 1879.[55]

As stated in the Introduction, Hing Kee's management of hotel businesses serves as a good example of the international characteristics of the Hong Kong compradors. In his old age, Hing Kee was involved in an auction and ice depot business. As a valuer and commission agent, Hing Kee's business went well. After Hing Kee's death in 1911, his son, Peter Hing Kee, took over his father's enterprises. Peter Hing Kee worked for the China Mutual Insurance Company Limited, the Canton Navigation Co. Ltd, the Hong Kong Ice Co. Ltd., and the

Daily Farm throughout 1916.[56] Hing Kee worked with a variety of foreign merchants throughout his entire career. His international background, including his expertise in four languages – French, English, Chinese and Portuguese – might have been an advantage for him in managing prestigious hotels for foreign and Chinese customers.

Collaborating with multi-national traders and merchants, the compradors conducted international business in Hong Kong from the 1860s to the 1880s. To conduct a large-scale business in Hong Kong, it was necessary for the entrepreneurs to have access to both Western technology and the Chinese commercial network. For this, the Chinese and foreign entrepreneurs had to collaborate with one another. However, due to language issues and differences in business practices, the foreign and Chinese merchants needed commercial intermediaries, namely the comprador merchants. Therefore, the compradors were involved in the formation and the management of joint Sino-foreign ventures, such as sugar refining and hotel businesses. The comprador merchants involved in these international businesses tended to have previous experience working with foreigners and had often spent time in foreign countries.

Diversification of business

The third attribution of Hong Kong compradors' commercial activity was their handling of multiple businesses. As described above, the majority of the compradors were involved in multiple businesses. The wills of notable compradors suggest what kind of companies they ran, invested in and owned. According to the will of Lo Pak Sheung (Luo Bochang), the head comprador to the Hong Kong and Shanghai Banking Corporation, he was involved in the management of at least nine companies and shops in Hong Kong in 1877. Kwok Acheong stated in his will, 'I have been trading in Hong Kong and carrying different kinds of businesses (large and small).'[57] It was common for the compradors to diversify their business. Therefore, this section explores the multiplicity of the compradors' economic activities to trace the inception of the Hong Kong style of business.

Primarily, most of the Hong Kong compradors invested in land and properties. In 1876, Kwok Acheong was the third highest ratepayer ($6,906.36) to the colonial government. His sons, Kwok Ying Kai and Kwok Ying Shew, were the seventh and thirteenth highest ratepayers in 1881. The sum paid by the Kwok brothers was approximately $10,448. Ng Sang (Wu Sheng), a comprador to Douglas Lapraik & Co., was the sixteenth highest ratepayer, at $2,572.80 in 1876. In 1881, Ng Sang became the second highest ratepayer, paying a total sum of $10,240.[58] In 1881, a list of the 20 top ratepayers of Hong Kong included 17 Chinese. Of them, seven Chinese were compradors or family members of the compradors and six were merchants.[59] Mok Sze Yeung operated a real estate company and owned approximately 10 buildings in Lyndhurst Terrace.[60] Robert Hotung made large sales of his 21 properties on Wellington Street, Cochrane Street, and Stanley Street in October 1899.[61] Land and property investment was a major source of income for compradors throughout the nineteenth century.

In addition to working with foreign traders, the compradors conducted businesses targeting Chinese customers and merchants in Hong Kong. Kwok Acheong was also known as an owner of a slaughterhouse in Hong Kong. Because of his cattle-importing business, Kwok was called Ngau Lan Atsung (Niulan Yaxiang), meaning 'Cattle-market Atsung'.[62] Kwok also managed a general merchant house called Fat Hing Hong (*Faxing hang*).[63] Lum King Wong, a comprador at Deetjen & Co., carried out a business as a dyer under the name of Yan Loong in Jerovois Street in collaboration with other Chinese merchants. Tong Kingsing owned profitable pawnshops in Hong Kong during the late 1850s and received 25 to 45 per cent of his money from the shops every year while he was working for Jardine.[64] Wei Akwong lent quicksilver to people who needed it and also sold it when the price rose. Lee Yu Chow (Li Ruzhou) of Sz Yik Firm and a dealer in quicksilver borrowed 200 flasks of it from Wei Akwong, a Mercantile Bank comprador, in 1877.[65] At that time, 200 flasks were valued at $10,631.25, and to borrow them, Lee paid $7,312.50 for 2 months as well as a 1 per cent commission of $50. When the price of the quicksilver sharply fell soon after that, Wei claimed that Lee had purchased the quicksilver rather than borrowed it. However, Lee had already left the colony in August and Wei could bring the case only against Lee's sureties to make the full payment of the quicksilver; ultimately, Wei's claim was not accepted in court.[66] All of these examples demonstrate how the compradors carried out multiple businesses in the Chinese community of Hong Kong.

The Hong Kong compradors emulated both Chinese and foreign merchants' businesses. This was possible because as intermediaries, the compradors had multiple functions in different communities and societies. Though the compradors were styled intermediaries and business associates for foreign merchants, they also acted as Chinese traders and merchants in the treaty port world and the local community. By the beginning of the 1880s, shipping, sugar refining, management of hotels, and property and land investments had become major industries in Hong Kong. It was common for the compradors to conduct small-scale sideline businesses in addition to playing a role in large-scale modern enterprises. In this context, Robert Hotung transformed himself into a business magnate in Hong Kong in the late nineteenth and the early twentieth century. Hotung was Jardine's principal comprador; he was called 'Hong Kong's Grand Old Man' due to his contribution to the development of multiple businesses in Hong Kong during the period. After serving in the Customs, he started working in Jardine, Matheson & Co. as Junior Assistant to the Comprador of Messers in the early 1880s. In 1900, he became the Chief Comprador; he held this position for 6 years. He resigned from the position only due to health issues, after which point he let his brother take it over. Hotung was engaged in a variety of businesses on his own and was remarkably successful in all of them. In 1931, Robert Hotung invested in real estate in Hong Kong and Macau and handled several businesses, including the management of a hotel. He also served on the board of directors of more than ten companies. The *Daily Press* wrote:

> [H]e serves on the Board of Directors of the Hong Kong and Whampoa Dock Co., Ltd., Hong Kong Electric Co., Ltd., Chairman, Hong Kong, Canton and Macao Steamboat Co., Ltd., Indo-China Steam Navigation Co., Ltd. Canton Insurance Co., Ltd., Hong Kong Fire Insurance Co., Kam Hing Knitting Co., Hong Kong Rope Manufacturing Co., Hong Kong and Shanghai Hotels, Peak Tramways Co., Douglas Steamship Co., Green Island Cement Co, Hong Kong Engineering and Construction Co., China Light and Power Co., China Provident Loan and Mortgage Co., and chairman of the United Photoplay Service. Ltd . . .[67]

In a similar manner to earlier compradors, Robert Hotung carried out multiple businesses and had become a 'Financial Magnate' of Hong Kong by 1931.[68] Running multiple businesses, the compradors became an influential class in the commercial world of Hong Kong from the 1860s to the 1880s. These commercial activities of the early generation of the compradors contributed to the fundamental business structure of Hong Kong and enabled the rise of Robert Hotung.

One reason for the diversification of business was to reduce the risk of going bankrupt due to the failure of one business. The instability of the market enabled the compradors to make huge amounts of money in a short period of time. However, over-reliance on one business sector carried a high risk of bankruptcy. Therefore, the compradors dispersed the risk by diversifying their businesses. On 17 July 1933, in an article titled as 'How to Become Rich: Advice from China's Richest Man' in *The South China Morning Post*, Robert Hotung stated, 'There were many men who have a good idea. That is not enough. A man should have two good ideas in case one fails.'[69] Whether consciously or unconsciously, the majority of the comprador merchants understood this kind of business rule. The diversification of business is still a feature of the Hong Kong businessmen's commercial behaviour.[70]

The groups of the compradors

The fourth feature of the Hong Kong compradors was the formation of their own commercial network. By the 1870s, it became evident that the company compradors, especially principal compradors, constituted an influential group in the commercial world of Hong Kong. The compradors were integrated with each other through their economic activities and marriages. There were Chinese businessmen who became compradors as well as compradors who turned into entrepreneurs in Hong Kong during the late nineteenth century. Lau Wai Chun (Liu Weichuan) had already been a well-to-do merchant before he became a comprador to the Hong Kong and Shanghai Banking Corporation in 1892.[71] Choa Chee Bee, Jardine's sugar refinery comprador, was from a traditional Chinese merchant family in Southeast Asia before he came to Hong Kong. Choa Chee Be and his nephew transitioned into the position of comprador because it was beneficial for their commercial activities. From the end of the 1860s to the early 1870s, the role of comprador became an attractive occupation for Chinese merchants. This was because the position brought business networks and financial resources from other comprador merchants.

The compradors gradually formed their own commercial network by doing business with one another from the 1870s to the 1880s. This could be particularly observed in the compradors' involvement in the sugar refining business during the period. On 18 July 1879, Lo Hok Pang made a contract with Jardine, Matheson & Co. and let Jardine take his premises in Victoria. He also agreed to the company continuing the sugar refining business on these premises for a year under Lo's name.[72] Before selling the property to Jardine, Lo had once made a contract to sell it to the commissariat comprador Hing Kee in 1879. However, this plan eventually failed. On 5 June in 1879, in the Supreme Court, Lo Hok Pang (Luo Hepeng), a comprador of the Hongkong and Shanghai Banking Corporation, and Hing Kee sued each other over the payment of the properties of the Oriental Sugar Refinery. Hing Kee made a contract to purchase the premises and plant of the Oriental Sugar Refinery for about $170,000. However, later, Hing Kee found that he was unable to complete the payment, as one of his partners for the purchase of the refinery withdrew from the project. Messrs Sharp, Toller and Johnson, partners of Hing Kee, withdrew from the project. Then Lo Hok Pang and his friends who were also on the list of financial backers withdrew together. Therefore, Hing Kee was not able to pay the total cost of the premises to Lo, who sued Hing Kee for the enforcement of the contract. At the same time, Hing Kee sued Lo for a refund of the $20,000 that he had paid already, along with another $20,000 for Lo's failure to fulfil the contract. Eventually, the Chief Justice ordered Lo to pay back $16,000 to Hing Kee to settle the issue.[73]

Another incident illustrating the compradors' collaboration in business activities was Jardine's takeover of the Lee Yuen Sugar Refining Company in 1886. Choa Chee Bee, the China Sugar Refinery Co. comprador, played a mediating role in the case. When the Lee Yuen Sugar Refining Company was dissolved in 1886, Andrew Johnston, Li King Ting (Li Jingting) and Lau Wai Chun were appointed as liquidators. In the meeting of the company for the liquidation, although Johnston had managed the company since its foundation, Chun Yat Son and his partner, Choa Chee Bee of the Hip Tai Hong, told the court that they had doubts about Johnston's performance. Johnston insisted that Choa Chee Bee 'brought influence on the Directors' to sell the company to Jardine, Matheson & Co. He also suggested that the company properties should be advertised first for public sale rather than by private arrangement.[74] The details of how Jardine made a deal with the Lee Yuen Sugar Refining Company are explained in the transcripts of the meeting. On 20 February, when the directors were looking for a purchaser for the Lee Yuen Refinery, and were asking a price of $180,000, William Keswick first offered $170,000 for that purpose. On 21 February, when the directors were negotiating with other possible purchasers, Choa Chee Bee appeared and told them that he could give them a better offer. Then Choa Chee Bee immediately went to see Keswick and came back with an offer of $190,000 and a cheque for $30,000 as a guarantee. Johnston was not satisfied with the process of the negotiation and suspected the 'sincerity' of the Hip Tai Hong, which was a partner of the Lee

Yuen Refining Company. What Johnston pointed out was that Choa Chee Bee could access the internal information of the Lee Yuen Refining Company as a business partner, while he had a position as comprador in Jardine's sugar refining company.[75]

Eric Peter Ho, whose paternal grandfather was Ho Fook, explored the Jardine side of this case by drawing on family materials. According to his account, Robert Hotung was involved in the negotiations between Jardine, Matheson & Co. and the Lee Yuen Sugar Refining Company. Primarily, Choa Chee Bee and Choy Sing Nam, compradors working for Keswick, were interested in the purchase of the Lee Yuen Sugar Refining Company. Given that they wanted to know how much it would cost to make a tender for the sugar refining company on behalf of Keswick, Hotung investigated potential competitors for the purchase of the company. Hotung discovered that a well-known Chinese merchant was interested in it and convinced him not to be a bidder. Then Hotung suggested to Keswick that rather than waiting for the formal tender process, he should make a pre-emptive offer to the refinery 'with cash on the table'. Keswick took Hotung's suggestion, which proved successful in securing the purchase of the Lee Yuen Sugar Refining Company at a lower than estimated cost. Since Keswick believed that entering the tender would have cost Jardine Matheson & Co. $50,000 to $100,000 more, he rewarded Hotung, who had made the deal, with $20,000. Of this, Hotung took only $1,900 for himself, giving $1,900 to Choy Sing Nam and distributing the remaining money among his colleagues.[76] Jardine's takeover of the Lee Yuen Sugar Refining Company highlighted the compradors' dual function for the foreign traders. From the viewpoint of Keswick, the compradors were valuable intermediaries who offered external market intelligence and spontaneously made deals with other Chinese merchants for the expansion of business. On the other hand, from the viewpoint of Johnston, the compradors were gatekeepers who prevented direct business with other economic actors in Hong Kong. If a foreign merchant succeeded in establishing a constructive relationship with his comprador and understood the importance of drawing on the compradors' commercial networks, the merchant was able to conduct effective business. But if he did not, it meant exclusion from the commercial network and financial resources of the compradors.

Outside of the sugar refining business, the compradors and Chinese merchants also managed a variety of companies together. *Xunhuan Ribao* was a Chinese newspaper established by Chinese merchants, the majority of whom were compradors, in 1874. The early directors of the publishing company (*Zhonghua yingwu ju*) of the newspaper mainly consisted of comprador merchants. One of them was Fung Ming-shan, a comprador to A. H. Hogg and Co., and later to the Mercantile Bank.[77] Another two were Leung On, a comprador to Gibb, Livingston and Co., Chen Ruinan, alias Chen Guishi, a comprador to Arnhold & Karberg & Co.[78] The newspaper printed a number of notices written by Chinese merchants and compradors in the 1870s and 1880s.[79] Mok Sze Yeung and others borrowed $47,000 under deed of mortgage from the Hong Kong Fire Insurance Company in February 1872.[80] On 23 October 1877, the Hong Kong

Fire Insurance Company notified Mok Sze Yeung, Chun Quan Ee, Ng Chop Qing and Mok Kee Cheong that their mortgage of $47,000 was due for payment on 1 November.[81] Of these individuals, Chun Quan Ee could be identified with Chan Quan-ee (Chen Guanyi), another comprador to Augustine Heard & Co., during the period.[82] The ties between different comprador families were thus strengthened by conducting joint businesses.

Different comprador families were connected with one another through marriage and that strengthened the commercial ties between them. Robert Hotung's mother, Shi Si, meaning Ms. Shi (Shi Shi), became a concubine to Kwok Acheong after Hotung's father, Charles Henri Maurice Bosman, left Hong Kong in 1868.[83] The Choa family formed strong marriage ties with the Ho family during the 1910s and the 1920s.[84] Wong Kam Fuk married Hotung's fourth daughter, while Xie Jiabao, a comprador to the Nippon Yūsen Kaisha, married Ho Fook's fifth daughter.[85] Mok Sze Yeung's daughter married a member of the Tongs (Tong King Sings' family). It was said that Mok Sze Yeung was educated in business under Wu Jianzhang, a Shanghai Daotai and a comprador. Mok's eldest son, Yunshang, married Wu's niece.[86] A son of a comprador took over his father's work, while a daughter married another comprador and merchant. In this manner, through marriages, the compradors strengthened their integrity and collectivity. It should be noted that ties between different comprador and merchant families were also strengthened simply through business and personal friendship. Close business associates usually inherited a comprador's properties and estates alongside family members. In his will, Ng Sang stated that he would bequeath all his property and estate to four Chinese merchants.[87] Ng Hip (Wu Ye), a comprador to Butterfield, Swire & Sons, bequeathed his real and personal estate to Mok Koon Yuk (Mo Guanwu), alias Mok Cho Chuen (Mo Zaoquan), the second son of Mok Sze Yeung.[88]

Conclusion

The compradors played contradictory roles as collaborators with and competitors to foreign companies. Hong Kong commercial activities accelerated the development of Sino-foreign enterprises, including the steam-shipping, sugar refining and publishing businesses. Sufficient knowledge of both Chinese and foreign business practices made it possible for the compradors to launch and manage Sino-foreign joint ventures. A noticeable feature of the commercial activities of the Hong Kong compradors was their conduct of business beyond China. Overseas Chinese or Chinese compradors came to Hong Kong from Southeast Asia, America, and other regions. The business partners of the compradors were internationally diverse, including American, British, Chinese and Parsee merchants.

These comprador merchants diversified their businesses to minimise risk and maximise profit. They invested in multiple ventures together, and made business deals with one another. An intriguing point is that the compradors' commercial behaviours resembled those of well-to-do foreign traders and businessmen like Jardine and Heard. Through working as internal staff for foreign companies, the

Table 4.1 Ships of Kwok Acheong & Sons[1]

Name	*Year*	*Type*	*Size (ton)*	*Location*	*Captain*
Bombay	1878–1880	British	749	Inter ports	
China	1882	German	648		Sohoer
Cricket	1876				
Lintin[2]	1869–1875		69		
Mandarin	1865				
Mirage	1871	British			J. W. Flinch
Norna	1875–1879	British	606	Inter ports	
Olympia[3]	1878	German			
Prince Albert[4]	1869		180	Pearl River Delta	
Sir Jamsetjee Jeejeebhoy	1875–1879		184	Pearl River Delta	
Yotsai	1875–1882		180		Browne
Yottung[5]	1875	British	324		Riddell

1 From the shipping record of the *China Mail* and the *Hong Kong Daily Press*, 1869–1882.
2 *China Mail*, 6 November 1875, 8.
3 *Hong Kong Daily Press*, 1 October 1878.
4 The ship was seized by Chinese customs in 1866.
5 *China Mail*, 4 September 1875, 8.

Table 4.2 Sugar refining companies in nineteenth-century Hong Kong

Company	*Active years*	*Compradors who were involved in the business*
Wahee Smith, Co.	1869–1875	Choa Chee Bee
Oriental Sugar Refinery[1] (Jardine)	1876–1878[2]	Ng Chuck Chee
China Sugar Refinery Co.	1870s–1928	Choa Chee Bee, Lo Hok Pang, Choy Sing Nam
Lee Yuen Sugar Refining Company	1880s–1886	Lau Wai Chuen
Taikoo Sugar Refinery Company (Swire)	1881–1972	Mok Cho Chuen, Mok Kon Sang

1 Successor of Wahee, Smith & Co, at Swatow. Partnership with Oriental Sugar Refining Company of Hong Kong, Ltd. Directors were James Bingham Alliot, James Beattie, Joseph Clever, James Connell, John Hope Gordon. *London And China Telegraph*, 8 September 1877, 809.
2 *Government Gazette*, 23 November 1878, 579.

compradors observed and learnt the foreign principals' methods of conducting international and innovative enterprises and their techniques for risk management and the diversification of business. Many of the compradors applied these methods to their own businesses. At the same, the compradors emulated the commercial activities of general Chinese merchants. Following this model, many compradors turned into successful merchants who integrated Chinese and foreign business practices.

Last but not least, the compradors were interconnected, and they conducted joint ventures together. By formulating their own commercial network, the compradors acted as essential commercial intermediaries, and as gatekeepers of information and of financial and human resources at once. For foreign businessmen, the integrity of the compradors and their internal commercial network appeared to be a barrier to conducting direct trade with Chinese merchants. On the other hand, the compradors could provide foreign entrepreneurs in Hong Kong with financial resources and access to commercial networks. This way, by the end of the 1880s, the company compradors became a well-to-do class of commercial intermediaries and independent businessmen. Furthermore, they actively worked for political and public causes to secure their social position.

Notes

1 Liu, *Anglo-American Steamship*; Hao, *Comprador*, 120–124; Zhu, *Zhongguo jindai lunchuan*; Zhaoshangju shi yanjiuhui, Yì and Hu, *Zhaoshangju yu jindai zhongguo*, eds; regarding Cantonese merchants and the steam shipping business in South China, see Ye, 'Yueshang yu guangdong'.
2 *China Mail*, 22 April 1880.
3 *China Mail*, 22 June, 23 June, and 26 June 1871, 3, 3, and 3.
4 NCH, 30 December 1880, 611.
5 Smith, *Chinese Christians*, 124.
6 P&O Heritage, ship fact sheet 'Sir Jamsetjee Jeejebhoy'.
7 P&O Company Records: P&O/65/72, Individual Ships: Bombay, Miscellaneous material, 1852.
8 *XHRB,* 10 June 1874. Kwok Chung was another name of Kwok Acheong.
9 See Table 4.1.
10 *The China Directory* recorded that the P&O comprador was Kwok Acheong in 1872 and Wong Sü Tong in 1873. Wong could be identified as Wong Shu-tong (Huang Shutang); whose father, Wong Yook (Huang Yu), had business ties with Kwok Acheong. Carl T. Smith suggested that he was also a comprador to the P&O (Smith, *Chinese Christians*, 163–164).
11 Tsang, *Modern History of Hong Kong* (London and New York: I.B. Tauris, 2004), 61.
12 For instance, J.W. Flinch was the captain of the *Mirage* and Browne was the captain of the *Yotsai* in the 1870s. See Table 4.1.
13 JMA: B7/15/11726, Hong Kong 17 September 1875, Kwok Acheong to the *Hong Kong Times*.
14 Cassel, *Grounds of Judgment* 164–165.
15 HSBC Archive, London: HSBCS 0019/0001, Comprador File.
16 JMA: C36/23, Letters to local correspondents, Canton Insurance Office to Kwok Achoeng, 19 December 1879.
17 *NCH*, 30 December 1880, 611.
18 *Government Gazette*, 20 March 1869, 130.

19 Fok, 'Lineage', 159.
20 Lee, *Gourmets in Land*, 48–49. Hop Kee ran a British steamer, *Paladin*, between Singapore and Hong Kong, and Yuen Fat Hong ran a British steamer, *Danube*, between Hong Kong and Bangkok in 1878 (*Hong Kong Daily Press*, 19 September 1878).
21 Hao, *Commercial Revolution*, 247; Carroll, *Edge of Empires*, 101.
22 Hao, *Commercial Revolution*, 248–249.
23 *NCH*, 30 December 1880, 611.
24 Xu, *Xuyuzhai zixu nianpu*, 4.
25 *Hong Kong Daily Press*, 18 and 21 January 1869, *London and China Telegraph*, 28 August 1867, 445–446; *Government Gazette*, 20 March 1869, 130.
26 *London and China Telegraph*, 30 August 1875, 701.
27 *Hong Kong Daily Press*, 21 January 1869.
28 Liu, *Anglo-American Steamship*; Ye, 'Yueshang yu Guangdong', 327–331.
29 Hutcheon, *Wharf: First Hundred Years*, 27–28; *Hong Kong Daily Press*, 14 December 1931.
30 Wright, Twentieth Century Impressions, 178.
31 JMA: L14/9, The Pamphlet of The Golden Wedding of Sir Robert and Lady Ho Tung, 1932–1933, 'Sir Robert and Lady Ho Tung Celebrating Their Golden Wedding' Reprinted from *Hong Kong Daily Press*, 30 November, 1931.
32 *Singapore Free Press*, 29 June 1932, 12.
33 *Hong Kong Daily Press*, 13 May 1880.
34 *Wellington Independent*, Issue 3137, 2 March 1871, 3.
35 JMA: F10/5, Deed of partnership of Shanghai merchants. A copy of a deed of co-partnership between William Francis Brown Sams, Tong King Sing, William McGregor Smith and Wahee, all merchants of Shanghai, for a joint trade as sugar crushers and refiners at Hong Kong or Swatow, 7 March 1867.
36 Smith, *Chinese Christians*, 163–164; HKPRO: HKRS 144–4-354, Will of Wong Yook, Kwok Acheong was one of the witnesses, dated 12 January 1876.
37 Smith, 'Formative Years', 92.
38 *Government Gazette*, 22 January 1870, 37. The company went into bankruptcy and stopped its service in the beginning of 1875. See *Hong Kong Government Gazette*, 20 February 1875, 55.
39 *Hong Kong Daily Press*, 17 July 1869.
40 In the mid-1860s, Smith went to England to purchase machinery. Smith, *Chinese Christians*, 50. *China Mail*, 12 May 1868, Wahee and Others v Henderson 2.
41 *China Mail*, 31 May 1869, 3.
42 *China Mail*, 27 May 1869, 3.
43 *China Mail*, 28 May 1869, 3.
44 China Directory 1872.
45 Wright, *Twentieth Century Impressions*, 176–178.
46 Ibid., 176.
47 Ibid., 176; Smith, *Chinese Christians*, 163.
48 Feng, *Housheng liqun*, 30, 45.
49 *Hong Kong Daily Press*, 19 September 1878; Feng, Rao and Law, *Enriching Lives*, 43.
50 Notification regarding the launch of the *Xunhuan Ribao*. Included in the microfilm of the newspaper (11 February 1874).
51 Sinn, *Pacific Crossing*, 166–167.
52 Smith, *Chinese Christians*, 135.
53 Sinn, *Pacific Crossing*, 90–91.
54 JMA: C37/7, Letters re Hongkong Fire Insurance Co. Ltd, General Manager to Dorabjee and Hing Kee (Victoria Hotel), 12 March 1886, 311; *The Catholic World*, Vol. 39, No. 239, 161–162.
55 *Directory and Chronicle for China, Japan, Corea* (1879), 223.

56 England, *Quest of Noel Croucher*, 132.
57 HKPRO: HKRS 144–4-403, Will of Kwok Acheong, 6 November 1877.
58 *Government Gazette*, 4 March 1882, 241.
59 Ibid., Hui, 'Comprador Politics', 37–38; Yuan, *Xianggang shilue*, 130.
60 Zhang, *Maiban de qiyejia*, 72.
61 *Hong Kong Telegraph*, 19 October 1899; Zheng and Wong, *Xiangang dalao*, 104–105.
62 HKPRO: HKRS149–2-203, Indenture: Indenture of Lease of the Eastern Slaughter House. Between the Surveyor General of Hong Kong and Kwok Achoong, 30 June 1859.
63 Feng, *Xianggang huazi caituan*, 543; Holdsworth and Munn (eds), *Dictionary of Hong Kong Biography*, 233–234.
64 JMA: William Keswick (Shanghai), 4 January 1866 cited in Hao, *Compradors*, 112.
65 *Hong Kong Daily Press*, 14 December 1877.
66 *London and China Telegraph*, 18 March 1878, 245–246.
67 JMA: L14/9, The Golden Wedding of Sir Robert and Lady Ho Tung ('Hong Kong's Grand Old Man', reprinted from *Hong Kong Daily Press*, 30 November 1931).
68 Ibid.
69 *South China Morning Post*, 17 July 1933, cited in Zheng and Wong, *Xianggang dalao*, 350–352.
70 *Hong Kong Daily Press*, 30 May 1883.
71 King, *History of Hongkong and Shanghai Banking Corporation*, Vol. 1, 444, 515–516. Lau Wai Chun was educated in Vancouver, Canada.
72 JMA: F1/78, Agreement of Lo Hok Ping and Jardine Matheson, 1879–1880.
73 *China Mail*, 5 June 1879, 3; *London and China Telegraph*, 9 August 1879, 635.
74 *China Mail*, 12 March 1886, 3.
75 Ibid.
76 Ho, *Tracing My Children's Lineage*, 103.
77 Smith, *Chinese Christians*, 126; *China Directory* 1872 and 1873.
78 Notification regarding the launch of the *Xunhuan Ribao*; Feng, *Xianggang huazi caituan*, 42.
79 For instance, notifications regarding business and charitable activity of Leung On sometimes appeared in the *Xunhuan Ribao*.
80 *NCH*, 29 February 1872, 161–162.
81 JMA: C37/2 Letters re Hongkong Fire Insurance Co. Ltd, 23 October 1877, General Manager to Chun Quan Ee, 233.
82 Smith, *Chinese Christians*, 163.
83 Ho, *Tracing My Children's Lineage*, 46.
84 Ibid., 11, 298.
85 Zheng and Wong, *Xianggang dalao*, 211–212; Lee, 'Shijiu shiji maiban', 72.
86 *Jinding huitong moshi jiapu* cited in Ding 'Xinaggang moshiyang', 170, 186–187, n. 8.
87 HKPRO: HKRS 144–4-501, Ng Sang (Ng Ying Sang, Ng Chuk Sau), 20 July 1883.
88 HKPRO: HKRS 144–4-761, Ng A Heap (Ng Yung Ng), 14 October 1889; Mok, *Chenghuai gujin*, 34.

5 The compradors' social and political activities

The compradors coordinated triangular relationships between the local Chinese community, the colonial government and the Qing government in late nineteenth-century Hong Kong. The prominent compradors constituted a key element of the leading class of the local Chinese community from the 1850s onwards, together with the Chinese gentry and merchants. These Chinese representatives established public institutions and organisations for the management of the social order of the local Chinese community. Via both naturalisation as British subjects and by appointment to positions in the Legislative Council, some compradors were directly integrated into the British administrative structure. For the British colonial government, the compradors and other Chinese representatives were informal ancillary administrators of the Chinese society. It was necessary for the Hong Kong compradors to establish a mutually constructive relationship with the colonial authorities, since the majority of the compradors utilised British legal privileges and protections to conduct their trade in China. Although there were tensions and confrontations between the compradors and the Qing officials throughout the nineteenth century, some of the compradors successfully maintained cooperative relationship with the Qing officials. These compradors' non-economic activities allowed them to secure their social status in Hong Kong.

The compradors and the local Chinese community

The Chinese migrants formed several social associations in Hong Kong from the 1850s to the 1860s. For instance, the early Hong Kong residents formed commercial guilds, regional organisations (*huiguan*), temple committees and *kaifong* (*jiefang*) (neighbourhood associations).[1] In addition to other Chinese community leaders, the compradors played leading roles in the formation and the management of these associations. The early Chinese community leaders were more dubious than those of the Chinese leaders that emerged after the 1860s. Tam Achoy and Lo Aqui (Lu Yagui), a contractor and a landowner, accumulated their wealth by working with the foreigners. Moreover, Tam and Lo and their fellows, including the government compradors, increased their authority in the Chinese community using their close ties with government officials and by intermediating in the public issues between the local community and the colonial government.[2]

A small number of Chinese leaders dominated the communication channel to the colonial government from the 1840s to the 1850s, and this led to the corruption of the colonial officials and their collaborators. However, different kinds of Chinese leaders appeared after the 1860s. The variety of Chinese merchants and company compradors raised their social status as they obtained commercial successes in diverse areas; ultimately, they became social leaders of the Chinese communities, supplanting the government compradors and the early colonial government collaborators. A number of company and bank compradors participated in public activities in collaboration with the commercial and intellectual elites from the 1860s to the 1880s. The colonial government approved the social activities of the Chinese elite but their status was ambiguous. It was probable that Chinese citizens in general in Hong Kong regarded the leading Chinese figures as semi-officials of the Qing and the British colonial governments due to their obtaining Qing official titles and their collaboration with the colonial officials. This dual and semi-official status strengthened the social basis of the Chinese elites in Hong Kong, since the majority of Chinese businessmen in Hong Kong required support from the Qing and the colonial officials to protect and enhance their economic interests in China and the areas of the British Empire. Furthermore, intermediary elites such as the compradors were able to increase their influence by streamlining the communication between Chinese local leaders who did not understand English and the British authorities. In this way, the company compradors functioned as political and social intermediaries in Hong Kong from the late 1860s onwards.

One of the notable Chinese associations in early Hong Kong was the committee of the Man Mo Temple (*wenwu miao*). The Man Mo Temple was established by Lo Aqui, a former provision supplier to British battleships during the First Opium War, and Tam Achoy.[3] In 1847, Lo Aqui and Tam Achoy established the Man Mo Temple at Sheung Wan for the worship of the 'Gods of Literature and War'. The temple not only provided religious services, but also became a 'social centre' for Chinese residents. Moreover, the temple provided judicial services for the Chinese community by holding public trials. In 1851, Chinese merchants in Sheung Wan restored the temple and formed a committee, which made decisions regarding the public interests of the Chinese community.[4] Wai Kwan Chan observes that the Man Mo Temple was an archetype of social organisation integrating the wealthy public in Chinese society; this social integration, he suggests, culminated in the formation of the Tung Wah Hospital.[5] Another important feature of the committee of the temple could have been its function as an unofficial link to the Qing officials. In the 1890s, Eitel noted:

> [T]he Committee of the Man-moo temple (rebuilt and enlarged in May, 1851) now rose into eminence as a sort of unrecognised and unofficial local-government board (principally made up of Nampak-hong or export merchants). This Committee secretly controlled native affairs, acted as commercial arbitrators, arranged for the due reception of mandarins passing through the Colony, negotiated the sale of official titles, and formed an unofficial link between the Chinese residents of Hong Kong and the Canton Authorities.[6]

After 1870, the directors of the Tung Wah Hospital concurrently participated in the management of the temple. It was recorded that many of the prominent compradors were members of the temple committee in the 1880s. For instance, Fung Ming-shan, a comprador to the Mercantile Bank, and Leung On, a comprador to Gibb, Livingston & Co., were involved in the management of the temple as well as the Tung Wah Hospital and Po Leung Kuk.[7] The Man Mo Temple was an unofficial institution for the management of the Chinese community in the formative period of the colony. After the 1870s, one of the main functions of the temple, the management of Chinese public issues, was taken over by the Tung Wah Hospital, which became a semi-official public institution of the Chinese community.

Many well-to-do compradors served as directors on the Tung Wah Hospital committee in the 1870s and 1880s.[8] The colonial government formerly authorised the construction of the Tung Wah Hospital in 1870 and the hospital was opened on 14 February 1872. From the moment of its establishment, the prominent compradors of the time were engaged in its management. Wang Tao observed that Leung On and Chen Ruinan, who were both prominent company compradors, planned to establish the Tung Wah Hospital as they recognised the necessity for a new institution that could provide healthcare services to needy Chinese migrants and patients.[9] The colonial government formed the Chinese committee for the construction of the hospital by 1 June 1867. The members of the committee included Ho Asek (He Yaxi), alias Ho Fai-yin (He Peiran), and Ho In Kee, a leading figure of Chinese neighbourhood associations and a comprador to Lyall Still & Co., and Leung On. The number of members was originally around 20, but this soon increased to 125.[10] The compradors were one of the dominant social groups sending representatives to the committee. The compradors' guild, called *yanghang* in 1873 and *yanghang xulitang* in 1874, was a major subscriber to the hospital alongside the Nam-pak hong merchants, who were engaged in trade between southern and northern ports in China and Southeast Asian ports.[11] Between the 1870s and the 1880s, the committee members usually included at least one or two compradors.[12] When the governor officially visited the hospital in February 1878, notable compradors, including Leung On, Kwok Acheong, Wei Akwong, Fung Ming-shan, Ng Sang and Ng Chueck Chee, were all present.[13] As Elizabeth Sinn highlights, the Tung Wah committee was 'the first Chinese group' formally regarded as a leader of the Chinese community in Hong Kong by the colonial government.[14] In that sense, the prominent compradors became an external communication channel between the colonial government and the Chinese community through their involvement in the management of the Tung Wah Hospital.

In a similar vein, the compradors were involved in the development of the Po Leung Kuk. On 8 November 1878, leading figures of Chinese community such as Lo Lai-ping (Lu Liping), Fung Ming-shan, Shi Shang-kai (Shi Shengjie), and Tse Tat-shing (Xie Dasheng) petitioned Governor Hennessy to establish Po Leung Kuk in order to save kidnapped women and children. In 1879, Leung On, Fung Ming-shan, Kwok Acheong and other figures of the Chinese gentry again petitioned the government on the same issue.[15] In Hong Kong, the trafficking and abduction of women and children became a social issue in the late nineteenth century. The abduction of women was mainly caused by the *Mui Tsai* (*meizi*) system. *Mui Tsai* generally meant a female domestic servant working in a Chinese house or brothel who had often been sold by her poor family.[16] When Po Leung Kuk was officially acknowledged by the colonial government in 1882, the committee included Fung Ming-shan, the president, Wu Ting-fang, the vice-president, and Leung On, the treasurer.[17] Many prominent members of the Chinese elite were engaged in the administration of both Po Leung Kuk and Tung Wah Hospital over the long term.

The career of Ip Chuk-kai, comprador to Reiss & Co., illustrates how the merchant elites were constantly engaged in public organisations in late nineteenth-century Hong Kong.[18] Table 5.1 highlights how Ip Chuk-kai kept working for the management of the Po Leung Kuk and the Tung Wah Hospital by serving in different positions for many years. Rotating and sharing the leading positions in the public institutions, the Chinese compradors stayed engaged in the politics of Chinese society over long periods. In this manner, the company compradors were constantly involved in the formulation and management of public institutions in the Chinese society of Hong Kong.

These compradors' political activities were widely supported by local leading Chinese figures. According to the *Zhishilu* (the Minutes Book) of the Po Leung Kuk, the benevolent activities of the Po Leung Kuk were supported by the *kaifong*, the neighbourhood associations. On 24 July 1880, at the meeting of the *kaifong* associations, the participants discussed the establishment of the Po Leung Kuk and the Chinese club (*huashang huiguan*) together.[19] In 1873, the committee of the Tung Wah Hospital consisted of managers, assistant directors who belonged to various different commercial guilds, including compradors in the rice, opium, yarn and California trade business, and other individuals in different occupations.[20] Each guild contributed to the hospital yearly and usually sent one representative

Table 5.1 Credentials of Ip Chuk-kai from Chan, *Making of Hong Kong*, 86

Year	*Position*
1872	Zhishi*, Tung Wah Hospital
1873	Director, Tung Wah Hospital
1874	Xieli**, Tung Wah Hospital
1881	Chairman, Tung Wah Hospital
1882	Xieli, Tung Wah Hospital
1883	Director, Po Leung Kuk
1885	Director, Po Leung Kuk
1888	Principal director, Tung Wah Hospital
1889	Xieli, Tung Wah Hospital
1894	Chairman, Po Leung Kuk
1897	Director, Po Leung Kuk

**Zhishi* (Manager) ** *Xieli* (Consultant)

to the committee. Directors were elected from among the committee members. Because of the guild system, the Tung Wah Hospital committee obtained the legitimacy and authority to handle Chinese affairs, as well as to provide medical and healthcare services.[21] Due to its significant financial contribution to the hospital, the comprador's guild sent more than one representatives in the early 1870s.[22] In other words, the compradors became one of the most influential groups of Chinese elites during this period.

The compradors increased their influence by mediating in the communication between the British officials and the local Chinese elites. In particular, from the late 1860s to the early 1870s, on behalf of the Chinese merchants, the compradors expressed their dissatisfaction with the launch of the licensing system for gambling houses. Governor MacDonnell introduced the licensing system to control gambling in Hong Kong in 1866. By licensing a few gambling houses, the colonial government intended to close other illegal gambling places.[23] One of the owners of the licensed gambling houses was the comprador Ho Asek, who was working with Lyall Still & Co. in the late 1840s. After Lyall Still & Co ceased trading, Ho ran his own company, Kin Nam Hong (*jiannan mihang*), and engaged in the trade of rice and opium.[24] In 1871, Ho won a licensed monopoly on gambling houses in Hong Kong. It was estimated that he earned profits of $28,000 in a single year.[25] From the gaming house revenue, the Secretary of State permitted $50,000 to be spent on the general expenditure of police forces, and a grant of $13,000 was spent on the 'native hospital' of Tung Wah.[26] However, the corruption among the police force hindered the efficiency of the scheme. Daniel Richard Caldwell became a managing agent of the licenses; he had an annual salary of $20,000. Several officials doubted Caldwell's eligibility for the position. The Secretary of State spoke against the appointment of Caldwell and suggested that the licence should be provided by the highest bidder who was not under the influence of Caldwell.[27] Chief Justice Smale insisted that the system did not contribute to reducing illegal gambling and questioned its legitimacy.[28] When MacDonnell was on leave in 1870, Major General Whitefield took over his functions. During this period, conflict arose regarding the local anti-licensing system campaigns. The Secretary of State received a memo from the Chamber of Commerce suggesting the closure of licensed gambling houses. Whitefield notified them that the licensed gambling houses would be closed by the end of 1870, yet the Secretary of State suggested that the decision should wait until the governor's return.[29] The local Chinese populace generally criticised the licensed gambling system.

One of the means for the Chinese compradors and merchants to influence the policies of the colonial government was the submission of a petition. The colonial government received a petition from the Chinese community in early 1871 regarding the issue of the suppression of licensed gambling houses. The petitioners, calling themselves 'the Chinese merchants and residents of Hong Kong (*xianggangzhong shangmin*)' and 'the people of Hong Kong (*xianggang zhimin*)', asked the government to abolish the licensing system of gambling as it detracted from the moral values and practices of the Chinese citizens. The original Chinese petition was signed by numerous merchants and companies in Hong Kong, including prominent compradors and traders. The list of signatures included some famous leading Chinese figures, such as Kwok Acheong, Ho Fook Tang, Lo Kam Song, Choi Long Chi and Ko Man Hua.[30] These petitioners attempted to transform the colonial government's policy on gambling by insisting that the licensing system produced more 'corruption, bankruptcy, robbery, suicide and the selling of children into slavery'.[31] The Register General, Cecil Clementi Smith, insisted that the anti-licensing of gambling opinions were formulated by missionaries, and leading petitioners were mainly failed applicants for a license.[32] Yet with more than 800 signatures, the petition put pressure on the colonial government to change its policies on the gambling houses.[33]

One comprador expressed his opinions on the licensed gambling system in a newspaper. At the beginning of February 1871, a person describing himself as 'a comprador' wrote a letter to *The China Mail* regarding the licensed gambling houses and pointed out the problems caused by the system. For instance, he emphasised the increase in crime because the Chinese who lost money from gambling turned to robbery.[34] For the elimination of secret gambling, he suggested an establishment of regulations which put emphasis on the responsibilities of the landlords who were the owners of illegal gambling houses.[35] Due to the severe criticisms from both the foreign and Chinese population, the colonial government abolished the licensing gambling system by the end of January 1873 and gambling became illegal again.[36] In this sense, the compradors became opinion leaders of the Chinese society in the anti-licensing of gambling campaign.

Beginning in the early 1840s, the Chinese local leaders, the compradors, and the merchants managed the Chinese social and communication network in Hong Kong for the mobilisation of the Chinese people and provided mutual assistance. In 1844, the colonial government issued the first Registration Ordinance; however, the Chinese community was strongly against it. The ordinance incited small strikes and riots, and the foreign authorities suspected the company compradors and called a meeting of Chinese to mobilise the Chinese workers.[37] In 1852, Chinese shopkeepers and compradors gathered more than $150 for the construction of a Chinese Hospital in Sheung Wan as a replacement for the one destroyed by fire.[38] Table 5.2, the list of the subscribers presented in *The China Mail*, shows that out of a total of 26 subscribers, 8 were company compradors and 2 were government compradors. Then, six shopkeepers and two merchants followed the group of compradors. Others included merchants, builders and a teacher.[39] The Chinese merchants, compradors and members of the local gentry established a community in which they provided financial support to one another. For example, in April 1880, Wang Bingsheng, a Chinese businessman, who had difficulty paying his debts, showed his gratitude to the Chinese merchants who helped him avoid prosecution because of the debt of his shop. Collectively, 51 Chinese individuals, Leung On and 2 compradors' offices had provided financial assistance to Wang.[40]

In this manner, in the late nineteenth century, based on public associations and ties among the Chinese community, Chinese leaders, including the compradors, efficiently developed their own system for the management of the Chinese community in Hong Kong. The superstructure of the management system consisted of institutions such as the Tung Wah Hospital, functioning as an executive council, the Po Leung Kuk providing welfare service, and the District Watch Force, which was a policing organisation. Then its substructure system comprised multiple occupational guilds and *kaifong* neighbourhood associations in each district.[41] The intermediary elites integrated the activities of this range of interest groups and local organisations through establishing and managing the institutions of the superstructure. The establishment of these synthetic institutions, which coordinated the interests of small and local associations, was one of the features of the Chinese society of Hong Kong. In Shanghai, for example, the Chinese elite established *huiguan*, the native tie-based organisations and commercial guilds, which played an important role in the management of the Chinese community in the city. Cantonese merchants established *Guangzhao gongsuo*, while Swatow (*Shantou*) merchants, who mainly conducted the opium trade, organised the Swatow Opium Guild (*shantou yapian hanghui*) to serve the interests of each group.[42] The intermediary elites in Shanghai had to handle the different interests of distinct groups, as the Chinese community in Shanghai was quite diverse due to the regional

Table 5.2 A list of subscribers for the establishment of a Chinese hospital, 1852 (*The China Mail*, 23 September 1852, 154)

Name	*Occupation*	*Amount of the contribution ($)*
Yeong Lan-ko	Dent & Co.'s comprador	15
Low Ye-hin	Williams, Anthon & Co.'s comprador	15
Chang On-kee	Merchant	15
Ko Pooi-shing	Merchant	15
Tam Ah-choy	Building contractor	15
Wei Ah-kwong	Bowra & Co.'s comprador	15
Loo Ah-qui	Gentleman	15
Chun Mow-sang	Commissariat contractor	15
Lee Tong-suck	Shopkeeper	10
Soon Wo	Navy comprador	10
Tye Chong	Hong merchant	10
'Ng Tuck-hung	Lindsay & Co.'s comprador	10
Leong Po-wan	Gibb, Livingston & Co's comprador	10
'Ng Tye Gong	Rawle, Drinker & Co.'s comprador	10
Ho Teen-leong	Shopkeeper	10
Fong Suck	Builder	10
Cun-wo Ah-kwi	Merchant	5
Com Cheong	Shopkeeper	5
Sang Loong	Shopkeeper	5
Ho Sa-ke	Lyall, Still& Co,'s comprador	5
Chow Oan	Treasury comprador	5
Che Loong	Shopkeeper	5
Leong Chee	P & O's comprador	5
Cheong Loong	Shopkeeper	5
Tye Loong	Shopkeeper	5
Yang	Teacher	7

diversity of the population. On the other hand, adjacent to Guangzhou, the Chinese population of Hong Kong was predominantly Cantonese. Although the Cantonese population included various ethnic communities, including Cantonese, Punti (*bendi*), Hakka (*kejia*), Tanka and Hoklo (*fulao*), the regional diversity was still less than that of Shanghai.[43] In Hong Kong, benevolent institutions such as the Tung Wah Hospital obtained authority instead of *huiguan*. Moreover, by institutionalising the social associations, the Hong Kong compradors and other English-speaking members of the Chinese intellectual elite, such as Wu Ting-fang and Wong Shing, occupied indispensable positions as communication channels to the colonial government.

The commercial compradors and the colonial government

The leading figures of the Chinese community, especially the compradors, were generally keen to work with the colonial government, and this enabled them to be indispensable collaborators to the foreign residents in Hong Kong. The British officials recognised the wealth of Chinese merchants and their indispensability to the commercial development of Hong Kong. In the early 1870s, the Reverend Dr. James Legge noted that, 'there is a large body of Chinese merchants who have as great a stake in the colony as the British and merchants of other nationalities have.'[44] Chinese merchants became competitors against the foreign businessmen in property investment. Governor Hennessy stated that from January 1880 to May 1881, foreign properties worth $1,710,000 were transferred to the Chinese.[45] Based on their financial resources, the compradors and Chinese merchants improved their social status in Hong Kong.

However, the compradors also needed to increase their importance in foreign society as well as in the Chinese community, because their group identity and nationality were obscure and could easily be excluded and suppressed by both the British and Chinese governments. As explained above, the compradors became the representatives of the local Chinese community during the formative period of the city. In addition, the company compradors established strong ties with British administrators in the colony from the 1860s onwards. Thereafter, the compradors acted as intermediaries between the British and the local Chinese community. The compradors also drew on British legal prestige to secure their economic interests and protect themselves and their relatives in China. Therefore, this section specifically explores how the compradors established their close ties with the British officials in Hong Kong as well as how they obtained 'protection' from the British colonial government in the late nineteenth century.

The Hong Kong compradors had established a communication link with the British authorities by the late 1860s. On 13 May 1867, on the day of Acting Governor and Colonial Secretary William Thomas Mercer's departure, the Chinese community sent silk 'about 20 feet long by 4 deep'. Stitched into the silk was a message from the Chinese mercantile leaders that showed their gratitude to Mercer.[46] *The China Magazine* in 1868 reported that Chinese leading figures, including Kwok Acheong, Cheung A-Shau, Wo-Hang and Tso-Tak, presented a

Chinese cup to Mercer as well. The cup was inscribed with 'long shall we remember you like the genial sun; your ocean-like kindness constantly benefits us.'[47] Later, this cup was evidently exhibited at Lee Ching's place on Queens Road in the winter of 1868.[48] This practice of sending memorials and gifts to the governors was continued by successive Chinese merchant elites. The eighth governor, John Pope Hennessy, received a memorial from prominent Chinese merchants, including Wei Yuk and Leung On, in 1881. In a similar manner, the tenth governor, William Des Voeux, received a memorial when he left Hong Kong in 1890.[49] For the Chinese intermediary elite, British high-ranking officials who protected their commercial and political interests were an effective substitute for Qing officials.

The colonial government gradually integrated Chinese representatives in its formal administrative apparatus. In particular, Western-educated and Eurasian compradors worked closely with the government officials. One of them was Wei Yuk, a comprador to the Mercantile Bank. James Stewart Lockhart, the Register General and the Colonial Secretary in 1891, proposed the formation of a District Watch Committee based on ideas suggested by Wei Yuk.[50]

From the 1860s to the 1940s, a District Watch Force (*tuanfangju*) operated in Hong Kong. This force was spontaneously organised by the local Chinese, and it functioned as a Cantonese policing system for the Chinese community.[51] Stewart Lockhart's District Watch Committee became an official organisation in 1891. The committee consisted of prominent Chinese members, including Wei Yuk, Ho Kai and Ho Fook, a Eurasian comprador to Jardine, Matheson & Co.[52] The government's strong ties with Western-educated compradors and Chinese intellectuals could also be observed in the ceremony of the Jubilee of Hong Kong in 1891. The committee for the jubilee celebrations included some Chinese members, including Lo Hok Pang and Wei Yuk.[53]

The integration of the Chinese representatives into the colonial government further developed after the colonial government started appointing a few representatives of the Chinese elite as unofficial members of the Legislative Council. Governor Robinson (1891–1898) appointed Wei Yuk as an unofficial member of the Hong Kong Legislative Council in 1896, and Wei served as a chairman of the Tung Wah Hospital twice, in 1880 and 1887.[54] In 1917, Ho Fook took over Wei Yuk's position in the Legislative Council.[55] Before Wei Yuk's appointment, Wu Ting-fang, a barrister, Wong Shing, a journalist, and Ho Kai, a doctor, were the unofficial members of the Legislative Council.[56] These unofficial Chinese members of the Legislative Council had received a Western education and were familiar with British society and the political system. That is to say, in the late nineteenth century, there was an emergence of several compradors acting as intellectual elites who had a deep knowledge of Western culture.

In a symbolic sense, the compradors were also integrated into the British official administrative structure through the conferment of knighthoods and their appointment as Justice of the Peace after the 1880s. Wei Yuk was made a Justice of the Peace in 1883 and knighted in 1910.[57]

In a similar manner, Robert Hotung was appointed a Justice of the Peace in 1890 and awarded a knighthood in 1915.[58] A number of compradors were appointed as Justice of the Peace between the late nineteenth and the early twentieth centuries. For instance, Lau Wai Chun, a comprador to Hongkong and Shanghai Banking Corporation, and Wong Kam Fuk, the comprador to Hongkong and Kowloon Wharf and Godown Co., had been appointed Justices of the Peace by 1905.[59] Although Mok Sze Young and his son, Mok Cho Chuen, did not receive official honours from the colonial government, Cho Chuen's son, Mok Kon Sang (Mo Gansheng), a comprador to the Butterfield & Swire from 1917 to 1931, was made a Justice of the Peace in 1921.[60] During the 1880s, the colonial government started attempting to integrate leading Chinese figures into the political system of the British Empire to formalise the informal social and political status of the compradors.

Kwok Acheong was a well-known comprador who sought British judicial protection in Chinese port cities, as his commercial activities were often hindered by the Qing officials. In March 1866, Kwok's ship, *The Prince Albert*, was seized at the port of Shui Tung (*Shuidong*) near Canton. Soon after that, British Consul Robertson was requested to call the owner of the ship to make a payment to Customs. Kwok Acheong petitioned the governor of Hong Kong and the governor consulted with the British minister in Beijing.[61] Kwok's ship was seized by a Chinese Customs cruiser because it was operating in a non-treaty port. However, at the mixed court of Canton, it was adjudged to have been confiscated.[62] Eitel recorded that the Consul Robertson only managed to acquire the release of the ship by paying the fine of $4,000.[63] On 7 May, *The Hong Kong Daily Press* criticised the British consul's reluctant approval of the seizure of the ship.[64]

The Hong Kong merchants recognised the problems caused by the confiscation of their properties by Qing officials. On 12 June 1874, an editor of *Xunhuan Ribao* wrote an article reporting that 'British officials were planning to establish a law to protect Chinese Merchants'. It stated that investigation cruisers run by the Guangdong governor had seized more than 300 ships from Hong Kong in the past 5 years, and the Chinese merchants were afraid of the cruisers. Then the article stated that the colonial government recognised the issue, had reported it to London, and had already started discussing a law for the protection of Chinese merchants.[65] In fact, in the late 1860s and the early 1870s, British officials and businessmen carefully observed and discussed the issue of the establishment of the office of Chinese Customs near Hong Kong and the seizure of Chinese ships under gunboats.[66] In this vein, on 14 September 1874, a public meeting was held in Hong Kong, and there the issues of the Chinese armed customs cruisers and the tax imposed on Chinese vessels were discussed.[67] Kwok Acheong had been running ships registered as British and benefitting from the British judicial protection in Hong Kong. Chinese compradors such as Kwok avoided leaving Hong Kong even when Chinese Customs summoned them.[68] However, at the same time, it was necessary for him to deal with the risk of collaborating with British merchants and officials. Therefore, Kwok and the other Hong Kong merchants were keen to see how they could obtain better legal protection from the colonial government.

In 1878, Kwok Acheong's son, Kwok Yao, was detained by Qing officials when he travelled to Canton, and the colonial government made an effort to obtain Kwok Yao's release.[69] On 18 September 1878, *The China Mail* reported that the son of Kwok Acheong was arrested when he was on a boat trip up beyond Canton, and Chinese officials demanded 35,000 taels for his release. It seemed that there was no particular reason for Kwok Yao's arrest. *The China Mail* reported that the man merely carried '10 taels of prepared opium' for himself, for which duty was already paid at Canton and a few 'tins of biscuits' and 'bottles of raisins and some figs' and other necessities for travel. He also held a pass issued from the Likin office certifying his destination of travel and the commodities he carried. Kwok Yao made an application to the British consul at Canton, who referred it to the colonial government. On 9 September, Kwok Acheong appealed the case to the governor.[70] Governor Hennessy and the British consul in Canton negotiated with the Qing officials, and Kwok's son was eventually released in early October.[71]

The detention of Kwok's son raised a question for the British community: 'What makes a Chinaman a British subject in this colony?'[72] Rutherford Alcock's statement in *The Government Gazette* in 1868 mentioned that a Chinese person who was wearing Western clothes could be regarded as a British subject. However, he further pointed out this was not applicable to the case of Hong Kong, as all inhabitants of Hong Kong were declared to be British subjects in 1841. The editor did not argue the issue further; but he did suggest that the rescuing of Kwok's son should be prioritised to protect the interests of the colony.[73] For the British community, the protection of Kwok's interests was a priority, and this illustrates the indispensability of collaborative Chinese intermediaries in Hong Kong.[74] As such, Kwok Acheong was a popular figure in the foreign community in Hong Kong until Western-educated elites appeared after the 1880s.

Since the early 1880s, the Chinese merchants had been applying for naturalisation to obtain British judicial protection. After John Eitel became the first non-Briton to be naturalised in 1880, several Chinese, including compradors, applied for naturalisation to become British subjects.[75] Fung Ming-shan was the second person to be naturalised as British in Hong Kong. In 1881, there were about 10 additional Chinese who were naturalised. They were Wong She-tai (Huang Shedai), Shi Shang-kai (Shi Shengjie), P'ang Im (Peng Yan), Ip Him-kwong (Ye Qianguang) and Un Man-tsoi (Yuan Mincai).[76] Of them, Fung Ming-shan, P'ang Im and Wong She-tai were compradors to the foreign firms.[77]

Furthermore, the compradors made financial contributions to a variety of benevolent British activities. Ho Kam Tong, a Eurasian assistant comprador of Jardine, made a contribution to bereaved families of British soldiers killed in the Boer War as well as to the London Tropical School of Medicine. Kam Tong's brother, Robert Hotung, was an administrator of Queen Victoria's Diamond Jubilee Fund, and of the South African War Fund.[78] The compradors, provision purveyors to British troops, were particularly indispensable collaborators for the British officials from the 1840s to the 1860s. Practically speaking, the compradors' material assistance was important for the conduct of the wars in China. Depicting Kwok as a victim of the pressure and suppression that Qing officials exerted while emphasising the colonial government as his protector, the British created a narrative to legitimise the British rule of the Chinese community in Hong Kong. In this vein, from the 1860s to the 1880s, British officials worked with the Western-educated compradors and intellectuals on various public and diplomatic issues. Although the pattern of collaboration was different and evolving throughout the period, the compradors consistently collaborated with the British administrators from the 1840s to the 1880s.

However, this collaboration did not necessarily mean that all the compradors were supportive of British policies. Leung On would often show opposition to the policies of the colonial government. In 1869, the acting Register General Alfred Lister witnessed the deaths of Chinese residents around Kwong Fook I-tsz (*guangfu yici*), a Chinese ancestral hall on Tai Pin Shan Street.[79] Lister prohibited removing a dying patient from his room at I-tsz temple, as he thought it was a cruel practice. However, the Tung Wah committee, supervising the practice of I-tsz temple, opposed Lister's actions. Leung On, who led the members of the committee, petitioned the governor to explain that the removal of a dying man from his room was Chinese Custom. The petition indicated the possibility that the Chinese leaders would withdraw from the project if the government allowed Lister's action. The petition threated the possibility of the withdrawal of the Chinese leaders from the project of establishing the hospital, if the government allowed Lister's action.[80] In August 1876, at an interview of the Committee of the Tung Wah Hospital, Leung On stated that Chinese patients were scared to receive European treatment, which they feared would involve the amputation of their limbs. This misconception was representative of the general impressions of Western surgery shared by the majority of the Chinese citizens at that time.[81] In that sense, Leung On styled himself a spokesman of the Chinese community of Hong Kong.

In 1876, when Ernst Johann Eitel, then a member of the London Missionary Society, gathered prominent compradors to raise funds to build a school in Wanchai, Leung On opposed the proposal for Christian education and suggested secular education without the use of the Bible or other Christian texts.[82] Elizabeth Sinn observes that Leung On, the first chairman of the Tung Wah committee, was 'a perfect illustration of the assertive Chinese representative' who demanded that the government allow Chinese leaders to manage Chinese matters.[83] In contrast to Kwok Acheong, Leung On was a comprador who was passionate about preserving Chinese tradition, and who acted as an opposition leader to the British officials.

Some of the foreign residents were suspicious of the socio-political activities of the leading Chinese figures. The tension between the Chinese and foreign communities escalated with the great public meeting held on 10 October 1878. The main purpose of the meeting was to show the collective opposition among the foreign representative to Governor John Pope Hennessy's policies on the commutation of the punishment of Chinese criminals. Governor Hennessy was well known for his favourable policies towards the Chinese populace, and he succeeded in obtaining support from the Chinese mercantile and intellectual leaders in Hong Kong, though he was less popular among the foreign community.

The foreign elite regarded Hennessy's attempts to reduce the severe punishment of Chinese prisoners as worsening the security of the colony. In late September 1878, an armed Chinese gang of about 40 to 80 attacked and ransacked a shop in Winglok Street. The gang managed to escape from the scene after fighting the police force. This incident shocked European inhabitants, and led by William Keswick, prominent foreign figures decided to hold a public meeting to discuss the insecurity of the colony.[84] The notification of the meeting was circulated to the foreign community as well as to prominent Chinese merchants.

On 7 October, *The China Mail* pointed out that Wu Ting-fang and Leung On encouraged the Chinese to attend a public meeting at the City Hall.[85] On the same day, *The Daily Press* criticised the Tung Wah Hospital as 'the Chinese Government Offices for this colony', at which Chinese leaders made the decision to participate in the meeting. At the meeting in City Hall, the participants had to move to the Cricket Ground as the Chinese had secured most of the seats. However, the majority of the Chinese participants, except Wu Ting-fang, did not understand English, and they were unable to understand in order to vote for resolutions.[86] Kwok Acheong was in a complicated position in terms of his participation at the public meeting. It seemed he had once signed a paper calling for the public meeting. However, later he wrote to *The China Mail* that he would have refused to do so if he understood the purpose of the meeting because his son was 'causing so much trouble to H. E. the Governor'.[87] When the public meeting was held, Kwok's son was still detained in Canton, and Kwok was asking for Hennessey's support to settle the issue. Division in the foreign community, anti-Governor Hennessy or not, complicated Kwok's attempts to obtain general support from the foreigners in Hong Kong.

In the late nineteenth century, a variety of compradors established different commercial and political networks with different communities. Due to their diversity, the prominent compradors formed an indispensable social group in Hong Kong. Leung On acted as a representative of the Chinese community while Kwok Acheong acted as a pro-British Chinese. This division of roles enabled the Chinese community to protect their interests while developing formal political ties with the colonial government. Throughout these confrontations and collaborations, the colonial government and the prominent Chinese, including the compradors, improved the administration system of Hong Kong. Although Kwok Acheong was outside of the official hierarchy of the Qing government, some of the other compradors managed to construct a practical relationship with the Qing officials.

The compradors and the Qing government

The group of compradors in Hong Kong strengthened ties with Qing officials in China from the 1860s onwards. Hui Po-Keung argues that the compradors cultivated informal and formal political ties with British authorities to avoid 'being "squeezed"' by Qing officials in mainland China. At the same time, the compradors were required to play a 'double-sided game', as they had to establish a constructive relationship with both the Western and Chinese authorities.[88] This was in part because of the transition of the policies of the Qing government towards overseas Chinese after the 1860s. Due to the fiscal difficulties caused by floods, droughts, wars against foreign countries, and military action against rebels, the Qing government started accepting financial support from overseas Chinese merchants.[89] In particular, the North China Famine in the late 1870s shifted the Qing government's attitudes towards overseas Chinese merchants, who were valuable providers of moral and financial support.[90] The Hong Kong compradors were thereby able to build close ties with the Qing authorities through donations for disaster relief, supporting the industrialisation of Chinese business, and purchasing titles.

The activities of the Hong Kong compradors can be found in Qing historical records. In 1878, it was recorded that members of the Chinese gentry such as Liang Yun Han (another name for Leung On) managed to collect more than 30,000 taels in donations to the Qing government in Hong Kong and port cities in Southeast Asia.[91] Leung On also worked with high-ranking officials in the project to Westernise commerce. In 1881, Leung On and other Chinese merchants established the Zhaoxing company (*zhaoxing gongsi*) in London, which was suggested and planned by Li Zhaotang, Qing's reformist official.[92] Leung On was a director in Canton, with Liu Shaozong and Liang Shaogang dealing with business in London.[93] Liu Shaozong was a former comprador to Augustine Heard & Co. at Hankow in the mid-1860s.[94] The Zhaoxing Company was established in order to conduct direct trade between Europe and China. However, due to the insufficiency of funding, the firm ceased business after 3 years.[95] The Qing government hired numerous comprador merchants during the period of the Self-Strengthening Movement, the Qing elites' reformation efforts at the modernisation of the military and industry, from the 1860s to the early 1890s. For instance, Tong Kingsing, a former comprador to Jardine in Tianjin, and Wu Nan'gao, a former comprador to the Hongkong and Shanghai Banking Corporation in Tianjin, worked with reformist officials who undertook modernisation projects, including the opening of the Kaiping mines and the construction of the China Railway Company.[96] Leung On was among the comprador merchants who collaborated with the Qing officials in their attempts to industrialise and Westernise the Chinese commercial system.

During the period of the Second Sino-British War (1856–1860), the compradors faced severe difficulties in their activities in China. The Qing officials in Guangdong issued warrants for the arrest of Chinese collaborators with the British in Hong Kong during this period. In April 1858, *The China Mail* reported:

> [T]he Sub-Prefect of Caza Branca has issued warrants of arrest against Cheong-Achew – the well-known carpenter; Tsun-Atow – Messrs Augustine Heard & Co.'s compradors, Lum Ayow – owner of the *lorcha Good Chance*; and Wei Akwong – formerly comprador to Messrs Bowra & Co., and more lately interpreter in the Supreme Court. If such proceedings are permitted, we shall soon feel the effects of them, for not a single comprador, household servant, or even workman, will dare to remain in Hong Kong.[97]

During the war period, Qing officials again warned the compradors that they and their descendants would not be allowed to purchase official titles unless they quit their work for the foreigners and returned home.[98] The Qing government ordered the compradors to retreat from their work in a similar manner to their predecessors in the First Opium War.

To avoid friction with the Qing government, the Hong Kong compradors were eager to establish formal ties with Qing officials. In part, compradors accomplished this by purchasing official titles. Mok Sze Yeung, a comprador of Augustine, Heard & Co., was appointed 'Grand Master for Assisting towards Good Governance, Mandarin Second Rank' (*zizheng dafuxian*, *zhengerpin*) by the Qing government. He was also awarded the prestigious peacock plume. Mok Sze Yeung's second son, Mok Cho Chuen, a chief comprador to Butterfield & Swire, held the same title with his father and was awarded the same plume.[99] Mok Cho Chuen's son, Mok Kon Sang, took over his father's position of comprador in Butterfield & Swire, and also received the prestigious peacock plume; he was appointed 'Grand Master for Forthright Service' (Mandarin Fifth Rank, *zhidafu*, *zhengwupin*)' by the Qing government. As Eitel observed, the Man Mo Temple negotiated the sales of the official titles in the 1890s, and the prominent Chinese in Hong Kong, including compradors, were able to purchase official titles.[100] Aside from the Mok compradors, many of the directors of the Tung Wah Hospital, including compradors, were likely to hold official titles. At the ceremony to mark Governor Hennessy's visit to the hospital in February 1878, 50 to 60 prominent Chinese were 'in Mandarin costumes, some with blue buttons, some with crystal, and some with gold buttons, while a few had the additional honour of wearing the peacock's feather'.[101] At least 7 out of 14 prominent Chinese participants in the ceremony were compradors or former comprador merchants in Hong Kong, such as Kwok Acheong, Leung On and Wei Akwong.[102]

By 1870, the compradors in Hong Kong had constructed better relationships with the Qing government. When high-ranking Qing officials visited Hong Kong, they sometimes went to visit groups of prominent compradors. On 21 August 1873, *The London and China Telegraph* reported that the hoppo and general Pang Yuk from Canton had visited the Comprador's Club before the meeting with the governor. The club was located 'in Queen's Road, which was opposite the London Inn', and the hoppo was welcomed by notable compradors in Hong Kong.[103] In the late 1880s, Zhang Zhidong, Governor General in Guangdong and Guangxi (1884–1889), drew on the Hong Kong Chinese elites and the Tung Wah Hospital for information and funds.[104] Unlike the compradors, who had to maintain constructive ties with both Qing and British governments, Hong Kong Chinese merchants were able to openly collaborate with Qing officials. In the Sino-French War in 1884, Ho Amei (He Yamei), alias Ho Kwan-shan (He Kunshan), and Li Tak Cheong (Li Dechang) were prominent among Chinese merchants for their nationalistic activities in the war period. They contributed to the circulation of proclamations which supported the Qing government and were produced by Canton officials.[105] Ho Amei even reported on the movement of French vessels around Hong Kong to Zhang Zhidong.[106] In the 1880s, there was an emergence of Chinese traders and businessmen who had nationalistic minds and collaborated with the reformist officials in the Qing government.

Although each comprador had an individual political attitude towards Qing and British policies, most of them worked as negotiators in confrontations between the Chinese and foreign communities in Hong Kong. Once, a disturbance occurred between the Qing and foreign countries, and the compradors made efforts to settle the Chinese riots and strikes in Hong Kong between the middle of September and early October 1884. Responding to the Canton officials' proclamation forbidding Chinese to repair French ships in port cities, Chinese workers in shipyards refused to work for French warships in September 1884 during the period of the Sino-French War. Several cargo boat workers also refused to work for French employers. The boat workers were fined due to their refusal to work with the French. This incited the anger of other Chinese workers, and caused the strike to intensify and grow. Cargo boat people and workers left their work and several foreigners were attacked and injured. Eventually the colonial government sent troops to the Tung Wah Hospital on 3 October in order to control the situation and end the strike.[107]

Thereafter, prominent Chinese negotiated with the Chinese workers to convince them to return to work. At a meeting in the government offices, the prominent Chinese and British administrators discussed how to convince the workers to end the strike. The officials and the Chinese representatives discussed issuing a proclamation which pardoned the workers and encouraged them to return to work. Leung On was deputed to issue this proclamation. However, Acting Colonial Secretary Frederick Stewart objected to the use of the words 'the government, on the intercession of the merchants', as it could be interpreted as indicating that the colonial government officially approved of the political authority of the Chinese merchants. In the meeting, Leung On insisted that the British troops retreat from the Tung Wah Hospital, after which the members of the Tung Wah Hospital committee would assemble the workers and induce them to end the strike. However, Frederick Stewart was against this suggestion, emphasising that political matters were not the business of the Tung Wah directors.[108] On 5 October, staff of Butterfield & Swire went to Yau Ma Tei and convinced their boat workers to resume work. The police force kept working to disperse assemblies of Chinese workers and arrested several men. By 6 October, the strike was mostly over.[109]

The strike of 1884 highlights that the compradors were carefully balancing their political and social positions between the colonial government, the Qing Dynasty and the local Chinese people. Unlike Chinese merchants such as Ho Amei and Li Tak Cheong, as well as Chinese workers, it was not easy for the compradors to openly collaborate with the Qing officials. Even Leung On, an aggressive spokesman for the Hong Kong Chinese populace, did not refuse to work with the British officials to end the strike. To conduct Sino-foreign trade in China, the compradors needed British legal protection, and for that purpose, they had to maintain an amicable relationship with the colonial government. The compradors working with foreigners also had to deal with the resentment of nationalistic workers. In one incident, rioters targeted Wing Kee, a ship comprador's shop providing coal for foreign ships; they surrounded the shop on 5 October 1884. The police arrived soon and dispersed the crowds, preventing further mischief.[110] However, the prominent company compradors were able to gather information from the three groups effectively, and put themselves in neutral positions to avoid direct confrontations with any one group. The compradors thus acted as negotiators to settle disturbances; by drawing on the political networks they had established, they increased their authority and indispensability in the society of Hong Kong.

The physical insecurity of the compradors could also prompt them to establish political networks with foreign and Chinese authorities. Murders and attacks on the compradors were not uncommon in nineteenth-century Hong Kong. *The Friend of China* dated 4 May 1843 reported a robbery at Jardine's Bazaar. A large group of armed robbers broke into the houses and Jardine's comprador lost '$300 and nine catties of opium'.[111] In 1846, Lindsay & Co.'s comprador was murdered at East Point.[112] Hong Kong was not a safe place in the 1840s, and the compradors who handled large amounts of cash and notes were often easy targets for burglars. In the late 1870s, crime was still one of the major issues in Hong Kong, and the compradors had to be aware of that. In September 1878, burglars broke into Hine Kee, a commissariat comprador's house at No. 53 Queen's Road East, which was opposite the Commissariat Office, twice within a single week.[113] The compradors recognised their insecurity, and that could be one reason why they were keen to obtain protection from various political authorities, in particular, from both the British and Qing governments. They also attempted to improve their social positions in the local Chinese society.

The compradors gained certain *de facto* political power to deal with Chinese affairs in Hong Kong by establishing communication networks with the Qing officials. Until the Self-Strengthening Movement began in the early 1860s, the relationship between the Qing officials and the compradors was not necessarily amicable. In part, this was because of the compradors' tax avoidance throughout utilising their British legal status. Through purchasing official titles, establishing informal ties with the high-ranking Qing officials, and participating in the Westernisation of Chinese industry, the compradors gradually established a collaborative relationship with the Qing government. The Qing officials understood the importance of the compradors as watchmen over the foreigners. During the Sino-French War, by ordering the compradors to cease working, the Qing officials again attempted to control the foreigners' activities in the treaty ports and the colony, as they did in the First Opium War. Although some of the Chinese merchants and working people followed the Qing officials' orders and caused strikes and small riots in Hong Kong, the compradors were reluctant to respond to the Qing government's order. Instead, the compradors, including Leung On, chose to work with the British officials and the other Chinese elites to end the disturbances. As the Hong Kong compradors were able to obtain British judicial protections, they were outside the control of the Qing authorities.

Compared to the case of the Shanghai compradors in the late nineteenth century, it is possible to say that the Hong Kong compradors were more integrated into the formal political system of the British Empire. In the case of Shanghai, Qing and foreign administrators drew on personal networks of reliable Chinese leading figures, including compradors, for the administration of the Chinese community in Shanghai. The Shanghai compradors established complex, informal, commercial and political ties with foreign and Qing authorities.[114] Yet the administration system was not clearly institutionalised. This difference in the political functions between the Hong Kong and Shanghai compradors could have been caused by the differences in the status of the colony and the foreign settlement. To put it simply, in Hong Kong, it was evident that the colonial government had sole authority to rule the city. On the other hand, in Shanghai, it was unclear whether foreign or Chinese authorities had political hegemony. The British, the Qing, and other imperial political and social systems co-existed in nineteenth-century Shanghai. Because of the lack of a single clear foreign authority that could provide legal protection, the Shanghai compradors more actively worked with the Qing government and officials than did the Hong Kong compradors. For the compradors in Shanghai, it was crucial to establish a constructive relationship with the Qing authorities to conduct their business as well as for their social security and safety. However, the Hong Kong compradors were more able to rely on the British legal system. Being integrated into the formal social structure of the British Empire, the Hong Kong compradors stabilised their social status.

Even after the consolidation of the comprador system in the 1880s, the Hong Kong compradors continued to be actively engaged in the social and political affairs of the city, mainly because they had to maintain social recognition to uphold their social status as representatives of the Chinese community. Responding to the anti-Mui-tsai campaign led by British opinion leaders, Ho Fook and Lau Chu Pak, a comprador of A. S. Watson and Co., and other prominent Chinese, organised a mass meeting at the Tai Ping Shan Theatre in July 1921 to discuss the issue of female domestic servants in China.[115] The successive compradors' public functions could be represented by Robert Hotung's various benevolent activities. For instance, Hotung contributed a total of $260,000 to the Endowment Fund of Hong Kong University. He was the chairman of the Tung Wa Hospital in 1898 and contributed to the settlement of the seamans' strike in 1922. Hotung's benevolent activities were recognised by both the British and Chinese governments. He was honoured with a knighthood in 1915, and made a Justice of Peace in Hong Kong; he was also awarded 'several Chinese Decorations'.[116] In the 1880s, the socio-political significance of the compradors culminated in Hong Kong due to their ability to balance their alliances with the Chinese and the British government.

In the early twentieth century, the compradors that worked within the different foreign political systems became significant in Hong Kong. One such prominent comprador was Sum Pak Ming (Cen Boming). Sum was a Chinese agent of Java-China-Japan Lijn, a Dutch company, and a former comprador to Bornemann & Co., a German firm in Hong Kong. In 1917, he was made a Justice of Peace. In 1926, he received the Order of Orange-Nassau from Queen Wilhelmina of the Netherlands for supporting the work of Dutch companies, including opening the Java–China–Japan Line. Before his death in 1939, he was connected with various public activities in Hong Kong and had served both the Tung Wah

Hospital and Po Leung Kuk as a director.[117] In that sense, Chinese intermediaries in early twentieth-century Hong Kong inherited and developed the legacy of nineteenth-century compradors in Hong Kong.

Conclusion

To improve and maintain their economic and social status in Hong Kong, the compradors cooperated with the local Chinese populace, the British officials and the Qing authorities. After the rise and the decline of the government compradors, the early commercial compradors emerged as leading figures of the Chinese society through their extensive economic activities by the late 1860s. The compradors also served as informal communication conduits between the Chinese citizens and the British officials, as they had already established ties with well-to-do foreigners in the 1850s and the 1860s. Thereafter, the compradors and other prominent Chinese were engaged in the institutionalisation of the social associations and groups in Hong Kong.

The compradors contributed to bridging Chinese social institutions and the administrative structure of the colonial government. This enabled them to act as pivotal intermediaries for the colonial government. In return, the government provided British judicial protection for the compradors' conduct of trade in China. Concurrently, the compradors were vigorously improving their social position in the Qing society through working with Qing officials and obtaining official titles of the Qing government. As a group, the compradors were in a politically marginal position. Yet each comprador had unique political views and thoughts. For example, Leung On had a relatively pro-Qing political stance, while Kwok Acheong was a more pro-British comprador. Despite the differences in their sense of belonging, the compradors worked together to maintain the political and social stability of Hong Kong since it was a necessary condition for the economic prosperity of the city. In doing so, the compradors contributed to merging foreign society and Chinese society in nineteenth-century Hong Kong.

Last but not least, Hong Kong's peculiar status as a formal British colony in China served as a main factor enabling compradors to be a key constituent of the class of Chinese intermediary elites. To make money to improve their daily lives, numerous local Chinese lived and worked with foreigners in Hong Kong. They were in marginal positions between Chinese and foreign societies in a similar manner as the compradors. Thus, the compradors did not merely represent the interests of local Chinese populace; they but also symbolised them, acting as intermediaries between foreign and Chinese communities in the city.

Notes

1 Sinn, *Power and Charity*, 13.
2 Munn, *Anglo-China*, 76–78.
3 Hao, *Comprador*, 195. Loo Aqui was also known as Loo King, Loo Aking (Lu Jing), Lo Aqui and Sz-man-king or see mun king (Si Wenjing).
4 Chan, *Making of Hong Kong*, 76; Ting, 'Native Chinese Peace Officers', 152.

5 Chan, *Making of Hong Kong*, 76.
6 Eitel, *Europe in China*, 282.
7 *Government Gazette*, 23 April 1881, 274; Li, ed., *Xianggang Donghua sanyuan*, 116, 292.
8 Tsai, *Hong Kong in Chinese History*, 87.
9 Wang, 'chuanjian donghua yiyuan'.
10 Sinn, *Power and Charity*, 39–40; Smith, *Chinese Christians*, 125–126.
11 TWM: *Zhengxinlu* 1871 and 1874.
12 TWM: *Zhengxinlu*, 1873, 1885, and 1886.
13 *Government Gazette*, 16 February 1878, No. 7.
14 Sinn, *Power and Charity*, 40.
15 Po Leung Kuk Museum: *Chengwen*, 1878–1881, 11.
16 Po Leung Kuk Museum: *Chengwen*, 1878–1881, 1.
17 *Government Gazette*, 5 August 1882, 653–654 and 12 August 1882, 666.
18 Wright, *Twentieth Century Impressions*, 184.
19 Po Leung Kuk Museum: *Zhishilu*, 1880–1885, 12.
20 Sinn, *Power and Charity*, 54–55.
21 Tsai, *Hong Kong in Chinese History*, 67.
22 TWM: *Zhengxinlu*, 1873.
23 Endacott, *Biographical Sketch-book*, 99.
24 Smith, *Chinese Christians*, 123; *China Mail*, 19 December 1871, 3.
25 *China Mail*, 7 February 1872, 3.
26 Collins, *Public Administration,* 113. CO No. 4 of January 1870.
27 Ibid. 111–112. CO No. 76, 10 July 1867, 129 of 14 October 1867, CO Nno. 13 of 25 January 1868, and 159 of 7 October 1869.
28 Munn, *Anglo-China*, 361–362; Collins, *Public Administration,* 113. The Secretary of State in his dispatch No. 26 of 7 March 1871.
29 Collins, *Public Administration*, 113. Dispatch No. 19 of 6 February 1871, to the Secretary of State.
30 TNA: CO129/149, Government House to Lord Kimbaly, 'Licensed Gambling Gaming Houses – transits memorial from the Chinese Community of Hong Kong', 208–232.
31 Carroll, *Concise History*, 52.
32 Munn, *Anglo-China*, 362.
33 TNA: CO129/149, Government House to Kimberley, 6 March 1871, 232.
34 *China Mail*, 1 and 2 February 1871, 3 and 3.
35 *China Mail*, 2 February 1871, 3.
36 Munn, *Anglo-China*, 362.
37 Eitel, *Europe in China*, 224–225; TNA: CO129/7, extracts from newspapers, 209, 211.
38 *China Mail*, 1 July 1852, 106.
39 The emerging company compradors started participating in the social issues in Hong Kong in the 1850s and a few government compradors, including Chow Aaon, the treasury comprador followed their activities. Yet, in the early 1850s, more numbers of company compradors participated to the public activities than government compradors and the social importance of the government compradors was fading.
40 *XHRB*, 19 April 1880. *Guiji banfang* and *Bilina banfang* were listed as financial supporters.
41 For Kaifong, see Hayes, *Hong Kong Region*, 64–66.
42 For the functions of *huiguan* in Shanghai, see Goodman, *Native Place.*
43 Munn, *Anglo-China*, 71.
44 Tsai, *Hong Kong in Chinese History*, 89; Legge, 'Colony of Hong Kong,' 180.
45 Chan, *Making of Hong Kong*, 107.

46 *Addresses Presented*, 17–19.
47 *China Magazine*, 174–176; *London and China Telegraph*, 25 January 1869, 37.
48 *London and China Telegraph*, 25 January 1869, 37.
49 Carroll, *Edge of Empires*, 67–68; *Government Gazette*, 23 April 1881, 274–278; Des Voeux, *My Colonial Service*, Vol. 2, 280–282.
50 Carroll, *Edge of Empires*, 64–65; Lethbridge, *Hong Kong, Stability and Change*, 109.
51 Tsang, *Modern History*, 70.
52 Carroll, Edge of Empires, 64–65; Wright, *Twentieth Century Impressions*, 109.
53 *Fifty Years of Progress*, 32. The Chinese members of the committee for the jubilee celebrations were Ho Kai, Ho Amei, Lo Hok Pang, Poon Pong, Wei Yuk, and Wong Shing. Poon Pong was a director of the Hong Kong, Canton, and Macao Steam Boat Company.
54 Sinn, *Power and Charity*, 201; Wu, *Prominent Chinese*, 4; Wright, *Twentieth Century Impressions*, 109.
55 Cheng, 'Chinese Unofficial Members', 20.
56 Ibid., 17.
57 Wu, *Prominent Chinese*, 3–4.
58 Wright, *Twentieth Century Impressions*, 176; *Hong Kong Daily Press*, 30 November 1931 included in JMA: L14/9, The Golden Wedding of Sir Robert and Lady Ho Tung; Zheng and Huang, Xianggang dalao, 235–236.
59 Smith, *Chinese Christians*, 165; Wright, *Twentieth Century Impressions*, 178.
60 Mok, *Chenghuai gujin*, 32–35.
61 Correspondence Respecting Revision of Treaty of Tien-tsin, 15.
62 *Sydney Mail*, 23 June 1866; *Overland China Mail*, 28 April 1866.
63 Eitel, *Europe in China*, 414.
64 *Hong Kong Daily Press*, 7 May 1866, 2.
65 *XHRB*, 12 June 1874.
66 TNA: CO129/156, MacDonnell to Kimberley, 20 May 1872, 427–435; CO129/129. MacDonnell to Duke of Buckingham and Chandos, 22 February 1868, 248–255.
67 *Blockade of Port and Harbour*.
68 TNA: CO129/167, Chinese customs stations in the vicinity of Hong Kong, 25 August 1874, 645–646.
69 *NCH*, 10 October 1878, 344.
70 *China Mail*, 18 September 1878, 2.
71 *China Mail*, 14 October 1878 2.
72 *China Mail*, 19 September 1878, 2.
73 Ibid.
74 *China Mail*, 24 September 1878 and 1 October 1878 and 14 October 1878, 3 and 2.
75 Weng, *Bainian maishen*, 56.
76 Weng, *Bainian maishen*, 57–58; Leach, *Ordinances of Legislative Council*, Ordinances 5–10 in 1881, 1589–1591; Un Man-tsoi was manager of the Branch Stamp Office, *Government Gazette*, 12 August 1882, 666.
77 Wong She-tai was Wong Yook's eldest son and the comprador to Belilios and Company in Hong Kong. Smith, *Chinese Christians*, 164.
78 Carroll, *Edge of Empires*, 74; Wright, *Twentieth Century Impressions*, 174–176; Wu, *Prominent Chinese*, 1–3.
79 Sinn, *Power and Charity*, 39–40; Smith, *Chinese Christians*, 125–126.
80 Sinn, *Power and Charity*, 41.
81 *Hong Kong Daily Press*, 30 August 1876.
82 Archives of the London Missionary Society, SOAS: South China, Box 8, 23 September 1876.
83 Sinn, *Power and Charity*, 47.
84 Hennessy, *Verandah*, 202.

85 *China Mail*, 7 October 1878, 2.
86 *Hong Kong Daily Press*, 'The Insecure Condition of the Colony of Hong Kong, Report of a great Public Meeting Held at Victoria, Hong Kong, on Monday, the 7th Day of October, 1878' (Hong Kong, 1878), 4, 11.
87 *China Mail*, 7 October 1878, 3; *Hong Kong Daily Press*, 7 October 1878.
88 Hui, 'Comprador Politics', 39.
89 Ibid., 39; Lin and Zhang, *Xinjiapo Malaxiya huaqiao*, 180–183.
90 Sinn, *Power and Charity*, 99.
91 *Daqing Dezong Jing*. Vol. 71, The fourth month of the fourth year of Guangxu, 7–8 in Rao, Xinjiapo gushiji, 2.
92 Zhao, *Qingshigao, juan 150 zhi yibai ershiwu, jiaotong er, lunchuan* (draft history of Qing, Vol. 150, zhi 125, transportation 2, steamship).
93 Nie, *Zhongguo hangyunshi ziiliao*, ed., Vol. 1, 1102.
94 Hao, *Commercial Revolution*, 172.
95 Ibid., 172.
96 Xu. *Xu Yuzhai zixu*, 57–58; Pomerantz-Zhang, *Wu Tingfang*, 82–83.
97 *China Mail*, 30 April 1857, 70; Casa Branca (White House) was located north west of Macau. Qing officials who were responsible for the area of Macau stayed in there.
98 *NCH*, 7 August 1858, cited in Hao, *Comprador*, 287, n. 25.
99 Mok, *Chenghuai gujin*, 32.
100 Eitel, *Europe in China*, 282.
101 *Government Gazette*, 16 February 1878, No. 7 'The Tung Wah Hospital, Hong Kong', 47.
102 Ibid.
103 *London and China Telegraph*, 21 August 1873, 545.
104 Sinn, *Power and Charity*, 137–141.
105 Tsai, *Hong Kong in Chinese History*, 82; *China Mail*, 8 October 1884, 3.
106 Tsai, *Hong Kong in Chinese History*, 82.
107 Tsai, 'Hong Kong Insurrection', 5–6; *China Mail*, 26 September 1884, 3, 30 September 1884, 1, 2, 3, 4, 6 October 1884; *Hong Kong Daily Press*, 1, 3, 4 October 1884.
108 Tsai, '1884 Hong Kong Insurrections', 9–10; CO 129/217, Marsh to Derby, 6 October 1884, 434–438.
109 *China Mail*, 26 and 30 September and 1, 3, 4, and 6 October 1884; *Hong Kong Daily Press*, 4, 15, and 19 September and 3, 4, 6, and 7 October 1884.
110 *Hong Kong Daily Press*, 6 October 1884, 2.
111 *Friend of China*, 4 May 1843.
112 *Hong Kong Register*, 1 September 1846, 139.
113 *Hong Kong Daily Press*, 30 September 1878.
114 Tong Kingsing and Tong Mow-chee establishd certain formal and informal ties with Qing officials and foreign intellectuals and merchants in late nineteenth-century Shanghai. For instance, in 1883, they attempted to petition the high ranking officials of the Qing court, including Li Hongzhang, to obtain his approval for the construction of a school of western knowledge and technology. *NCH*, 18 April 1883, 431–432; Throughout the late nineteenth century, the Tong brothers often worked with a British barrister, William Venn Drummond, in many public projects and court cases in which Chinese merchants were involved. *The North China Daily News*, 'The Late Mr W.V. Drummond', 24 March 1915.
115 Smith, *Sense of History*, 246–250.
116 JMA: L14/9, The Golden Wedding of Sir Robert and Lady Ho Tung (1932–1933).
117 *The Straits Times*, 1 December 1940, 2; *Hong Kong Daily Press*, 21 August 1939; *Hong Kong Telegraph*, 16 August 1939, 4; *Cen Boming xiansheng*.

Conclusion

Intermediaries in Hong Kong, China and the British Empire

This monograph has focused on the socio-economic activities of compradors in nineteenth-century Hong Kong by addressing five key questions. Where did the early generation of compradors come from? What were the functions of the government compradors? How did company compradors emerge in Hong Kong? How did the compradors conduct their own businesses? What did prominent compradors do in the political and diplomatic fields? I described the period of the emergence and the consolidation of the comprador system in Hong Kong from the 1830s to the 1880s. The first chapter explained the licensed comprador system during the Canton trade period and its collapse due to the First Opium War, leading to the privatisation of the comprador system. The second chapter investigated the rise and fall of the government compradors from the 1840s to the 1850s. Despite their privatisation, the early compradors in Hong Kong retained their position as public servants; some chose to work with the British officials instead of the Qing officials. The third chapter examined the emergence of the company compradors alongside the decline of the government compradors. The fourth chapter further explored the company compradors' businesses, which underpinned the economic development of Hong Kong as a commercial centre in East and South East Asia. The fifth chapter discussed the compradors' involvement in local politics and in diplomatic issues between the British and the Qing governments. These five chapters provided a narrative of the formulation of the durable system of intermediation in nineteenth-century Hong Kong.

This study contributes to a wide range of areas. As Motono Eiichi points out, studies on the compradors will enable us to understand further the commercial activities of the Chinese business elites operating in present-day China. Motono suggests that Chinese business elites emerged after the economic reforms of China in the 1980s that resembled the nineteenth-century compradors. These new Chinese business elites succeeded in the commercial world and elevated their social status by intermediating business between Chinese and foreign companies.[1] Margaret M. Pearson also focuses on the Chinese 'new business elite', a class of prominent businessmen who often drew on foreign capital for their commercial activities in post-Mao China; they were called 'the national bourgeoisie, the comprador elite, the managerial bourgeoisie'.[2] She discusses the emergence of the Chinese 'foreign sector managers', especially in the 1980s and the 1990s, and their political and economic autonomy from the state. When compared with the state-owned companies, Chinese managers working with foreign companies benefited from the foreign companies' relative freedom from the economic and political control and regulations of the state.[3] At the same time, these new business elites were keen to construct productive relationships with the state officials, especially local cadres for their commercial success.[4]

In Hong Kong, these Chinese business elites have played key roles in the internationalisation of Chinese business as intermediaries. In the nineteenth century, Hong Kong was one of the port cities in which the compradors actively engaged in international trade and the brokering business, benefitting from the city's unique position as a British colony adjoined to China. By the late nineteenth century, Hong Kong prospered because of intermediary business and the compradors embodied this key feature of Hong Kong. However, the system of intermediation had not been established quickly. It took more than 40 years to consolidate the comprador system, a symbiotic employment relationship between foreign companies and Chinese intermediaries.

This research highlights the commonality and uniqueness of the local intermediaries in the areas of European empires from the eighteenth to the twentieth centuries. In the broader historiography of European empires, the emergence of the compradors in nineteenth-century Hong Kong has many similarities with other cases of the rise of intermediary elites in other colonial societies, especially in the areas of the British Empire in Asia from the eighteenth to the twentieth centuries. For instance, it is possible to find many similarities between the socio-economic activities of Hong Kong compradors and local intermediaries to the British administrators in the Persian Gulf in the modern period. James Onley says that in the pre-twentieth century Persian Gulf, due to the insufficiency of the number of British officers, the British employed local intermediaries to secure their political and economic interests and also for the effective administration of the local society.[5] These intermediaries mainly consisted of Bania merchants (Indian Hindu merchants), members of local elite families, and Muslim merchants who had a strong commercial and political network with local authorities. These intermediaries chose to work with the British to improve their social position as well as for their economic and political prosperity. Drawing on political and economic intermediaries, the British officials in Persia and Arabia were able to maintain their political hegemony in these regions. The local intermediaries sometimes became political and economic competitors to the British. Nevertheless, the British administrators continued to employ the local intermediaries because of the usefulness of their extensive commercial and political network in the local society and their contribution to the protection of British interests.[6]

The Hong Kong compradors' economic and political cooperation with the British officials and businessmen resembled that of the intermediaries operating in British Burma and India. Robert H. Taylor focuses on the rise of the middle class who emerged in the period of the British rule of Burma in the early twentieth century. The new middle class included former local officials who had served the government of Imperial Burma before the British colonisation and English-educated students. These intermediaries worked with the British officials, and made wealth from investments in land and the property business. The children of the early generation of the middle class were often sent to London or India to receive an English education, which could enable their commercial and political success in their future career.[7] In terms of British India, David L. White underlines the local brokers' work for the EIC; they were keen to accumulate wealth, improve their social status, and obtain protection from the company in the seventeenth and eighteenth centuries. These brokers mediated in buying and selling between the foreign traders and local producers of trading commodities, and obtained between 0.5 and 1 per cent commission from both sides.[8] Bayly argues that a variety of local information agents in British India underpinned the maintenance of the system of information gathering and transmission for the administration of the colony in the eighteenth and nineteenth centuries.[9] In a similar manner to these intermediaries in the British Empire, the Hong Kong compradors acted as commercial and political brokers and information agents.

One of the most significant and unique characteristics of the Hong Kong compradors was the consolidation of their social status and the establishment of their legitimacy to function as leaders of the local communities. When compared with the cases of local intermediaries in India, Burma and the Gulf, primarily the compradors in Hong Kong emerged from the migrant society in relatively small islands, in which the number of pre-colonial local leaders and authorities were not large. Most of the population consisted of migrants from China who were seeking business opportunities with foreigners. In that sense, a large number of the Chinese population were more or less intermediaries between Chinese and foreign commerce and culture, and the compradors were typical representatives of this variety of intermediaries, such as intellectuals, contractors, servants and boat workers operating in Hong Kong. Therefore, the Hong Kong compradors had a strong advantage in acting as representatives of the local intermediaries' commercial and social interests in nineteenth-century Hong Kong. This contributed to the establishment and the consolidation of the social, political and commercial system of intermediation in late nineteenth-century Hong Kong.

The evolution of the comprador system

This study also helps to clarify the inception of the intermediate business system in Hong Kong and provides a valuable case study on the compradors in terms of the historiography of modern China for comparative purposes. The comprador system was different in each port city, and continued evolving through the nineteenth and twentieth centuries. As most research has concentrated on mainland China, this study highlights the diversity of the comprador system as well as its commonalities throughout the Chinese world. For the history of the British Empire, this research suggests a symbiotic relationship between the British and Chinese intermediary elites that challenges the simplistic view that colonial society consisted merely of colonisers and colonised.

The reassessment of the licensed comprador system suggests that a certain number of local Chinese people, including the compradors, obtained profits from the foreign trade, legally or illegally, before the First Opium War. This could be one of the reasons why a number of Chinese compradors and provision purveyors collaborated with the British and came to Hong Kong both during and after the war. The licensed compradors, consisting of ship and house compradors, mainly operated in the Pearl River Delta, and especially in Canton, which was the only Chinese port open to Western traders. Under the Canton Trading System designed by the Qing government, the foreign traders were required to hire compradors licensed by Qing officials, and they were not permitted to hire someone without a licence. The main duties of these licensed compradors were providing provisions for the foreigners. Ship compradors provided provisions to foreign vessels, while house compradors dealt with both procuring of provisions and accounting for the foreign firms. Along with the licensed compradors, linguists, hong merchants and sampans had permission to work with foreigners. Some of the licensed Chinese merchants and compradors made their living by working with foreigners on a long-term basis. They also acted as the Qing's supervisors to the foreigners. By overseeing the activities of the licensed Chinese merchants and workers, Qing authorities attempted to control foreigners' commercial activities in China. Once the Qing officials ordered the compradors to withdraw from their services, the foreigners in Canton faced great difficulty in their daily lives because of the lack of food and water. However, by the end of the 1830s, the licensed comprador system had already started dissolving due to the increase in the number of unlicensed compradors.

From the late 1830s to the early 1840s, a number of local Chinese became compradors and provided provisions without permission from the Qing officials. This led to the privatisation of the comprador system. Before the First Opium War in 1839, the compradors and the linguists were already involved in the contraband trade with foreigners. The Qing authorities were aware of the existence of unlicensed compradors and attempted to capture them, yet due to the extensive corruption of local officials, unlicensed compradors managed to continue conducting their business. The foreigners also preferred to trade with the unlicensed compradors, as they could sell provisions at cheaper prices because of inflation. By the end of the 1830s, the Qing government started losing control of foreigners' and local people's commercial activities. The confusion of the First Opium War provided further opportunities for local Chinese people who did not have a licence to work with foreigners. They were likely to regard the British officials and traders arriving in Hong Kong as new customers. Because of the 1842 Treaty of Nanking, Hong Kong formally became a British crown colony, and the Canton Trading System and its licensed comprador system was dismantled. Despite the privatisation of the licensed comprador system, some new compradors in Hong Kong remained employees of government officials. However, they did not work for the Qing, but rather for the British.

The government compradors became influential intermediaries between the colonial government and the local Chinese populace in Hong Kong in the 1840s and the 1850s. The institutions of the colonial government directly employed government compradors, or the colonial officials personally employed compradors to support their official duties. As a communication conduit between the colonial officials and the Chinese society, the government compradors exercised and sometimes abused their authority to obtain profits from their own business. In particular, the involvement of the treasury comprador, Chow Aaon, and his colleagues in the corruption of the colonial government was well known. In addition to the treasury comprador, this research found various government compradors who were working with the colonial officials from the 1840s to the 1850s. The duties of the government compradors were different in each colonial institution. However, the diversity and ubiquitousness of the government compradors suggest that the colonial government depended heavily on support from the Chinese intermediaries in its formative period. The rise of government compradors instead of company compradors before the 1860s was in part because the term *maiban* had been used as a verb meaning 'buying provisions at government expense' since the Ming period.[10] In that sense, it was natural for the government compradors to work with the British officials as they regarded the colonial government as a substitute for the Qing government.

Nevertheless, the government compradors lost their significance in the political and commercial world of Hong Kong by the end of the 1850s. The number of compradors employed by the organisations of the colonial government declined, while the total number of Chinese staff increased. The work of the government compradors was broken up and taken over by other types of Chinese staff. After nearly 20 years of experience in the administration of Hong Kong, the colonial officials understood what types of Chinese personnel were required. Therefore, they did not necessarily need to rely on the compradors' support in their daily work.

Furthermore, in the 1860s, the Hong Kong Cadetship, introduced by Governor Robinson, contributed to the reduction of government dependency on Chinese middlemen. Recruiting British graduates who had studied Cantonese and Mandarin, the colonial government was able to secure personnel who could deal directly with Chinese matters.[11] Another possible factor in the decline of the government compradors was the corruption and recurrent scandals caused by the compradors and their principals. Several formal investigations into the corruption cases threw doubt on the symbiotic relationship between the compradors and the colonial officials during the 1850s. It may have become difficult for the colonial officials to let their personal compradors assist their work in the colonial government. Moreover, after the mid-1860s, a class of Chinese mercantile and intellectual elites emerged and became political intermediaries between the colonial government and the local Chinese community.[12] Because of the transformation of the employment system for Chinese staff, the government compradors' loss of credibility, and the rise of different intermediaries, including the company compradors, the government compradors lost their significance in politics and business by the mid-1860s.

Along with the fall of the comprador system within the colonial government, the company comprador system was consolidated between the 1860s and the

1880s.[13] In addition to the government compradors, house compradors and ship compradors operated in the private sector in Hong Kong from the 1840s to the 1860s. The commercial success of the compradors employed by foreign firms and banks became evident by the late 1860s. Both foreign and Chinese merchants required the intermediation of the compradors for effective business operations in China during that period. Starting in the late 1850s, due to the Second Opium War and the Taiping Uprising, wealthy Chinese merchants were exiled to Hong Kong from southern China, promoting the importance of Hong Kong as a trading centre. The influx of Chinese merchants to Hong Kong also increased the demand for middlemen. By the mid-1870s, more than 60 principal compradors operated in Hong Kong.[14] Not only successful as compradors, they were also well-to-do merchants, traders and leading figures in the Chinese community. In the 1860s, the term 'comprador' was more frequently used to refer to company compradors rather than government or house compradors. However, the duties of the company compradors were not yet clearly defined, and foreign companies struggled to clarify them throughout the nineteenth century.

The dual functions of the compradors created difficulties in defining the compradors' position in foreign firms. The company compradors were internal staff of the foreign companies, but concurrently they were external business partners. A company comprador was responsible for the management of Chinese matters in the foreign company. The main duties of the company compradors were hiring Chinese staff, intermediating in business with Chinese firms, and dealing with accounting, marketing and financial transactions for Chinese customers. Large trading firms such as Jardine, Matheson & Co. usually established a compradors' office in which chief and assistant compradors, shroff and other Chinese staff worked. In many cases, the main compradors served the foreign firms long-term, until their death or retirement. The comprador's position was often taken over by the next generation of relatives or close friends, because a security bond and a recommendation from credible guarantors were required to employ a new comprador. The company compradors had turned into indispensable internal staff of the foreign firms and banks by the early 1870s.

At the same time, many of the compradors acted as external business partners as well as competitors to their foreign employers. Obtaining financial means, information and human resources by working with foreign companies, the Hong Kong compradors were engaged in a wide range of international, innovative and entrepreneurial businesses including shipping, sugar refining and publishing. To put it simply, the compradors emulated the foreign companies. A representative case is Kwok Acheong, a comprador to the P&O steamship company, who established his own steamship company, Kwok Acheong & Co. The compradors also emulated the businesses of Chinese merchants. Drawing on the commercial network of overseas and general Chinese merchants, the compradors were able to conduct large-scale trade across South East Asia, East Asia and the Pacific Ocean. Meanwhile the compradors conducted a variety of local business in Hong Kong, for instance, the management of pawnshops and investment in land and property. By diversifying their business, the compradors reduced the risk of failure and survived the competitive and rapidly changing Hong Kong market. The diverse range of the compradors' commercial activities helped to establish a durable Sino-foreign business system in Hong Kong.

The company comprador system had benefits and disadvantages. As an independent merchant and investor, a comprador was able to gather market intelligence and an extensive commercial network, which was useful for his employers. Jardine, Matheson & Co. expanded its sugar refining operation in collaboration with its compradors and their commercial network in the 1880s. However, the comprador could leak his employers' internal information and embezzle the company's money. Conflict between the compradors and foreign firms because of embezzlement was constantly reported in newspapers in Hong Kong in the latter half of the nineteenth century. Lawyers, foreign businessmen and journalists pointed out the ambiguities and problems of the comprador system. Some argued for the abolishment of the comprador system, as it hindered direct trade with Chinese merchants.

Nevertheless, the company compradors increased their influence from the 1860s to the 1880s, and the comprador system continued to exist until the mid-twentieth century. This was partly because the foreign firms and the compradors managed to establish constructive relationships. Major foreign firms avoided direct competition with the compradors by consultation and negotiation, as well as the differentiation of their businesses from the compradors. For foreign traders, a key to conducting profitable business in Hong Kong was obtaining a comprador who was a credible employee as well as a successful merchant. As such, the company comprador system became an indispensable basis for collaboration between Chinese and foreign firms from the 1870s to the 1880s.

From the 1840s to the 1880s, the compradors were eager to increase their socio-political status in the local Chinese community, as well as in British and Qing society. As marginal men working for both foreigners and Chinese, the compradors were often disrespected and could be an easy target of discrimination in foreign and Chinese communities. Due to their unstable position in society, the compradors engaged in public activities to gain respect from the local Chinese populace. In particular, the principal compradors were keen to establish and manage semi-official organisations providing public services, including health care, policing, and rescuing kidnapped children and young women, in collaboration with other members of the local Chinese mercantile and intellectual elites. These prominent compradors attempted to establish a mutually productive relationship with the Qing government by purchasing official titles and financially contributing to charitable institutions and activities for disaster relief in China.

In parallel, the compradors were eager to secure their position in foreign communities, and especially with the British. For instance, they obtained titles and honours from the British by contributing to public activities and ceremonies in the foreign community, and some applied for naturalisation. After achieving commercial success, the compradors attempted to secure and improve their position in multiple societies.

The multiplicity of the company compradors' social functions enabled them to be effective political intermediaries between the colonial government and the Chinese community. This could be observed in the compradors' efforts to end the cargo boat workers' strikes in 1884. Each comprador had different political attitudes towards the Qing and British authorities; however, most of them were practical about political issues and avoided serious confrontation with either government. They prioritised maintaining social order in Hong Kong for their commercial activities. The compradors also benefited from their ambiguous position. When the Hong Kong compradors encountered trouble with the Qing officials, they were able to obtain legal support from the British side. By collaborating with local Chinese elites and acting as representatives of the Chinese mercantile community, they were able to influence the politics of the colonial government. Working with the British and Qing governments and with local Chinese leaders, the compradors succeeded in improving and securing their social status.

The compradors' commercial and political activities contributed to the coordination of financial, human and information resources between China and foreign countries that occurred in Hong Kong. Hisasue Ryoichi states that the main function of Hong Kong has been the integration, intermediation and distribution of these resources since the late nineteenth century, which has underpinned the prosperity of the city as one of the most important commercial centres in the world.[15] Drawing on his argument, it is possible to say that the compradors played key functions in the formulation of the system of intermediation in Hong Kong, whereas Chinese workers, merchants and intellectuals played key functions in the integration and distribution of these resources. Although there was an overlapping in functions, the core of the compradors' behaviour was seen as their consistent commitment to coordinating the interests of different stakeholders. By the late 1880s, the compradors' socio-economic activities enabled the formulation of the system of intermediation, which became a basis of Hong Kong society.

The Hong Kong compradors continued to be an influential class in the commercial and political sector from the 1890s to the 1930s. Successive generations of compradors continued to adapt to new technologies, knowledge and the evolving business structure of Hong Kong while they were working with foreign firms. In a manner similar to the Hong Kong compradors in the nineteenth century, twentieth-century compradors were keen to run general trade, shipping, banking and sugar refining businesses, and to manage electric companies.[16] Concurrently, they were influential in politics. During that period, several compradors served the Legislative Council as unofficial members.[17]

The Compradors' Association (*Yanghang banfang lianhehui*) was formally established in 1925. The Shanghai Branch of the East Asian Research Centre (Tōa Kenkyūjo Shanhai Shisho), a Japanese research institution established pre-war, estimates that the number of guild members in Hong Kong was 39. It also reports that 19 compradors who were non-guild members were active in Hong Kong. About 60 compradors were operating in Hong Kong before the Second World War. However, the members of the guild included non-compradors, such as Tse Yu

Chuen (Xie Yuchuan), a Chinese manager for Melchers & Co.[18] This suggests the Chinese managers gradually took over the functions of the compradors.

Although the compradors were successful in the commercial world of Hong Kong in the first half of the twentieth century, the decline of the comprador system started as early as in the 1890s. Foreign firms restricted the external commercial activities of the compradors, and changed the name of the position of comprador to the Chinese term for manager (*huajingli*). By teaching Japanese staff the Chinese language, the Japanese trading firm Mitsui Bussan succeeded in abolishing its comprador system in 1899.[19] The sons of compradors also became lawyers, doctors and soldiers, because they received a Western higher education in Hong Kong and the United Kingdom. The emergence of different types of intermediary elites reduced the indispensability of the compradors. Moreover, from the 1900s onwards, the compradors were often criticised as traitors to their home country, alongside the rise of Chinese nationalism. In the 1920s, the Hong Kong compradors' commercial and political influence declined, which could be one reason for the establishment of the guild in order 'to protect the compradors' right and to attempt to reduce and resist deficits'.[20] The Japanese occupation of Hong Kong hindered the commercial activities of the compradors and foreign companies from 1941 to 1945. In the post-war period, the number of compradors continued to decrease. When the last comprador, Peter Lee of the Hongkong and Shanghai Banking Corporation, was re-designated Chinese manager in 1960, the comprador system ended.[21]

Nevertheless, this does not mean the end of the system of intermediation. From the 1860s to the present, Hong Kong business elites were consistently engaged in international commerce, especially in intermediating business between Chinese and foreign companies. The commercial and political behaviour of Hong Kong business elites had many similarities with that of the compradors. Contemporary Hong Kong business elites collaborate with both Chinese and foreign firms, diversify their business and contribute to benevolent activities in a manner that resembles the nineteenth-century compradors. Li Ka-shing (Li Jiacheng), one of the wealthiest businessmen in Asia and a well-known philanthropist, made his fortune operating multiple businesses such as plastic manufacturing, real estate, mobile phone and internet businesses.[22] The compradors' unique function as economic, social and cultural intermediaries can still be seen in the activities of contemporary Hong Kong business elites. Hong Kong's status as a settlement for both Chinese and foreign businessmen, and as a former British colony, and its lack of an established social order pre-1841 shapes this system of intermediation, as do the features of the Hong Kong compradors.

When compared with compradors in other port cities in East Asia, the Hong Kong compradors were more integrated into the British commercial and political structure. For the compradors in Chinese treaty ports, the British and other imperial powers were less likely to be long-term patrons of their business activities. As such, treaty port compradors were required to establish close ties with the Qing authorities for the protection of their economic interests. For instance, Shanghai and Tianjin compradors invested in the industrialisation project for Chinese businesses led by bureaucratic reformers from the 1860s to the 1880s.[23] Meanwhile, it was practical for the Hong Kong compradors to establish a constructive relationship with British officials to conduct profitable business in Hong Kong. It would have been almost impossible for treaty port compradors to act like Kwok Acheong, who heavily supported British military action in China and drew on British protection. In Hong Kong, a number of compradors came from areas of the British formal or informal empire in South East Asia, including the Straits Settlements. Some of the Hong Kong compradors were able to run their business without being deeply integrated into the Qing social order. Yet the greater part of the Hong Kong compradors were Cantonese whose hometowns were in southern China. For them, it was also necessary to elevate their social status in Qing society.

The Hong Kong compradors, especially those who were Cantonese, had many similarities with the treaty port compradors. The compradors in China also attempted to secure their social position in the nineteenth century by working with Qing officials and foreign businessmen, contributing to local Chinese communities, and organising regional and commercial associations. Both the Hong Kong and treaty port compradors purchased official titles to streamline their work with Qing officials.[24] During that period, a majority of the compradors in the treaty ports were Cantonese, and therefore their commercial behaviour had many similarities with that of the Cantonese Hong Kong compradors from the 1840s to the 1860s. Migrating to the treaty ports and to Hong Kong, the Cantonese compradors synchronised their business tactics.

However, from the 1860s onwards, in the case of Tianjin and Shanghai, the number of Suzhou and Ningbo compradors gradually increased and broke the dominance of the Cantonese.[25] By 1880, Fujian, Shandong and Hebei compradors also formulated their own group in the treaty ports, and this diversified the treaty port compradors. Their areas of specialty and social backgrounds were not similar to that of the Cantonese compradors.[26] Nevertheless, it is possible to say that the fundamental commonality of these compradors was their cooperation with multiple political and economic authorities. In part this was because the compradors were often disregarded in both Chinese and foreign communities.

However, the Chinese public in Hong Kong had a moderate, if not approving, attitude to the compradors. When Hong Kong was ceded to the British, it did not have an established class of Chinese elites who could criticise the compradors as collaborators with the foreigners. Hong Kong society largely consisted of Chinese immigrants, the majority of them were working with foreigners. In that sense, the compradors were not a minority in Hong Kong, but were representative of the variety of Chinese intermediaries. In nineteenth-century Hong Kong, the English media produced a critical discourse on the comprador system as a hindrance to direct trade with Chinese merchants. Meanwhile, the Chinese media in Hong Kong maintained a neutral tone on the compradors. Well-known Chinese opinion leaders, including Wang Tao, worked with the compradors in Hong Kong. The main founders of *Xunhuan Ribao* were comprador merchants.[27] *Xunhuan Ribao* provided useful information for Chinese workers in Hong Kong in the 1870s and 1880s, and in its articles the compradors were usually simply described as just one type employee in the foreign firms; their significance as the dominant intermediaries between foreign and Chinese businessmen was little highlighted. There could be some social discrimination against the Hong Kong compradors, but the Chinese critical discourse on the compradors was not primarily produced in Hong Kong.

In Chinese port cities, however, the compradors were often disregarded as servants of the foreigners (*yangnu*), 'Mister boy' (*xizai xiansheng*), or 'foreigners' dogs' in the late nineteenth century.[28] Wu Yueren (1866–1910), a novelist in late Qing China, wrote *Facai mijue*, which depicted compradors' lives in a cynical manner. The novel was first published in a monthly magazine in Shanghai, *Yueyue xiaoshuo*, in 1907.[29] In the novel, the author described Chinese workers and compradors serving foreigners, especially in Hong Kong, Canton and Shanghai, and criticised them for lacking proper moral values and for pursuing only economic prosperity.[30] Wu's description of the compradors is representative of their contemporary general perception in Shanghai, but not necessarily that of Hong Kong. In the early twentieth century, mainly in Shanghai, nationalistic novelists, opinion leaders and journalists facilitated the critical discourse against the compradors by inheriting and combining the English discussion about the comprador system, the Qing officials' view of traitors, the public resentment of the collaborators with foreigners, and Japanese researchers' analysis of the comprador system.

However, in nineteenth-century Hong Kong, the public critical discourse on the compradors evidently did not exist. There could have been social discrimination against the compradors in nineteenth-century Hong Kong; however, most of the Chinese intermediary elites in Hong Kong seemed to avoid drawing criticism. As Hong Kong was primarily a migrant society, based on intermediation between Chinese and foreigners, and as the compradors were sponsors of publishing firms in Hong Kong, it was not beneficial for the local intellectuals to overtly criticise the comprador system. As such, the Hong Kong compradors were able to style themselves as representatives of the social and economic interests of the Chinese community and to stabilise the social system of intermediation by the late 1880s.

This research, discussing the establishment of the modern comprador system in Hong Kong, produces two broad questions and themes for future research. The first theme is the dissolution of the comprador system in China during the first half of the twentieth century. The establishment of the PRC certainly terminated the comprador system in China, yet it was not clear how the compradors survived a politically difficult time for them: the 1910s to the 1940s, from the establishment of the Republic of China to the birth of the PRC. Other factors contributed to the decline of the compradors. The foreign companies reformed the comprador system while Chinese merchants learnt how to conduct direct business with the foreigners. The interconnections between these factors are not clear. Moreover, to explain why the comprador intermediary elites seemingly vanished in the 1940s and quickly returned after the 1980s, research on the dissolution of the comprador system is required.

The second theme relates to the Chinese compradors abroad. Previous scholars mainly focus on the comprador system in China, while the amount of research on the compradors operating outside China, including in Taiwan, Japan and Singapore, is limited. There should be more macro-scale research exploring the compradors' transnational and transregional interconnections, as well as case studies highlighting the unique traits of and commonalities between compradors in different places. In this way, it will be possible to illustrate the broader picture of the comprador system, a Chinese system of intermediation that existed for over a century in East Asia and Southeast Asia.

The Hong Kong compradors played a significant role in the production of the fundamental social structure of Hong Kong – that is, the system of intermediation – from the 1830s to the 1880s. The licensed comprador system was dismantled and was privatised from the late 1830s to the early 1840s in the Pearl River Delta. The existing local intermediaries who had economic interests in trade with foreigners largely promoted this. Then, from the 1840s to the 1850s, the government compradors obtained hegemonic authority in intermediation between the colonial government and the local Chinese community. However, by the late 1860s the socio-economic success of the company compradors had eclipsed them, and at this point the government comprador system was dismantled. Working with foreign firms, the company compradors collected market information and financial resources as well as cultivating human networks. The compradors' resources were indispensable for foreign employers and Chinese merchants, and this was one of the reasons why the comprador system flourished in Hong Kong. Based on accumulated wealth, a strong network, and access to information, the compradors were able to run large-scale businesses, and many of the principal compradors became successful merchants, investors and entrepreneurs. Commercial resources also underpinned the compradors' elevation as representative elites in Hong Kong and as political intermediaries between the colonial government and the local Chinese community. In this manner, the Hong Kong compradors formed a social system of intermediation that is maintained by Hong Kong business elites today.

Notes

1 Motono 'Baiben', 227.
2 Pearson, *China's New Business Elite*, 5–6.
3 Ibid., 65–66, 99, 101.
4 Ibid., 100–101, 115.
5 Onley, *Arabian Frontier*, 103.
6 Ibid., 103.
7 Taylor, *State in Burma,* 134–135.
8 White, *Competition and Collaboration*, 16–19.
9 Bayly, *Empire and Information*, 369–370.
10 Motono,'Baiben', 227.
11 Tsang, *Modern History*, 25–26.
12 In terms of the emergence of the Chinese elites in Hong Kong, see Carroll, *Edge of Empires*, 51–53; Smith, *Chinese Christians*, 103.
13 It should be noted that in this research, the term 'company compradors' is utilised to mean compradors working both in foreign companies and in banks.

14 *China Directory 1874*, 47; See Table 3.3.
15 Hisasue, 'Honkon', 291–293.
16 Cox, Huang, and Metcalfe, 'Compradors, Firm Architecture', 9–10; JMA: L14/9, The Golden Wedding of Sir Robert and Lady Ho Tung ('Hong Kong's Grand Old Man', reprinted from *Hong Kong Daily Press*, 30 November 1931); Carroll, *Edge of Empires*, 85–86.
17 Cheng, 'Chinese Unofficial Members', 7–30.
18 Toyo Bunko: Tōa Kenkyūjo Shanhai Shisho, *Honkon no baiben.*
19 Ma, 'Shanghai maiban de shenghuo', 21–22; Walter, *Present Day Impressions*, 572–601.
20 Toyo Bunko: Tōa Kenkyūjo Shanhai Shisho, *Honkon no baiben.*
21 HSBC Archive, London: HSBCS 0019/0001, Comprador File.
22 Zhang and Alon, eds, *Biographical Dictionary*, 81–83.
23 Hao, *Comrpador*, 120–136; Song, *Huashuo Jinshang*, 51–53.
24 Hao, *Comprador*, 180–206.
25 Lu, *Beyond Neon Lights*, 57; Song, *Huashuo Jinshang*, 40–41.
26 For research on the different regional groups of compradors, see Yu 'Xiangshanji maiban', 127–134.
27 Notification regarding the launch of the *Xunhuan Ribao.*
28 Song, *Huashuo jinshang*, 41; *Shenbao*, January 14, 1874 cited by Goodman, *Native Place*, 107; Ye, *Dianshizhai*, 128; *Dianshizhai huabao*, Vol. Jia, 81 xia.
29 A Ying, ed., *Wanqing xiaoshuoshi*, 93.
30 Wu, *Facai mijue*.

Bibliography

Primary – Archival

British Library, London

IOR/G/12/249	China and Japan: Canton Factory Consultations, India Office Records, 1831–1833

Jardine Matheson Archive, Cambridge University Library, Manuscripts Department

A2	Journals, 1811–1900
A6	Invoices, 1810–1852
A7	Miscellaneous bound accounts and papers, 1802–1941
A8	Miscellaneous loose accounts and papers, 1812–1934
B6/2	Business letters: America, 1821–1898
B7/2	Business letters: Canton, 1814–1904
B7/15	Business letters: Hong Kong, 1833–1905
B11	Business letters: unplaced, 1813–1900
C25	Letters re agreements and contracts, 1887–1903
C36	Letters re Canton Insurance Office, 1835–1894
C37	Letters re Hongkong Fire Insurance Co. Ltd, 1874–1891
F1	Agreements and contracts, 1819–1935
F10	Deeds of partnership, 1821–1913
H1	Chinese documents, Commercial documents, 1809–1914
L14/9	Miscellaneous printed papers, the Pamphlet of The Golden Wedding of Sir Robert and Lady Ho Tung, 1932–1933

Baker Library, Harvard Business School, Boston

Forbes Family Business Records

Series E	Robert Bennet Forbes papers, 1825–1883

Heard Family Business Records

Series I. Heard family business records, 1734–1901

GQ-1 and GQ-2	Miscellaneous Books and Papers, 1845–1877
FM-4–1	Letters to John Heard from A.F. Heard, 1846–1863
FM-5–1	Letters from John Heard, A. Heard, Jr. from A.F. Heard, 1864
HM-6	Letters from China and Japan. Original Letters. From John Heard at Ningpo and Hong Kong, 1860–1861
HM-28–3	Letters received from George B. Dixwell (a partner) at Macao, Hong Kong, Galle, Shanghai, 1862–1863

Series II. Augustine Heard & Company China records, 1827–1892

Carton 1	Vouchers, 1843–1875
Carton 6-A and Carton 6-B	Bills of Exchange, 1844–1866
Vol. 55–59	Accounts with Hong Kong and Shanghai Banking Corp., Cot d'Escompte de Paris and the Comprador, Hong Kong, 1869–1875

HSBC Archives (London), HSBC Holdings, plc.

HSBCS 0019/0001	Comprador File
MB 1225	Deed of Covenant and Security

Hong Kong Public Record Office

HKRS77	Documents relating to the appointment of staff and the supply of provisions to Victoria Gaol, 1847–1916
HKRS144	Probate Jurisdiction Will Files, 1840 – 1990
HKRS149	Legal documents relating to staff, supply of goods and services, and property, 1841–1928

National Archives, Kew

CO129	War and Colonial Department and Colonial Office: Hong Kong, Original Correspondence
CO133	War and Colonial Department and Colonial Office: Hong Kong, Miscellanea *Hong Kong Blue Book*
FO233	Northern Department and Foreign Office: Consulates and Legation, China: Miscellaneous Papers and Reports
FO1048	East India Company: Select Committee of Supercargoes, Chinese Secretary's Office: Chinese-language Correspondence and Papers, 1793 – 1834

P&O Archives, National Maritime Museum, Greenwich

P&O/16/1–7	Oriental correspondence, 1867–1899
P&O/65	P&O individual ship information files

Po Leung Kuk Museum, Hong Kong

Chengwen 呈文 (petitions), 1878–1881
Zhishilu 誌事錄 (minutes book), 1880–1885

Royal Mail Archive, London

POST 4/15	Colonial and Foreign Allowance Book, Salaries and Allowances to Postmasters, Agents and Other Post Office Employees Overseas, 1844–1857.

School of Oriental and African Studies Library, London

Council for World Mission: archives and library of the London Missionary Society (CWM/LMS) South China Incoming Correspondence, London Missionary Society

Collection of David McLean's letters

MS 380401/02	Transcripts of McLean's Letterbooks, Vol. 1–3

John Swire & Sons Collection

JSS/1	Papers of John Swire and Sons Limited 1869–1980

Toyo Bunko (The Oriental Library), Tokyo

Tōa Kenkyūjo Shanhai Shisho 東亜研究所上海支所, *Hong Kong no baiben kumiai nit suite: daitoa senso mae ni okeru* 香港の買辦組合について：大東亜戦争前に於ける (Compradors' guild in Hong Kong before the Greater East Asia War) (Shanghai, date unknown).

Tōa Kenkyūjo *Shanghai ni okeru baiben no keizaiteki seiryoku* 上海に於ける買辦の経済的勢力 (Comprador's economic influence in Shanghai) (Shanghai, Estimated to be written before before beginning of the Second Sino-Japanese War in 1937).

Tung Wah Group of Hospital's Archives

Zhengxinlu 徵信錄 (Annual Reports), 1871–1933

Primary – Published

Addresses Presented to William T, Mercer, M.A., Oxon. (London: E. Stanford, 1867).

Anstey, Thomas Chisholm, *Crime and Government at Hong Kong* (London: Eggingham Wilson, Loyal Exchange, 1859).

The Asiatic Journal and Monthly Register for British and Foreign India, China and Australasia, Vol. 25 (London: Parbury, Allen and Co., 1828).

Ballou's Monthly Magazine, Vol. 24 (Elliott, Thomes and Talbot, 1866).

Birmingham University Calendar for the Session 1911–1912 (Birmingham: Cornish Brothers, New Street, 1911).

Birmingham University Calendar for the Session 1912–1913 (Birmingham: Cornish Brothers, New Street, 1912).

The Blockade of the Port and Harbour of Hong Kong (London: Kent and Co.; and Norwich: Fletcher and Son, 1874).

Blunt, Joseph, *The Merchant's and Shipmaster's Assistant: Containing Information Useful to the American Merchants, Owners, and Masters of Ships* (New York: E. and G.W. Blunt, 1829).

Bourne, F.S.A., *Report of the Mission to China of the Blackburn Chamber of Commerce, 1896–7, F.S.A. Bourne's Section* (Blackburn: The North-East Lancashire Press Company, 1898).

British Parliamentary Papers, Published.

—— China. Vol. 39, *General correspondence, dispatches and reports relating to the rules, regulations, and other aspects of the trade between Great Britain and China*, 1831–1899.

—— *Reports from Committee, Select Committee on Mortality of Troops Together with the proceeding of the Committee, Minutes of Evidence, and Appendix*, Vol. 10 (1866).

—— *House of Commons Papers*, Vol. 48, China: Hong Kong, Session 24 January to 28 August 1860.

The Canton Press (Canton, 1835–1844).

The Canton Register (Canton, 1827–1843).

The Catholic World.

Cen Boming xiansheng fushu 岑伯銘先生訃書 (The obituary of Mr Cen Bobing) (Hong Kong: Cen Shuncheng tang, 1939).

The China Directory 1861 (Hong Kong: A. Shortrede & Co., 1861).

The China Directory 1874 (Hong Kong: A. Shortrede & Co., 1874).

The China Mail.

The China Magazine, A Weekly Miscellany, Illustrated with Photographs (Hong Kong: Noronha & Sons, Government Printers, 1868).

The Chinese Repository (Canton, 1832–1851).

The Chronicle and Directory for China, Japan and the Philippines (Hong Kong; Hong Kong Daily Press, 1870, 1879).

Chouban yiwushimo 籌辦夷務始末 (The management of foreign affairs) (Taibei: Wenhai chubanshe, 1970–1971).

Cooke, George Wingrove, *China and Lower Bengal: Being 'The Times' Correspondence from China in the years* 1857–58 (London: Routledge, Warne, & Routledge, 1861).

Correspondence respecting the revision of the treaty of Tien-tsin [signed 1858], presented to the House of Lords by Command of Her Majesty, in Pursuance of Their Address Dated 24 March 1871 (London: Harrison and Sons, 1871).

Daqing Dezong Jing (Guangxu) huangdi shilu, 大清德宗景 (光緒) 皇帝實錄, Vol. 71.

Davis, John Francis, *The Chinese: A General Description of China and its Inhabitants*, Vol. 1 (London: C. Knight, 1844).

Des Voeux, George William, *My Colonial Service in British Guiana, St Lucia, Trinidad, Fiji, Australia, Newfoundland, and Hong Kong with Interludes* (London: John Murray, 1903).

The Desk Hong List; A General and Business Directory for Shanghai and the Northern & River Ports, Japan, etc. 1875, 1876, 1878, 1884, 1903 (Shanghai, North China Herald, 1875–1903).

Dianshizhai huabao 點石齋畫報 (The Dianshizhai pictorial) (Guangdong: Guangdong renmin chubanshe, 1983).

The Directory and Chronicle for China, Japan, Corea, Indo-China, Straits Settlements, Malay States, Siam, Netherlands, India, Borneo, the Philippines (Hong Kong: Hong Kong Daily Press Office, 1879).

Dobell, Peter, *Travels in Kamtchatka and Siberia; With a Narrative of a Residence of China* (London: Henry Colburn and R. Bentley, 1830).

Eitel, E.J., *Europe in China: The History of Hong Kong From the Beginning to the Year* 1882 (London: Lozac & Co., 1895).

Elliot, John Bingham, *Narrative of the Expedition to China from the Commencement of the War to Its Termination in 1842: With Sketches of the Manners and Customs of that Singular and Hitherto Almost Unknown Country*, Vol. 1 and 2 (London: Henry Colburn, 1843).

Feldwick,Walter, *Present Day Impressions of the Far East and Prominent & Progressive Chinese at Home and Abroad: the History, People, Commerce, Industries and Resources of China, Hongkong, Indo-China, Malaya and Netherlands India* (London: Globe Encyclopedia, 1917).

Fifty Years of Progress: The Jubilee of Hongkong as a British Crown Colony, being an Historical Sketch, to Which is Added an Account of the Celebrations of 21st to 24th January, 1891 (Hong Kong: Daily Press, 1891).

Forbes, Robert Bennet, *Remarks on China and the China Trade* (Boston: Samuel N. Dickinson, printer, 1844).

Foster, Warren W., 'Things Chinese: A Comparative Study of Human Nature', *The Editorial Review*, Vol. 1, 1909 August–December, 117–130.

The Friend of China. 1842–1869.

Gützlaff, Karl Friedrich August, revised by Andrew Reed, *China Opened; or, A Display of the Topography, History, Customs, Manners, Arts, Manufactures, Commerce, Literature, Religion, Jurisprudence, etc, of the Chinese Empire*, Vol. 2 (London: Smith, Elder and Co., 1838).

Hall, William Hutcheon and Bernard, William Dallas, *The Nemesis in China: Comprising a History of the Late War in that Country; with a Complete Account of the Colony of Hong-Kong*, 3rd edn (London: Henry Colburn, 1846).

The Hong Kong Daily Press.

The Hongkong Directory, and Hong List for the Far East, etc (Hong Kong: R. Fraser-Smith, 1883–1895).

Hong Kong General Chamber of Commerce, Report for the Year, 1887 (Hong Kong, Noronha & Co., 1888).

Hong Kong Government Gazette.

Hong Kong Government, *Hong Kong Administrative Reports*.

The Hong Kong Register.

The Hong Kong Telegraph.

Huazi ribao 華字日報.

Hunter, William C., *The 'Fan kwae' at Canton before Treaty Days, 1825–1844* (London: Kegan Paul, Trench & Co., 1882).

Jarman, Robert L. (ed.), *Hong Kong Annual Administration Report 1841–1941*, Vol. 1–6 (Great Britain: Archive Editions, 1996).

Jinding huitong moshi jiapu 金鼎會同莫氏家譜 (The family records of the Moks).

Liang Tingnan 梁廷枏, *Yifen wenji 夷氛聞記* (Stories of the foreigners) (Beijing: Zhonghua shuju, 1959).

London and China Telegraph.

Mayers, W.F., and King, C., *The Treaty Ports of China and Japan: A Complete Guide to the Open Ports of Those Countries, Together with Peking, Yedo, Hongkong and Macao* (1867).

Medhurst, Walter Henry, *China: Its State and Prospects, with Special Reference to the Spread of the Gospel* (London: J. Snow, 1838).

Minutes of Inquiry into Civil Service Abuses before the Executive Council. 1860–61. Hong Kong. Executive Council (Hongkong, 1861).

The Monthly Chronicle of Events, Discoveries, Improvements, and Opinions, Vol. 2 (Boston: S.N. Dickinson, 1841).

Morrison, John Robert, *A Chinese Commercial Guide, Consisting of a Collection of Details Respecting Foreign Trade in China*, 4th edn (Canton: Albion Press, 1834).

The North-China Herald, Supreme Court and Consular Gazette (The North-China Herald (later, The North China Daily News 1850–1941).

Norton-Kyshe, James William, *The History of the Laws and Courts of Hong Kong From the Earliest Period to 1898*, Vol. 1–2 (London: T. Fisher Unwin, 1898).

The Ordinances of Hongkong (London: G.E. Eyre and W. Spottiswoode, 1866).

Overland China Mail.

Phipps, John, *A Practical Treatise on the China and Eastern Trade: Comprising the Commerce of Great-Britain and India Particularly Bengal and Singapore with China and the Eastern Islands* (Calcutta: Sold by Thacker, 1835).

Qu, Qiubai 瞿秋白, 'Shanghai maiban jieji de quanwei yu shangmin' 上海買辦階級的權威與商民 (Authority of the comprador class in Shanghai and merchant people), Xiangdao zhoubao *嚮導週報* (The guide weekly), 1926 (162).

Report of the Commission, with Minutes of Evidences, etc. (Hong Kong, 1858).

Ridgway, Archibald R., 'Letters from Hong Kong and Macao', *The New Monthly Magazine*, Vol. 70 (London: Henry Colburn, 1844).

Sha Weikai 沙為楷, Zhongguo maibanzhi *中國買辦制* (China's comprador system) (Shanghai, Shangwu yinshuguan, 1927).

Shenbao 申報. (1872–1948).

Shepherd, Bruce, *The Hong Kong Guide 1893* with *an Introduction by H.J. Lethbridge* (Oxford: Oxford University Press, 1982).

The Singapore Free Press and Mercantile Advertiser.

Sirr, Henry Charles, *China and the Chinese: Their Religion, Character, Customs, and Manufacturers: the Evils Arising from the Opium Trade: with a Glance at our Religious, Moral, Political and Commercial Intercourse with the Country*, Vol. 2 (London: W.S. Orr & Co., 1849).

The South China Morning Post.

The Straits Times.

The Sydney Mail.

Tarrant, William, *Hong Kong: Part 1, 1839 to 1844* (Canton: Friend of China, 1861).

Wang Tao 王韜, 'chuanjian donghua yiyuan xu 創建東華醫院序 (Introduction of the establishment of the Tung Wah Hospital)' in Wang Tao, *Taoyuan wenlu waibian 弢園文錄外編*, Vol. 8 (1870).

Wang Tao 王韜, 'My Sojourn in Hong Kong', in Barbara-Sue White, *Hong Kong: Somewhere between Heaven and Earth* (Hong Kong: Oxford University Press, 1996), 62–64.

Wellington Independent (1845–1874).

Wei Yuan and Parker, E.H., *A Chinese Account of the Opium War* (Shanghai: Kelly & Walsh, Shanghai, 1888).

Williams, S. Wells, *A Chinese Commercial Guide: Consisting of a Collection of Details and Regulations Respecting Foreign Trade with China, Sailing Directions, Tables*, 4th edn, revised and enlarged (Canton: printed at the Office of the Chinese Repository, 1856).

Williams, S. Wells, *The Chinese Commercial Guide*, 4th edn (Hong Kong: Shortrede & Co., 1863).

Wood, W.W, *Sketches of China* (Philadelphia: Carey & Lea, 1830).

Wright, Arnold, *Twentieth Century Impressions of Hong Kong, Shanghai, and Other Treaty Ports of China* (London: Lloyd's Greater Britain Publishing Company, 1908).

Wu Yueren 吳躍人, *Facai mijue youming huangnu waishi 發財秘訣 又名 黃奴外史* (Secret of wealth or, side history of slaves for gold) (originally published in 1907).

Xiangdao zhoubao 響導週報 (The guide weekly).

Xu Run 徐潤, *Xuyuzhai zixu nianpu 徐愚齋自敘年譜* (Self Biography of Xurun) (Xiangshan: self-published for the Xu family, 1927).

Xunhuan Ribao 循環日報 (Universal Circulating Herald) (Hong Kong, 1874–1947).

Zhao Erxun 趙爾巽, *et al.* (eds) *Qingshigao 清史稿* (Draft history of Qing) (Beijing: Zhonghua shuju: Xinhua shudian Beijing faxing suo, 1977).

Zhongguo diyi lishi danganguan 中國第一歷史檔案館 (First historical archives of China) (ed.), *Yapian zhanzheng dangan ziliao 鴉片戰爭檔案資料* (Archival materials of the Opium War), Vol. 1–7 (Shanghai: Shanghai renmin chuban she, 1987–1992).

Secondary – Western languages

Ball, Benjamin Lincoln, 'Diary of a Hong Kong Doctor', in Barbara-Sue White (ed.), *Hong Kong: Somewhere between Heaven and Earth* (Hong Kong: Oxford University Press, 1996).

Bayly, C.A., *Empire and Information: Intelligence Gathering and Social Communication in India, 1780–1870* (Cambridge, UK, and New York: Cambridge University Press, 1996).

Beeching, Jack, *The Chinese Opium Wars* (London: Hutchinson, 1975).

Bickers, Robert, *Britain in China: Community, Culture and Colonialism 1900–1949* (Manchester: Manchester University Press, 1999).

Bickers, Robert, *The Scramble for China: Foreign Devils in the Qing Empire, 1832–1914* (London: Allen Lane, 2011).

Birch, Alan, Jao, Y.C., and Sinn, Elizabeth (eds), *Research Materials for Hong Kong Studies* (Hong Kong: Centre of Asian Studies, University of Hong Kong, 1984).

Cassel, Pär Kristoffer, *Grounds of Judgment: Extraterritoriality and Imperial Power in Nineteenth-century China and Japan* (Oxford, UK, and New York: Oxford University Press, 2012).

Carroll, John M., *Edge of Empires: Chinese Elites and British Colonials in Hong Kong* (Cambridge, MA: Harvard University Press, 2005).

Carroll, John M., *A Concise History of Hong Kong* (Lanham, MD: Rowman & Littlefield, 2007).

Chan Kai Yiu, 'A Turning Point in China's Comprador System: KMA's Changing Marketing Structure in the Lower Yangzi Region, 1912–25', *Business History*, Vol. 43, No. 2 (2001), 51–72.

Clifford, Nicholas R., *Shanghai, 1925: Urban Nationalism and the Defence of Foreign Privilege* (Ann Arbor, MI: Center for Chinese Studies, The University of Michigan, 1979).

Chan Wai Kwan, *The Making of Hong Kong Society: Three Studies of Class Formation in Early Hong Kong* (Oxford, UK: Clarendon Press; and New York: Oxford University Press, 1991).

Chang Hsin-pao, *Commissioner Lin and the Opium War* (Cambridge, MA: Harvard University Press, 1964).

Cheng T.C., 'Chinese Unofficial Members of the Legislative and Executive Councils in Hong Kong Up to 1941', *Journal of Royal Asiatic Society Hong Kong Branch*, Vol. 9 (1969), 7–30.

Cohen, Paul A., *Discovering History in China: American Historical Writings on the Recent Chinese Past* (New York: Columbia University Press, 1984).

Collins, Charles H., *Public Administration in Hong Kong* (London: Royal Institute of International Affairs, 1952).

Cox, Howard, Huang, Biao and Metcalfe, Stuart, 'Compradors, Firm Architecture and the "Reinvention" of British Trading Companies: John Swire & Sons' Operations in Early Twentieth Century China', *Business History*, Vol. 45, No. 2 (2003), 15–34.

Endacott, George Beer, *A Biographical Sketch-book of Early Hong Kong* (Hong Kong: Hong Kong University Press, 2005).

England,Vaudine, *The Quest of Noel Croucher: Hong Kong's Quiet Philanthropist* (Hong Kong: Hong Kong University Press, 1998).

Evans, Dafydd Emrys, 'The Origins of Hong Kong's Central Market and the Tarrant Affair', *Journal of Royal Asiatic Society Hong Kong Branch*, Vol. 12 (1972), 150–160.

Fairbank, John King, *Trade and Diplomacy on the China Coast: the Opening of the Treaty Ports, 1842–1854* (Stanford, CA: Stanford University Press, 1969).

Fay, Peter Ward, *The Opium War, 1840–1842: Barbarians in the Celestrial Empire in the Early Part of the Nineteenth Century and the War by Which They Forced her Gates Ajar* (Chapel Hill, NC: University of North Carolina Press, 1975).

Feng Bangyan, Meijiao, Rao and Law, Violet, *Enriching Lives: A History of Insurance in Hong Kong, 1841–2010* (Hong Kong: Hong Kong University Press, 2010).

Fok, K.C. 'Lineage Ties and Business Partnership: A Hong Kong Commercial Network' in S. Sugiyama and Linda Grove (eds), *Commercial Networks in Modern Asia* (Richmond, UK: Curzon, 2001), 159–170.

Garrett, Valery M., *Heavens is High and Emperor Far Away: Merchants and Mandarins in Old Canton* (Oxford: Oxford University Press, 2002).

Gibson, James R., *Otter Skins, Boston Ships, and China Goods: The Maritime Fur Trade of the Northwest Coast, 1785–1841* (Seattle, WA: University of Washington Press, 1992).

Goodman, Bryna, *Native Place, City and Nation: Regional Networks and Identity in Shanghai, 1853–1937* (Berkeley, CA: University of California Press, 1995).

Greenberg, Michael, *British Trade and the Opening of China, 1800–1842* (Cambridge, UK: Cambridge University Press: 1951).

Hacker, Arthur, *A Rare Photographic Record of the 1860s* (Hong Kong: Wattis Finer Art, 1997).

Hanes, William Travis and Sanello, Frank, *Opium Wars: The Addiction of One Empire and the Corruption of Another* (Naperville, IL: Sourcebooks, 2002).

Hao Yen-p'ing, *The Comprador in Nineteenth Century China: Bridge between East and West* (Cambridge, MA: Harvard University Press, 1970).

Hao Yen-p'ing, *The Commercial Revolution in Nineteenth-century China: The Rise of Sino-Western Mercantile Capitalism* (Berkeley, CA: University of California Press, 1986).

Hao Zhidong, *Macau History and Society* (Hong Kong: Hong Kong University Press, 2011).

Hay, Douglas and Craven, Paul (eds), *Masters, Servants, and Magistrates in Britain and the Empire, 1562–1955* (Chapel Hill, NC: University of North Carolina Press, 2004).

Hayes, James, *The Hong Kong Region, 1850–1911: Institutions and Leadership in Town and Countryside* (Hamden, CT: Archon, 1977).

Ho, Eric Peter, *Tracing My Children's Lineage* (Hong Kong: Hong Kong Institute for the Humanities and Social Sciences, University of Hong Kong, 2010).

Ho Pui-yin, *The Administrative History of the Hong Kong Government Agencies, 1841–2002* (Hong Kong: Hong Kong University Press; and London: Eurospan, 2004).

Holdsworth, May and Munn, Christopher (eds), *Dictionary of Hong Kong Biography* (Hong Kong: Hong Kong University Press, 2012).

Hui Po-Keung, 'Comprador Politics and Middleman Capitalism' in Ngo, Tak-Wing, *Hong Kong's History: State and Society Under Colonial Rule* (London and New York: Routledge, 1999), 30–45.

Hurley, R.C., *Picturesque Hong Kong: British Crown Colony and Dependencies* (Hong Kong: Tillotson & Sons, 1925).

Hutcheon, Robin, *Wharf: The First Hundred Years* (Hong Kong: Wharf (Holdings), 1986).

Jardine, Matheson & Co., *Jardines and the Ewo Interests* (China: Jardine, Matheson; and New York: Charles A. Phelps, 1947).

King, Frank H.H., King, C.E. and King, David J.S., *The Hongkong Bank in Late Imperial China, 1864–1902: on an Even Keel. Volume 1 of The History of the Hongkong and Shanghai Banking Corporation* (Cambridge, UK, and New York: Cambridge University Press, 1987).

Leach, A.J., *The Ordinances of the Legislative Council of the Colony of Hongkong: From the Year 1844 to the End of 1890* (Hongkong: Noronha, 1891–1892).

Le Pichon, Alain, *China Trade and Empire: Jardine, Matheson & Co. and the Origins of British Rule in Hong Kong, 1827–1843* (Oxford: Oxford University Press, 2005).

Lee Seung-joon, *Gourmets in the Land of Famine* (Stanford, CA: Stanford University Press, 2011).

Legge, James, 'The Colony of Hong Kong', *Journal of the Royal Asiatic Society Hong Kong Branch*, Vol. 11 (1971), 172–193.

Legge, James, *Hong Kong, Stability and Change: A Collection of Essays* (Hong Kong: Oxford University Press, 1978).

Liu Kwang-ching, *Anglo-American Steamship Rivalry in China, 1862–1874* (Cambridge, MA: Harvard University Press, 1962).

Lockwood, Stephen, *Augustine Heard and Company, 1858–1862: American Merchants in China* (Cambridge, MA: Harvard University Press, 1971).

Lovell, Julia, *The Opium War: Drugs, Dreams and the Making of China* (London: Macmillan Distribution, 2011).

Lu Hanchao, *Beyond the Neon Lights: Everyday Shanghai in the Early Twentieth Century* (Berkeley, CA: University of California Press, 1999),

Luk Chi-hung, *The Opium War, Overlapping Empires, and China's Water Borders*, PhD Dissertation, University of Oxford (2016).

Luk Chi-hung, *Collaboration and Conflict: Food Provisioning in Early Colonial Hong Kong*, Thesis for MPhil, University of Hong Kong (2011).

Luk Chi-hung 'Monopoly, Transaction and Extortion: Public Market Franchise and Colonial Relations in British Hong Kong, 1844–58', *Journal of Royal Asiatic Society Hong Kong Branch*, Vol. 52 (2012), 139–188.

Mao Zedong, Michael Y.M. Kau, and John K. Leung (eds), *The Writings of Mao Zedong, 1949–1976: January 1956–December 1957*, Vol. 2 (Armonk, NY, and London: M.E. Sharpe, 1992).

Mao Zedong, 'Analysis of the Classes in Chinese Society' in *Selected Works of Mao Tse-tung*, Vol. 1 (Oxford: distributed by Pergamon, 1978), 13–22.

Morse, Hosea Ballou, *The Chronicles of the East India Company Trading to China, 1635–1843* (Oxford: Clarendon Press, 1926–1929), Vol. 1–5.

Morse, Hosea Ballou, Selected by Patrick Tuck, *Britain and the China Trade 1635–1842*, Vol. 4 (London and New York: Routledge, 2000).

Motono Eiichi, 'A Study of the Legal Status of the Compradors During the 1880s: With Special Reference to the Three Civil Cases Between David Sassoon Sons & Co. and Their Compradors, 1884–1887', *Acta Asiatica*, No. 62 (1992), 44–70.

Munn, Christopher, *Anglo-China: Chinese People and British Rule in Hong Kong, 1841–1880* (Hong Kong: Hong Kong University Press, 2009).

Munn, Christopher, 'Hong Kong, 1841–1870: All the Servants in Prison and Nobody to Take Care of the House', in Douglas Hay and Paul Craven (eds), *Masters, Servants, and Magistrates in Britain and the Empire, 1562–1955* (Chapel Hill, NC: University of North Carolina Press, 2004), 365–401.

Munn, Christopher, 'Colonialism 'in a Chinese atmosphere': The Caldwell affair and the perils of collaboration in early Colonial Hong Kong', in Robert Bickers and Christian Henriot (eds), *New Frontiers: Imperialism's New Communities in East Asia, 1842–1953* (Manchester, UK, and New York: Manchester University Press, 2000), 12–37.

Muter, Elizabeth McMullin, *Travels and Adventures of an Officer's Wife in India, China, and New Zealand*, Vol. 1 (London: Hurst and Blackett, 1864).

Ngo Tak-Wing, *Hong Kong's History: State and Society under Colonial Rule* (London and New York: Routledge, 1999).

Onley, James, *The Arabian Frontier of the British Raj: Merchants, Rulers, and the British in the Nineteenth-Century Gulf* (New York: Oxford University Press, 2007).

Osterhammel, Jürgen, 'Semi-Colonialism and Informal Empire in Twentieth-Century China: Towards a Framework of Analysis', in Wolfgang J. Mommsen (ed.), *Imperialism and After: Continuities and Discontinuities* (London: Allen & Unwin, 1986), 290–314.

Pao Kuang Yung, 'The Comprador: His Position in the Foreign Trade of China', *Economic Journal*, Vol. 21, No. 84 (December 1911), 636–641.

Pearson, Margaret M., *China's New Business Elite: The Political Consequences of Economic Reform* (Berkeley, CA: University of California Press, 1997).

Pomerantz-Zhang, Linda, *Wu Tingfang (1862–1922): Reform and Modernization in Modern Chinese History* (Hong Kong: Hong Kong University Press, 1992).

Pope-Hennessy, James, *Verandah; Some Episodes in the Crown Colonies: 1867–1889* (New York: Knopf, 1964).

Proud, Edward B., *The Postal History of Hong Kong*, Vol. 1, 1841–1958 (Heathfield, UK: Proud-Bailey, 1989).

Robinson, Ronald, 'Non-European Foundations of European Imperialism: Sketch for a Theory of Collaboration', in Roger Owen and Bob Sutcliffe (eds), *Studies in the Theory of Imperialism* (London: Longman, 1972), 117–140.

Sinn, Elizabeth, *Pacific Crossing: California Gold, Chinese Migration, and the Making of Hong Kong* (Hong Kong: Hong Kong University Press, 2013).

Sinn, Elizabeth, *Power and Charity: A Chinese Merchant Elite in Colonial Hong Kong* (Hong Kong: Hong Kong University Press, 2003).

Sinn, Elizabeth (ed.), *Between East and West: Aspects of Social and Political Development in Hong Kong* (Hong Kong: Centre of Asian Studies, 1990).

Sinn, Elizabeth, 'Materials for Historical Research: Source Materials on the Tung Wah Hospital 1869–1941: The Case of Historical Institution' in Alan Birch, Y.C. Jao and Elizabeth Sinn (eds), *Research Materials for Hong Kong Studies* (Hong Kong: Centre of Asian Studies, University of Hong Kong, 1984), 195–223.

Smith, Carl T., *A Sense of History: Studies in the Social and Urban History of Hong Kong* (Hong Kong: Hong Kong Educational Pub. Co., 1995).

Smith, Carl T., *Chinese Christians: Elites, Middlemen, and the Church in Hong Kong* (Hong Kong and New York: Oxford University Press, 1985).

Smith, Carl T., 'The Formative Years of the Tong Brothers: Pioneers in the Modernization of China's Commerce and Industry', *Chung Chi Journal* (崇基學報), Vol. 10, Nos 1 and 2 (1971), 81–95.

Spalding, William F., *Eastern Exchange, Currency and Finance* (London: Sir I. Pitman & Sons, 1920).

State Street Trust Company, *Other Merchants and Sea Captains of Old Boston* (Boston, MA: State Street Trust Company, 1919).

Stonequist, Everett V., *The Marginal Man: A Study in Personality and Culture Conflict* (New York: Russell & Russell, 1961).

Sugiyama S., and Grove, L. (eds), *Commercial Networks in Modern Asia* (Richmond, UK: Curzon, 2001).

Taylor, Robert H., *The State in Burma* (London: C. Hurst & Co., 1987).

Ting, Joseph S., 'Native Chinese Peace Officers in British Hong Kong, 1841–1861', in Elizabeth Sinn (ed.), *Between East and West: Aspects of Social and Political Development in Hong Kong* (Hong Kong: Centre of Asian Studies, 1990), 147–158.

Tsai Jung-fang, *Hong Kong in Chinese History: Community and Social Unrest in the British Colony, 1842–1913* (New York: Columbia University Press, 1995).

Tsai Jung-fang, 'The 1884 Hong Kong Insurrection: Anti-Imperialist Popular Protest During the Sino-French War', *Bulletin of Concerned Asian Scholars*, Vol. 16, No. 1 (January–March 1984), 2–14.

Tsang, Steve Yui-Sang, *A Modern History of Hong Kong* (London and New York: I.B. Tauris, 2003).

van de Ven, Hans J., *Breaking with the Past: The Maritime Customs Service and the Global Origins of Modernity in China* (New York: Columbia University Press, 2014).

van de Ven, Hans J., 'The Emergence of the Text Centered Party', in Tony Saich and Hans J. Van de Ven (eds), *New Perspectives on the Chinese Communist Revolution* (Armonk, NY: M.E. Sharpe, 1995), 5–32.

Van Dyke, Paul Arthur, *Americans and Macao: Trade, Smuggling, and Diplomacy on the South China Coast* (Hong Kong: Hong Kong University Press, 2012).

Van Dyke, Paul Arthur, *The Canton Trade: Life and Enterprise on the China Coast, 1700–1845* (Hong Kong: Hong Kong University Press, 2005).

Walker, Richard L., *China Under Communism: The First Five Years* (London: Allen & Unwin, 1956).

Waldron, Arthur, 'The Warlord: Twentieth-Century Chinese Understandings of Violence, Militarism, and Imperialism', *The American Historical Review*, Vol. 96, No. 4 (October 1991), 1073–1100.

Waley, Arthur, *The Opium War through Chinese Eyes* (Stanford, CA: Stanford University Press, 1982).

Wang, Jerry L.S., 'The Profitability of Anglo-Chinese Trade, 1861–1913', *Business History*, Vol. 35, No. 3 (1993), 39–65.

White, David L., *Competition and Collaboration: Parsi Merchants and the English East India Company in eightieth Century India* (New Delhi: Munshiram Manoharlal Publishers, 1995).

Wu, Xinglian, *The Prominent Chinese in Hong Kong* (Hong Kong: Wuzhou shuju, 1977).

Yeh Wen-Hsin, *The Alienated Academy: Culture and Politics in Republican China, 1919–1937* (Cambridge, MA: Harvard University Asia Center, 2000).

Yun, Lisa, *The Coolie Speaks: Chinese Indentured Laborers and African Slaves in Cuba* (Philadelphia, PA: Temple University Press, 2008).

Zhang, Wenxian and Ilan Alon (eds), *Biographical Dictionary of New Chinese Entrepreneurs and Business Leaders* (Cheltenham, UK: Edward Elgar, 2009).

Secondary – Chinese and Japanese languages

A Ying 阿英 (ed.), *Wanqing xiaoshuoshi 晚清小說史* (History of late Qing novel) (Taipei: Taiwan shangwuyin shuguan, 1996).

Bao Peizhi 包培之 (Pao, Kuang Yung), 'Shouzhou sunjia yu zhongfu yinhang 壽州孫家與中孚銀行 (Sun family from Shou and Zhongfu bank)', *Jianghui Wensh 江淮文史 (Jianghui Culture History)*, No. 4 (2000), 127–136.

Bao Peizhi, Gan, Zuolin, 甘作霖 (translate), 'Lun yanghang maibanzhi zhi lihai 論洋行買辦制之利害 (A discussion of pro and cons of the comprador system)', *Dongfang Zazhi 東方雜誌* (Oriental magazine), 16:11 (1919).

Chen Guowei 陳國威, 'Jindai zhongguo maiban de beiwei xinli fenxi 近代中國買辦的卑微心理分析 (Exploration on humble mentality of the comprador in modern China)', *Shixue yuekan 史學月刊* (Journal of historical science), 2007, No. 12.

Chen Jiyao 陳計堯, 'Jindai zhongguo maiban zhidu zaiyi – yi maiban qiyue wei fenxi zhongxin (1860–1940) 近代中國買辦制度再議——以買辦契約為分析中心 (1860–1940)', Zhang Zhongmín 張忠民, Lu Xinglong 陸興龍, Li Yixiang 李一 (eds), *Jindai Zhongguo shehuihuanjing yu qiyefazhan 近代中國社會環境與企業發展* (The development of the society, environment and company in modern China) (Shanghai: Shanghai shehui kexueyuan chubanshe, 2008), 347–358.

Ding Xinbao 丁新豹, 'Xianggang moshiyang jiazu chutan 香港莫仕揚家族初探 (First exploration of Hong Kong Moshiyang's family history)' in Chinese University of Hong Kong. Art Gallery; Chinese University of Hong Kong, Dept. of History, *Maiban yu jindai Zhonggue 買辦與近代中國* (Hong Kong: Sanlian shudian, 2009), 168–190.

Ding Xinbao 丁新豹, 'Lishi de zhuanzhe: Zhimin tixx de jianli he yanjin 歷史的轉折：殖民體系的建立和演進 (Turning point of history: establishment of the colonial system and its evolution)', in Wang Gungwu 王賡武 (ed.), *Xianggangshi xinbian 香港史新編* (Hong Kong history: new perspectives), Vol. 1 (Hong Kong: Sanlianshu dian (Xianggang) youxian gongsi, 1997), 59–130.

Feng Bangyan 馮邦彥, *Xianggang huazi caituan 香港華資財團, 1841–1997* (Chinese Financial Group in Hong Kong, 1841–1997) (Hong Kong: Sanlian shudian, 1997).

Feng Bangyan et al., *Housheng liqun: Xianggangbaoxianshi, 1841–2008 厚生利群: 香港保險史, 一八四一 – 二零零八* (History of Insurance in Hong Kong, 1841–2008) (Hong Kong: Sanlian shudian, 2009).

Guan Shiguang, 關士光, *Qishi nian lai jiaguo: yige lao Xianggang de huiyi 七十年來家國: 一個老香港的回憶* (Toronto, Ontario: University of Toronto-York University Joint Centre for Asia Pacific Studies, 1999).

Hao Yen-p'ing, 郝延平, translated by Li Rongchang 李荣昌 *Shijiu shiji de zhongguo maiban: dongxi jianqiao* 十九世紀的中國買辦: 東西間橋 (The comprador in nineteenth century China: bridge between East and West) (Shanghai: Shanghai shehuikexueyuan chubanshe, 1988).

Hisasue Ryoichi 久末亮一, 'Honkon doru kessaiken ni okeru gingou no yakuwari 香港ドル決済圏における銀号の役割 (Functions of yinhao in an area in which Hong Kong dollars were utilised)', *Ajia Keizai アジア経済*, No. 3 (2007), 29–46.

Hisasue Ryoichi 久末亮一, 'Honkon 香港 (Hong Kong)', in Okamoto Takashi 岡本隆司 (ed.), *Chugoku Keizaishi 中国経済史* (Economic history of China) (Nagoya: Nagoya daigaku shuppankai, 2013).

Huang Hongzhao 黃鴻釗, *Aomenshi gangyao 澳門史綱要* (Outline of the history of Macau) (Fuzhou: Fujian renmin chubanshe: Fujiansheng xinhua shudian faxing, 1991).

Huang Yifeng 黃逸峰, 'guanyu jiu zhongguo de maiban jieji de yanjiu 關於舊中國的買辦階級的研究 (Researches on compradors in the Republic of China)', *Lishi yanjiu 歷史研究 (Historical Research),* No. 3 (1964).

Huang Yifeng 黃逸峰 et al., *Jiu zhongguo de maiban jieji 舊中國的買辦階級* (A comprador class in the Republic of China) (Shanghai: Shanghai renmin Chubanshe, 1982).

Hu Bo 胡波, *Xiangshan maiban yu jindai zhong guo 香山買辦与近代中国* (Xiangshan's compradores and modern China) (Guangzhou: Guangdong renmin chubanshe, 2007).

Hu Bo 胡波, '香山買辦与開埠後的上海社会 Xiangshan comprador and Shanghai society after the opening to western countries', *Shilin 史林*, No. 4 (2004), 41–57.

Ishi Mayako 石井摩耶子 'Jiūkyū seiki kōhan no chūgoku ni okeru igirisu shihon no katsudō-Jādin Maseson Shōkai no bāi 19世紀後半の中国におけるイギリス資本の活動 - ジャーディン マセソン商会の場合 (British commercial activities in China during the latter half of nineteenth century, case of Jardine, Matheson & Co.)', *Shakaikeizaishigaku 社会経済史学*, Vol. 45 No. 4 (1979.12), 357–482.

Kuang Shinan, 鄺勢南 'Xianggang de maiban zhidu 香港的買辦制度', in Li, Jinwei (ed.), *Xianggang bainianshi* (*香港百年史*) (Centenary history of Hong Kong) (Hong Kong: Nanzhong bianyi chuban she, 1948).

Lee Pui-Tak 李培德, 'Shijiu shiji maiban de longduan diwei he yanshen wangluo 19世紀買辦的壟斷地位和延伸網絡 (The monopoly and extended networks of Chinese compradors in the nineteenth century)', *Guojia Hanghai 国家航海* (National maritime research), No. 2 (2012), 64–75.

Li Donghai 李東海 (ed.), *Xianggang Donghua sanyuan yibaiershiwunian shilüe 香港東華三院一百二十五年史略* (120 years of the history of Hong Kong Tung Wah Three Hospitals) (Beijing: Zhongguo wenshi chubanshe, 1998).

Lin Yuanhui 林遠輝, Zhang Yinglong 張應龍, *Xinjiapo Malaixiya Huaqiao shi 新加坡馬來西亞華僑史* (History of overseas Chinese in Singapore and Malaysia) (Guangzhou: Guangdong gaodeng jiaoyu chuban she, 1991).

Ma Xueqiang 馬學強, 'Shanghai maiban de shenghuo 上海買辦的生活 (lives of the shanghai compradors)', in Xianggang zhongwen daxue zhongwen wenhua yanjiusuo wenwuguan, xiangang zhongwen daxue lishixi hebian 香港中文大學中國文化研究所文物館, 香港中文大學歷史系合編 Chinese University of Hong Kong. Art Gallery; Chinese University of Hong Kong, Dept. of History (ed.), *Maiban yu jindai Zhongguo 買辦與近代中國* (Comprador and modern China), (Hong Kong: Sanlian shudian (Xianggang) youxian gongsi, 2009), 10–52.

Mao Haijian 茅海建. *Tianchao de bengkui: Yapian zhanzheng zai yanjiu 天朝的崩溃: 鸦片战争再研究* (The collapse of the Celestial Empire: a reanalysis of the Opium War) (Beijing: Sanlian shudian, 2005).

Mok, Christopher (ed.), *Chenghuai gujin: Mojia sandai zhencang 澄懷古今: 莫家三代珍藏* (Timeless legacy: the Mok family collections) (Hong Kong: Chinese University of Hong Kong, Art Museum, 2009).

Motono Eiichi 本野英一, 'Baiben 買辦 (comprador)' in Okamoto Takashi 岡本隆司 (ed.), *Chugoku Keizaishi 中国経済史* (Economic history of China) (Nagoya: Nagoya Daigaku shuppankai, 2013).

Motono Eiichi 本野英一, *Dentō Chūgoku shōgyō chitsujo no hōkai: fubyōdō jōyaku taisei to 'Eigo o hanasu Chūgokujin' 伝統中国商業秩序の崩壊: 不平等条約体制と「英語を話す中国人」* (Collapse of the traditional mercantile system in China) (Nagoya: Nagoya Daigaku Shuppankai, 2004).

Murakami Ei 村上衛, *Umi no kindai Chūgoku: Fukkenjin no katsudō to Igirisu Shinchō 海の近代<I> <I>中国: 福建人の活動とイギリス· 清朝 (Maritime history of modern China: local Fujian actors and the British and Chinese empires)* (Nagoya: Nagoya Daigaku Shuppankai, 2013).

Negishi Tadashi 根岸佶, *Baiben seido no kenkyu 買弁制度の研究* (A study on the comprador system) (Tokyo: Nihon Tosho, 1948).

Nie Baozhang 聂宝璋 (ed.), *Zhongguo hangyunshi ziiliao 中國近代航運史資料* Vol. 1 (Historical materials of modern Chinese steamship and shipping industries) (Shanghai: Shanghai renmin chubanshe, 1983).

Rao Zongyi 饒宗頤, *Xinjiapo gushiji 新加坡古事記* (Old stories of Singapore) (Hong Kong: Zhongwen daxue chubanshe, 1994).

Song, Meiyun, 宋美雲, *Huashuo Jinshang 話說津商* (Talks about Tianjin merchants) (Beijing: Zhonghua gongshang lianhe chubanshe, 2006).

Tsuchiya, Keizo 土屋計左右, *Baiben seido 買弁制度* (The comprador system) (Tokyo: Shina Keizai Kenkyūjo, 1940).

Uchida, Naosaku 内田直作, 'Baiben seido no kenkyu 買辦制度の研究 (Research on the comprador system)' *Shina Kenkyu 支那研究* (publisher and publication date unknown).

Wang, Jingyu 汪敬虞, *Tangtingshu yanjiu 唐廷枢研究* (Research on Tang Tingshu), (Peking: Zhongguo Shehui kexue chubanshe, 1983).

Wang, Shui 王水, 'Qingdai maiban shouru de guji ji qi zhuyao shiyong fangxiang 清代買辦收入的估計及其主要使用方向 (Estimated amount of compradors' income and the use of their wealth during the Qing period)', *Zhongguo shehui kexue xueyuan jingji yanjiusuo jikan 中國社會科學院經濟研究所集刊*, Vol. 5 (Beijing, zhongguo shehui kexue chubanshe 中國社會科學出版社, 1983), 298–324.

Weng, Jing jing 翁靜晶 (*Bainian maishen de huiyi: zhimindi shiqi Huaren xieleishi 百年賣身的回憶: 殖民地時期華人血淚史* (Memory of selling body for 100 years: history of Chinese crying bitter tears in the colonial period) (Hong Kong: Tiandi tushu youxian gongsi, 2011).

Xianggang Zhongwen Daxue Zhongwen Wenhua Yanjiusuo Wenwuguan, Xiangang Zhongwen Daxue Lishixi hebian 香港中文大學中國文化研究所文物館, 香港中文大學歷史系合編 Chinese University of Hong Kong. Art Gallery; Chinese University of Hong Kong, Dept. of History (ed.), *Maiban yu jindai Zhongguo 買辦與近代中國* (Comprador and modern China), (Hong Kong: San lian shu dian (Xianggang) you xian gong si, 2009).

Xie Wenhua 謝文華, 'Maiban yanjiu de huigu yu zhanwang 買辦研究的回顧與展望 (A review of the search for comprador)' www.tnfsh.tn.edu.tw/teach/his/paper/xie.doc accessed 25/11/2010. Originally published in *lishi xuebao 歷史學報* (Taiwan Shifan daxue 台灣師範大學) Vol. 22 (June 1994), 391–412.

Yamafuji Ryutaro, 山藤竜太郎, 'Mitusi bussan no baibensei haishi: Shanhai shiten ni Chūmoku shsite 三井物産の買弁制度廃止：上海支店に注目して (Abolishment of comprador system in Mitsui bussan with specific focus on the case of Shanghai branch),' *Keiei Shigaku*, 経営史学, Vol. 44, No. 2 (September 2009), 3–29.

Ye Xian'en 葉顯恩, 'Yueshang yu guangdong de hangyunye jindaihua: 1842–1911粵商與廣東的航運業近代化:1842–1911 (Cantonese merchants and the modernisation of shipping industry)' in Ye Xian'en 葉顯恩, *Huizhou yu Yuehai lungao 徽州與粵海論稿* (Hefei Shi: Anhui daxuechubanshe, 2004), 316–342.

Yu Heping, 虞和平, 'Xiangshanji maiban yu ningboji maiban tedian zhi bijiao 香山籍買辦與寧波籍買辦特點之比較 (A comparison of the features of Xiangshan and Ningbo comrpadors)', *Guangdong shehuikexue 廣東社會科學*, No. 1 (2010), 127–134.

Yuan Bangjian 元邦建 (ed.), *Xianggang Shilue 香港史略* (Hong Kong: Zhongliu chuban she, 1988).

Zhang Ping 張萍, 'Jindai maiban yanjiu zongshu 近代買辦研究綜述 (Summary of the researches on the compradors)', *Qingshi yanjiu 清史研究*, 1996 (1), 111–118.

Zhang Xiaohui 張曉輝, 'Maiban de qiyejia jingshen – jian lun maiban de lishi zuoyong 買辦的企業家精神—兼論買辦的歷史作用 (Comprador's entrepreneurial spirits: discussing the compradors' historical roles)' in Xianggang zhongwen daxue zhongwen wenhua yanjiusuo wenwuguan, xiangang zhongwen daxue lishixi hebian 香港中文大學中國文化研究所文物館, 香港中文大學歷史系合編 Chinese University of Hong Kong, Art Gallery; Chinese University of Hong Kong, Department of History (eds), *Maiban yu jindai Zhongguo 買辦與近代中國* (Comprador and Modern China), (Hong Kong: Sanlian shudian (Xianggang) youxian gongsi, 2009), 54–82.

Zhang Xiaohui 張曉輝, *Xianggang yu jindai zhongguo duiwai maoyi 香港與近代中國對外貿易* (Hong Kong and foreign trade of modern China) (Beijing: Zhongguo Huaqiao chuban she, 2000).

Zhaoshangju shi yanjiuhui; Yì Huili, Hu Zheng 招商局史研究會編; 易惠莉, 胡政主編. 易惠莉, 胡政 (eds), *Zhaoshangju yu jindai zhongguo yanjiu 招商局與近代中國研究* (The research on the China Merchants' Steam Navigation Company and modern China), (Beijing: Zhongguo shehui kexue chubanshe, 2005).

Zheng Hongtai 鄭宏泰 and Wong, Siu-lun 黃紹倫, *Hejia nūzi: sandai funū chuanqi 何家女子: 三代婦女傳奇* (Women in He family: stories of three generations) (Hong Kong: Sanlian Shudian, 2010).

Zheng Hongtai 鄭宏泰, *Xianggang dalao: He Dong 香港大老: 何東* (The Grand Old Man of Hong Kong: Robert Hotung), (Hong Kong: Sanlian shudian, 2007).

Zhu Yingui 朱蔭貴 *Zhongguo jindai lunchuan hangyunye yanjiu 中國近代輪船航運業研究* (The research on the modern Chinese steam shipping business) (Taizhong Xian: Gaowen chubanshee, 2006).

Glossary

Achun	亞松
Ahoy	亞開
Anji	安記
Antai baoxian gongsi	安泰保險公司
aomen tongzhi	澳門同知
Bailing	百齡
banfang	辦房
Bao Peng	鮑鵬
Bao Renguan	鮑人琯
Bao Yacong	鮑亞聰
Bao Zonghong	鮑宗鴻
baoshang	保商
Beijing	北京
Bilina banfang	鼻厘拿辦房
Boston Jack	波臣則
Bu Dingbang	布定邦
Chan Quan-ee	陳關意
Chen Duxiu	陳獨秀
Chen Ruinan/ Chen Guishi	陳瑞南/陳桂士
Choa Leep-chee	蔡立志
Chow Aaon	曹亞安
Choy Tsz Mee	蔡紫微
chuan maiban	船買辦
danjia	蛋家
Daqing huangjia haiguan zong shuiwusi	大清皇家海關總稅務司
Deng Yasu	鄧亞蘇
Deng Zhiang	鄧志昂
dibao	地保
Dinghai	定海
Fanbachen	嗃吧咗
Faxing hang	發興行
Feng Mingshan	馮明珊

Fujian	福建
Fung Achew	馮道照
Fung Tang	馮登
Gan Zuolin	甘作霖
Gao Manhua	高滿華
gonghang	公行
Guan Jidong	關濟東
Guan Zhunzhou	關准洲
Guangdong	廣東
Guangxi	廣西
Guangzhao gongsuo	廣肇公所
Guangzhou	廣州
Guiji banfang	癸記辦房
Guo Ganzhang	郭甘章
Hailingdao	海陵島
Hakka	客家
hangshang	行商
Hangzhou	杭州
He Kunshan	何崑山
Ho Amei	何亞美
Ho Asek	何亞錫
Ho Fai-yin	何裴然
Ho Kai	何啟
Ho Kam Tong	何甘棠
Hoklo	福佬
Hongqiao	虹橋
Howqua	伍秉鑒
huajingli	華經理
Huang Cheye	黃車葉
Huang Jinfu	黃金福
Huang Tianhua	黃添化
Huang Yifeng	黃逸峰
Huashang baoan gongsi	華商保安公司
huashang huiguan	華商會館
Hubei	湖北
hubu	户部
huiguan	會館
Hunan	湖南
Ip Him-kwong	葉謙光
Jiannan mihang	建南米行
Jiaqing	嘉慶
junfa	軍閥
kaifong	街坊
Kaiping	開平
Kwan Shi-kuang	關士光

Kwok Acheong	郭亞祥
Kwong Fook I-tsz	廣福義祠
Lang Akhuw	梁球
Lau Wai Chun	劉渭川
Lee Yu Chow	李汝舟
Leong A-ting	楊亞丁
Leong Akum	梁亞根
Li Hongbin	李鴻宾
Li Ka-shing	李嘉誠
Li King Ting	李敬亭
Li Songyun	李松筠
Li Tak Cheong	李德昌
Li Zhaotang	黎兆棠
Liang Shaogang	梁紹剛
Liangguang	兩廣
lijin	釐金
Lin Zexu	林則徐
Lingdingyang	零丁洋
Litu	唎吐
Liu Shaozong	劉紹宗
liutang	流糖
Lo Aqui /Loo King, Loo Aking/ Sz-man-king, see mun king	盧亞貴/盧景 /斯文景
Lo Een-teen	羅見田
Lo Hok Pang	羅鶴朋
Lo Pak Sheung	羅伯常
Lu Liping	盧禮屏
Lu Yajing	盧亞景
Ma Yinchu	馬寅初
maiban	買辦
Man Fook Tin	孟福田
Man Mo Temple	文武廟
Mao Zedong	毛澤東
maoyi shiwu shifei	貿易事務使費
Meiji	明治
Mo Gansheng	莫幹生
Mo Shiyang	莫仕揚
Mok Cho Chuen	莫藻泉
Mok Koon Yuk/ Mok Cho Chuen	莫冠鍌/莫藻泉
Mok Shing	莫勝/莫亞勝
Mui Tsai	妹仔
Nanhai	南海
Nanjing	南京
Neilingdingdao	內伶仃島
Ng Chook	吳祝

Ng Chuk-shau	吳竹修
Ng Hip	吳叶
Ng Sang	吳生
Ng Tuk hang	吳德衡
Ningbo	寧波
Nippon Yūsen Kaisha	日本郵船会社
Niulan Yaxiang	牛欄亞祥
Pang A Yim	彭炎
Panyu	番禺
Pao Kuang Yung's	包培之
Pedro Leung Hing Kee/ Pang Ahim, Pang A Yim	興記/彭炎
Po Leung Kuk	保良局
Punti	本地
Qichang yanghang	旗昌洋行
qinchai dachen	欽差大臣
Qishan	琦善
Qu Qiubai	瞿秋白
Shandong	山東
shangzhan	商戰
Shantou	汕頭
Shantou yapian hanghui	汕頭鴉片行會
Shaoyuan	紹元
Shau U	守愚
shengcheng hangnei shiyongfei	省城行內使用費
Shi Shang-kai	施笙階
Shi Shi	施氏
Shi Yusheng	石玉勝
Shui Tung	水東
Shuxinguan	書信館
Sum Pak Ming	岑伯銘
Sung Chin Tseung	宋展翔
Taiyuan	泰源
Tan Yacai	譚亞才
Tang Aming	唐寧
Tang Atim	唐添
Tang Neng	唐能
tangjiang	糖漿
Tianfu yinhao	天福銀號
Tōa Kenkyūjo Shanghai Shisho	東亜研究所上海支所
tongshi	通事
Tse Yu Chuen	謝雨川
Tsim Sha Tsui	尖沙咀
Tsoi Sing Nam	蔡星南
tuanfangju	團防局

Tuchanfu	吐嘽咈
Tungkoon	東莞
Un Man-tsoi	袁敏才
Wang Bingsheng	王炳生
Wang Jingyu	汪敬虞
Wang Tao	王韜
Wei Afoon	韋亞寬
Wei Aqui	韋亞貴
Wei Guang	韋光
Wei Yuan	魏源
Wei Yuk	韋玉
Whampoa	黃浦
Wong Ka-yau	黃家猷
Wong She-tai	黃社帶
Wong Shu-tong	黃樹堂
Wong Yook	黃玉
Wu Jianzhang	吳健彰
Wu Xiongguang	吳熊光
Wu Yaping	吳亞平
Wu Yueren	吳躍人
wuchang shifei	無常使費
wulai	無賴
Wusong	吴淞
Xianggang zhimin	香港之民
Xianggangzhong shangmin	香港衆商民
Xiangshan	香山
Xie Dasheng	謝達盛
Xie Jiabao	謝家寶
Xieli	協理
Xijiang	西江
Xin Qingnian	新青年
xingbu	刑部
xingu	新股
xizai xiansheng	西崽先生
Xu Run	徐潤
Xunhuan Ribao	循環日報
yahang	牙行
Yamao	亞茂
yanghang	洋行
yanghang banfang lianhehui	洋行辦房聯合會
yanghang xulitang	洋行敘理堂
yangnu	洋奴
yichuan maiban	夷船買辦
yiguan maiban	夷館買辦
yinhao	銀號

yinshuiren	引水人
Yongda yinhao	永打銀號
Yongde yinhao	永德銀號
yuanfa hang	元發行
yuehaiguandu	粵海關督
Yueyue xiaoshuo	月月小說
Zhan Guchuan	占谷船
Zhang Zhidong	張之洞
Zhao Ziyong	招子庸
Zhaoxing gongsi	肇興公司
Zhejiang	浙江
zhengerpin	正二品
zhengwupin	正五品
zhidafu	直大夫
Zhishi	值事
Zhishilu	誌事錄
Zhongfu yinhang	中孚銀行
Zhonghua yinwu ju	中華印務局
Zhoushan	舟山
Zhujiang	珠江
zizheng dafuxian	資政大夫銜

Index

For Product Safety Concerns and Information please contact our EU
representative GPSR@taylorandfrancis.com
Taylor & Francis Verlag GmbH, Kaufingerstraße 24, 80331 München, Germany

www.ingramcontent.com/pod-product-compliance
Ingram Content Group UK Ltd.
Pitfield, Milton Keynes, MK11 3LW, UK
UKHW022124190926
475702UK00013B/1634
9780367878078